W9-BHV-209

FOURTH EDITION

1

Series Director: **Diane Larsen-Freeman**

Grammar Dimensions

Form • Meaning • Use

Victoria Badalamenti
Carolyn Henner-Stanchina

THOMSON
HEINLE™

Australia • Canada • Mexico • Singapore • Spain • United Kingdom • United States

THOMSON
HEINLE

Series Director: Diane Larsen-Freeman
Grammar Dimensions 1: Form, Meaning, and Use
Victoria Badalamenti, Carolyn Henner-Stanchina

Publisher: *Sherrise Roehr*
Consulting Editor: *James W. Brown*
Director of Content Development: *Anita Raducanu*
Acquisitions Editor, Academic ESL: *Tom Jefferies*
Director of Product Marketing: *Amy Mabley*
Executive Marketing Manager: *Jim McDonough*
Senior Field Marketing Manager: *Donna Lee Kennedy*
Assistant Marketing Manager: *Caitlin Driscoll*
Assistant Editor: *Sarah Spader*
Editorial Assistants: *Katherine Reilly, Emily Dendinger*
Senior Production Editor: *Maryellen Eschmann-Killeen*
Senior Print Buyer: *Mary Beth Hennebury*
Development Editors: *Yeny Kim, Sarah Barnicle*
Production Project Manager: *Chrystie Hopkins*
Production Services: *Pre-Press Company, Inc.*
Interior Designer: *Lori Stuart*
Cover Designer: *Studio Montage*
Printer: *R.R. Donnelley*

Cover Image: © John Lawrence/Photographer's Choice/Getty

Copyright © 2007 Thomson Heinle, a part of The Thomson Corporation. Thomson, the Star logo, and Heinle are trademarks used herein under license.

All rights reserved. No part of this work covered by the copyright hereon may be reproduced or used in any form or by any means—graphic, electronic, or mechanical, including photocopying, recording, taping, Web distribution or information storage and retrieval systems—without the written permission of the publisher.

Printed in the United States of America.
1 2 3 4 5 6 7 8 9 10 — 11 10 09 08 07

For more information contact Thomson Heinle, 25 Thomson Place, Boston, Massachusetts 02210 USA, or you can visit our Internet site at http://elt.thomson.com

Credits appear on pages C-1–C-2, which constitutes a continuation of the copyright page.

For permission to use material from this text or product, submit a request online at http://www.thomsonrights.com

Any additional questions about permissions can be submitted by email to thomsonrights@thomson.com

ISBN 10: 1-4130-2740-7
ISBN 13: 978-1-4130-2740-2

International Student Edition
ISBN 10: 1-4130-2753-9
ISBN 13: 978-1-4130-2753-2

Library of Congress Control Number:
2006909606

CONTENTS

Unit 15 Present Progressive Tense 232

Unit 16 Adjective Phrases *Another, The Other, Other(s), the Other(s),* Intensifiers 252

Unit 17 Past Tense of *Be* 272

A Word from Diane Larsen-Freeman, Series Editor

Before ***Grammar Dimensions*** was published, teachers would ask me, "What is the role of grammar in a communicative approach?" These teachers recognized the importance of teaching grammar, but they associated grammar with form and communication with meaning, and thus could not see how the two easily fit together. ***Grammar Dimensions*** was created to help teachers and students appreciate the fact that grammar is not just about form. While grammar does indeed involve form, in order to communicate, language users also need to know the meaning of the forms and when to use them appropriately. In fact, it is sometimes not the form, but the *meaning* or *appropriate use* of a grammatical structure that represents the greatest long-term learning challenge for students. For instance, learning when it is appropriate to use the present perfect tense instead of the past tense, or being able to use two-word or phrasal verbs meaningfully, represent formidable challenges for English language learners.

The three dimensions of *form*, *meaning*, and *use* can be depicted in this pie chart with their interrelationship illustrated by the three arrows.

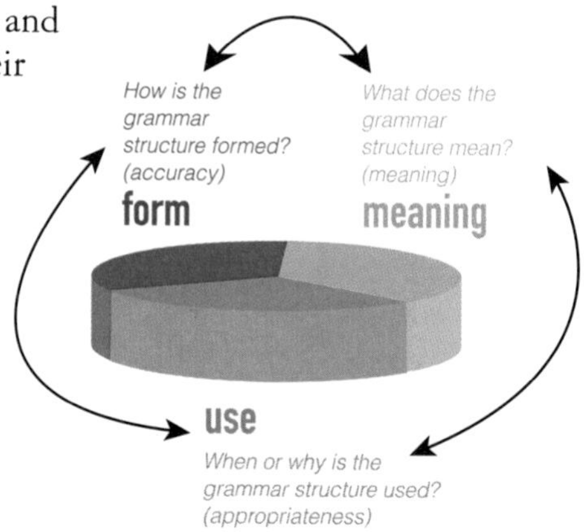

Helping students learn to use grammatical structures accurately, meaningfully, and appropriately is the fundamental goal of ***Grammar Dimensions.*** It is consistent with the goal of helping students to communicate meaningfully in English, and one that recognizes the undeniable interdependence of grammar and communication.

Enjoy the Fourth Edition of *Grammar Dimensions*!

To learn more about form, meaning, and use, read ***The Grammar Book: An ESL/EFL Teacher's Course,*** Second Edition, by Marianne Celce-Murcia and Diane Larsen-Freeman. ISBN: 0-8384-4725-2.

To learn about theory that has informed ***Grammar Dimensions,*** consult ***Teaching Language: From Grammar to Grammaring,*** also by Diane Larsen-Freeman. ISBN: 0-8384-6675-3.

Welcome to *Grammar Dimensions*, Fourth Edition!

The **clearest**, most **comprehensive** and **communicative** grammar series available! The fourth edition of *Grammar Dimensions* is more **user-friendly** and makes teaching grammar more **effective** than ever.

GRAMMAR DIMENSIONS IS COMPREHENSIVE AND CLEAR.

Grammar Dimensions systematically addresses the three dimensions of language—form, meaning, and use—through clear and comprehensive grammar explanations and extensive practice exercises. Each unit methodically focuses on each students' dimension and then integrates what they have learned in end-of-unit activities. In addition, grammatical structures are recycled throughout the series allowing students to practice and build upon their existing knowledge.

GRAMMAR DIMENSIONS IS COMMUNICATIVE.

Grammar Dimensions includes a large variety of lively communicative and personalized activities throughout each unit, eliciting self-expression and personalized practice. Interactive activities at the start of each unit serve as diagnostic tools directing student learning towards the most challenging dimensions of language structure. Integrated activities at the end of each unit include reading, writing, listening, and speaking activities allowing students to practice grammar and communication in tandem. New research activities encourage students to use authentic Internet resources and to reflect on their own learning.

GRAMMAR DIMENSIONS IS USER-FRIENDLY AND FLEXIBLE.

Grammar Dimensions has been designed to be flexible. Instructors can use the units in order or as set by their curriculum. Exercises can be used in order or as needed by the students. In addition, a tight integration between the Student Book, the Workbook, and the Lesson Planner makes teaching easier and makes the series more user-friendly.

GRAMMAR DIMENSIONS IS EFFECTIVE.

Students who learn the form, meaning, and use of each grammar structure will be able to communicate more accurately, meaningfully, and appropriately.

New to the Fourth Edition

- **NEW and revised grammar explanations** and examples help students and teachers easily understand and comprehend each language structure.
- **NEW and revised grammar charts and exercises** provide a wealth of opportunities for students to practice and master their new language.
- **NEW thematically and grammatically related Internet activities in book 1 and *InfoTrac® College Edition activities*** in every unit of books 2, 3, and 4 develop student research using current technologies.
- **NEW Reflection activities** encourage students to create personal language goals and to develop learning strategies.
- **NEW design, art, and photos** make each activity and exercise more engaging.
- **NEW Lesson Planners** assist both beginning and experienced teachers in giving their students the practice and skills they need to communicate accurately, meaningfully, and appropriately. All activities and exercises in the Lesson Planner are organized into step-by-step lessons so that no instructor feel overwhelmed.

SEQUENCING OF *GRAMMAR DIMENSIONS*

In *Grammar Dimensions* students progress from the sentence level to the discourse level, and learn to communicate appropriately at all levels.

Grammar Dimensions Book 1 → *Grammar Dimensions* Book 2 → *Grammar Dimensions* Book 3 → *Grammar Dimensions* Book 4

Sentence level → Discourse level

	Book 1	Book 2	Book 3	Book 4
Level	High-beginning	Intermediate	High-Intermediate	Advanced
Grammar level	Sentence and sub-sentence level	Sentence and sub-sentence level	Discourse level	Discourse level
Primary language and communication focus	Semantic notions such as *time* and *place*	Social functions, such as *making requests* and *seeking* permission	Cohesion and coherence at the discourse level	Academic and technical discourse
Major skill focus	Listening and speaking	Listening and speaking	Reading and writing	Reading and writing

Guided Tour of *Grammar Dimensions 1*

Unit goals **provide a roadmap** for the grammar points students will work on.

"**Opening Task**" can be used as a **diagnostic warm-up** exercise to explore students' knowledge of each structure.

UNIT 3

THE VERB *BE*

Information Questions, *It* with Time and Weather, and Prepositions of Location

UNIT GOALS

- Ask information questions with the verb *be*
- Use *it* to talk about the weather and the time
- Use prepositions of location

OPENING TASK

World Knowledge Game

Test your world knowledge. Work in groups of five. One person reads each answer aloud. The group makes the question. Use the pictures to help you.

Example: The Taj Mahal

One student reads the answer aloud: *The answer is "in India."*

The group makes the question: *Where is the Taj Mahal?*

28 UNIT 3

"**Focus**" **sections** present the **form, meaning,** and/or **use** of a particular structure helping students develop the skill of "**grammaring**"—the ability to use structures accurately, meaningfully, and appropriately.

Clear grammar charts present multiple examples, so teachers can have students work inductively to try to discover the rule on their own. More challenging grammar parts are accompanied by complete explanations.

FOCUS 1 Information Questions With *Be*

form meaning

We use *wh*-question words (such as *who, what, when, where, why* and *how*) to ask for specific information.

QUESTION WORD	*BE*	SUBJECT	ANSWER	MEANING
What	is 's	the Amazon?	a river	THING
Where	are	the Himalayas?	in India, Nepal, and China	PLACE
Who	is 's	the lead singer of U2?	Bono	PEOPLE
How	is 's	the weather in Argentina in June?	It's cold.	CONDITION
When	is 's	Thanksgiving in the United States?	on the fourth Thursday in November	TIME
It's 9:00 P.M.* in New York. What time	is	it in San Francisco?	It's 6:00 P.M.	CLOCK TIME
How old	are	the Pyramids in Egypt?	about 4,700 years old	AGE
Why	is 's	July 4th special in the United States?	because it's Independence Day	REASON

*P.M. = afternoon, evening, night

EXERCISE 1

Fill in the blanks with one of these *wh*-question words: *what, where, how, who, when, how old, what time,* and *why.* The first has been done for you.

Questions	Answers
1. How old is the Great Wall of China?	about 2,200 years old
2. ______ are the authors of *Grammar Dimensions, Book 1?*	Victoria Badalamenti and Carolyn Henner-Stanchina
3. ______ is Morocco?	in Africa
4. ______ is the weather in the summer in Washington, D.C.?	It's hot.

30 UNIT 3

Purposeful exercises provide a wealth of opportunity for students to practice and personalize the grammar.

EXERCISE 9

Work with a partner. Look at the map of the time zones in the United States. Take turns asking the time and answering the questions. Make two questions of your own.

Example: It's 7:00 A.M. in San Francisco. What time is it in Philadelphia? *10 A.M.*

1. It's 10:45 P.M. in Miami. What time is it in Salt Lake City?
2. It's 6:50 P.M. in Minneapolis. What time is it in New Orleans?
3. It's 10:30 P.M. in Santa Fe. What time is it in Chicago?
4. It's 2:15 A.M. in Los Angeles. What time is it in Boston?
5. It's 9:10 A.M. in Dallas. What time is it in Portland?
6. It's 10:20 A.M. in Atlanta. What time is it in Denver?
7. It's 10:05 A.M. in Seattle. What time is it in Cleveland?
8. It's 6:00 P.M. in New York. What time is it in your hometown in your country?
9. ______?
10. ______?

THE VERB *BE* Information Questions, *It* with Time and Weather, and Prepositions of Location 37

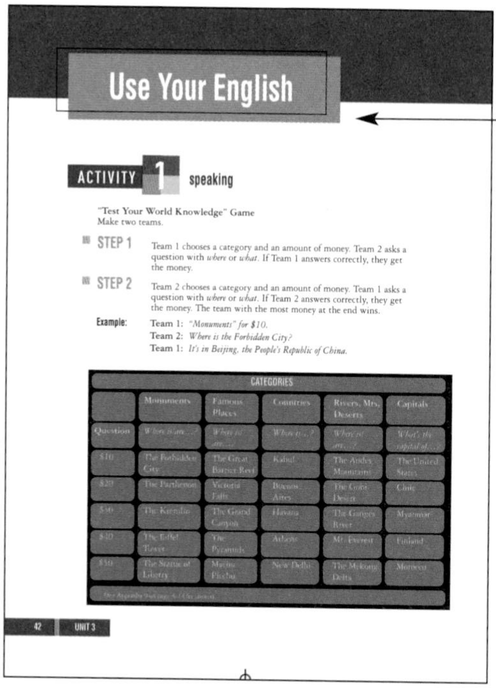

Use Your English

ACTIVITY 1 speaking

"Test Your World Knowledge" Game
Make two teams.

- **STEP 1** Team 1 chooses a category and an amount of money. Team 2 asks a question with *where* or *what*. If Team 1 answers correctly, they get the money.
- **STEP 2** Team 2 chooses a category and an amount of money. Team 1 asks a question with *where* or *what*. If Team 2 answers correctly, they get the money. The team with the most money at the end wins.

Example: Team 1: *"Monuments" for $10.*
Team 2: *Where is the Forbidden City?*
Team 1: *It's in Beijing, the People's Republic of China.*

CATEGORIES					
	Monuments	Famous Places	Countries	Rivers, Mts., Deserts	Capitals
Question	*Where is/are...?*	*Where is/are...?*	*Where is...?*	*Where is/are...?*	*What's the capital of...?*
$10	The Forbidden City	The Great Barrier Reef	Kabul	The Andes Mountains	The United States
$20	The Parthenon	Victoria Falls	Buenos Aires	The Gobi Desert	Chile
$30	The Kremlin	The Grand Canyon	Havana	The Ganges River	Myanmar
$40	The Eiffel Tower	The Pyramids	Athens	Mt. Everest	Finland
$50	The Statue of Liberty	Machu Picchu	New Delhi	The Mekong Delta	Morocco

42 UNIT 3

The "**Use Your English**" section (fondly known as the purple pages) offers communicative activities that **integrate grammar with reading, writing, listening, and speaking skills.** Communicative activities consolidate grammar instruction with enjoyable and meaningful tasks.

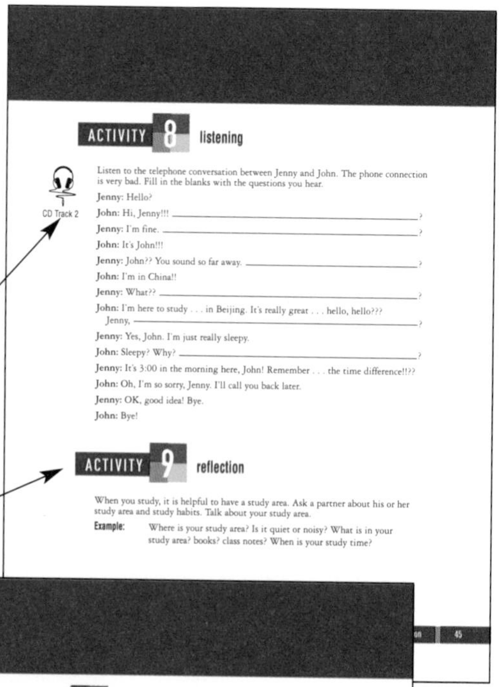

ACTIVITY 8 listening

CD Track 2

Listen to the telephone conversation between Jenny and John. The phone connection is very bad. Fill in the blanks with the questions you hear.

Jenny: Hello?
John: Hi, Jenny!!! ______________________?
Jenny: I'm fine. ______________________?
John: It's John!!!
Jenny: John?? You sound so far away. ______________________?
John: I'm in China!!
Jenny: What?? ______________________?
John: I'm here to study . . . in Beijing. It's really great . . . hello, hello???
Jenny, ______________________?
Jenny: Yes, John. I'm just really sleepy.
John: Sleepy? Why? ______________________?
Jenny: It's 3:00 in the morning here, John! Remember . . . the time difference!!??
John: Oh, I'm so sorry, Jenny. I'll call you back later.
Jenny: OK, good idea! Bye.
John: Bye!

ACTIVITY 9 reflection

When you study, it is helpful to have a study area. Ask a partner about his or her study area and study habits. Talk about your study area.

Example: Where is your study area? Is it quiet or noisy? What is in your study area? books? class notes? When is your study time?

45

Engaging listening activities on audio cassette and audio CD further reinforce the target structure.

Reflection activities help students understand their learning style and create learning strategies.

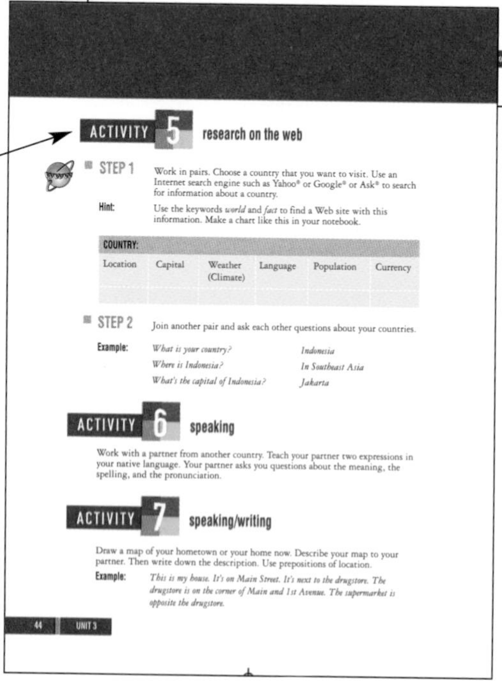

ACTIVITY 5 research on the web

- **STEP 1** Work in pairs. Choose a country that you want to visit. Use an Internet search engine such as Yahoo® or Google® or Ask® to search for information about a country.

Hint: Use the keywords *world* and *fact* to find a Web site with this information. Make a chart like this in your notebook.

COUNTRY:					
Location	Capital	Weather (Climate)	Language	Population	Currency

- **STEP 2** Join another pair and ask each other questions about your countries.

Example: *What is your country?* — *Indonesia*
Where is Indonesia? — *In Southeast Asia*
What's the capital of Indonesia? — *Jakarta*

ACTIVITY 6 speaking

Work with a partner from another country. Teach your partner two expressions in your native language. Your partner asks you questions about the meaning, the spelling, and the pronunciation.

ACTIVITY 7 speaking/writing

Draw a map of your hometown or your home now. Describe your map to your partner. Then write down the description. Use prepositions of location.

Example: *This is my house. It's on Main Street. It's next to the drugstore. The drugstore is on the corner of Main and 1st Avenue. The supermarket is opposite the drugstore.*

44 UNIT 3

Research activity using the Internet encourages students to read articles on carefully selected topics and use this information to reflect on a theme or on information studied in each unit.

Supplements

These additional components help teachers teach and student learn to use English grammar structures accurately.

The Lesson Planner

The lesson planner facilitates teaching by providing detailed lesson plans and examples, answer keys to the Student Book and Workbook, references to all of the components, and the tapescript for the audiocassette activities. The Lesson Planner minimizes teacher preparation time by providing:

- Summary of main grammar points for the teacher
- Information for the teacher on typical student errors
- Step-by-step guidelines for every focus box, exercise, and activity
- Suggested correlations between exercises and activities in the Use Your English pages
- Suggested timing for each exercise and each lesson
- Lead-in suggestions and examples for focus boxes
- Suggestions for expansion work follow most exercises
- Balance of cognitive and communicative activities
- Explanation for the teacher of the purpose of each activity, in order to differentiate cognitive from communicative emphasis
- Occasional methodology notes to anticipate possible procedural problems.

Assessment CD-ROM with *ExamView® Pro* Test Generator

The Assessment CD-ROM allows instructors to **create customized quizzes and tests** quickly and easily from a test bank of questions. Monitoring student understanding and progress has never been easier! The answer key appears with instructor copies of each quiz or test created.

Audio Program

Audio cassettes and CDs **provide listening activities for** each unit so students can practice listening to **grammar structures.**

Workbook

Workbooks **provide additional exercises** for each grammar point presented in the student text. Also offers editing practice and questions types found on many language exams.

Web site

Features additional grammar practice activities: elt.thomson.com/grammardimensions.

Empirical and Experiential Support for the *Grammar Dimensions* Approach

Opening Task Activities

The approach to teaching grammar used in the *Grammar Dimensions* series is well-grounded empirically and experientially. The Opening Task in each unit situates the learning challenge and allows students to participate in and learn from activity right from the beginning (Greeno 2006). In addition, students don't enter the classroom as empty vessels, waiting to be filled (Sawyer 2006). By observing how students perform on the Opening Task, teachers can analyze for themselves what students know and are able to do and what they don't know or are not able to do. Teachers can thus select from each unit what is necessary for students to build on from what they already bring with them.

Consciousness-Raising Exercises and Focus Boxes

Many of the exercises in *Grammar Dimensions* are of the consciousness-raising sort, where students are invited to make observations about some aspect of the target structure. This type of activity promotes students' noticing (Schmidt 1990), an important step in acquiring the grammar structure. The Focus Boxes further encourage this noticing, this time very explicitly. Explicit formulations of the sort found in the Focus Boxes can lead to implicit acquisition with practice (DeKeyser 1998). Moreover, certain learners (those with analytic learning styles) benefit greatly from explicit treatment of grammar structures (Larsen-Freeman and Long 1991).

Productive Practice and Communicative Activities

However, noticing by itself is insufficient. In order to be able to use the grammar structure, students need productive practice (Gatbonton and Segalowitz 1988; Larsen-Freeman 2003). Therefore, many of the exercises in ***Grammar Dimensions*** are of the output practice sort. Furthermore, each unit ends with communicative activities, where attention to the grammar is once again implicit, but where students can use the grammar structure in "psychologically authentic" or meaningful ways. Psychological authenticity is very important in order for students to be able to transfer what they know to new situations so that they can use it for their own purposes (Blaxton 1989) and so they are not left to contend with the "inert knowledge problem," (Whitehead 1929) where they know about the grammar, but can't use it.

The Three Dimensions of Grammar: Form, Meaning, and Use

Finally, applied linguistics research (Celce-Murcia and Larsen-Freeman 1999) supports the fundamental premise underlying ***Grammar Dimensions:*** that knowing a grammar structure means being able to use it accurately, meaningfully, and appropriately. Form focus or meaning focus by itself is insufficient (Larsen-Freeman 2001); all three dimensions—form, meaning, and use—need to be learned.

References

Blaxton, T. (1989). Investigating dissociations among memory measures: Support for a transfer-appropriate processing framework. *Journal of Experimental Psychology: Learning, Memory, and Cognition 15 (4): 657-668.*

Celce-Murcia, M. and D. Larsen-Freeman. (1999). *The grammar bbook: An ESL/EFL teacher's course.* Second Edition. Boston: Heinle & Heinle.

De Keyser, R. (1998). Beyond focus on form: Cognitive perspectives on learning and practicing second language grammar. n C. Doughty and J. Williams (eds.), *Focus on Classroom Second Language Acquisition.* Cambridge: Cambridge University Press, 42–63.

Gatbonton, E. and N. Segalowitz. (1988). Creative automatization: Principles for promoting fluency within a communicative framework. *TESOL Quarterly* 22 (3): 473–492.

Greeno, J. (2006). Learning in activity. In R. K. Sawyer (ed.), *The Cambridge handbook of learning sciences.* Cambridge: Cambridge University Press, 79–96.

Larsen-Freeman, D. (2001). Teaching grammar. In M. Celce-Murcia (ed.), *Teaching English as a Second or Foreign Language.* Third edition. Boston: Heinle & Heinle, 251–266.

Larsen-Freeman, D. (2003). *Teaching language: From grammar to grammaring.* Boston: Heinle & Heinle.

Larsen-Freeman, D. and M. Long. (1991). *An introduction to second language qcquisition research.* London: Longman.

Sawyer, R. K. (2006). Introduction: The new science of learning. In R. K. Sawyer (ed.), *The Cambridge handbook of learning sciences.* Cambridge: Cambridge University Press, 1–16.

Schmidt, R. (1990). The role of consciousness in second language learning. *Applied Linguistics* 11 (2), 129–158.

Whitehead, A. N. 1929. *The aims of education.* New York: MacMillan.

Acknowledgments from the Series Director

This fourth edition would not have come about if it had not been for the enthusiastic response of teachers and students using all the previous editions. I am very grateful for the reception ***Grammar Dimensions*** has been given.

I am also grateful for all the authors' efforts. To be a teacher, and at the same time a writer, is a difficult balance to achieve . . . so is being an innovative creator of materials, and yet, a team player. They have met these challenges exceedingly well in my opinion. Then, too, the Thomson Heinle team has been impressive. I am grateful for the leadership exercised by Jim Brown, Sherrise Roehr, and Tom Jefferies. I also appreciate all the support from Anita Raducanu, Amy Mabley, Sarah Barnicle, Laura Needham, Chrystie Hopkins, Mary Beth Hennebury, and Abigail Greshik of Pre-Press Company. Deserving special mention are Amy Lawler and Yeny Kim, who never lost the vision while they attended to the detail with good humor and professionalism.

I have also benefited from the counsel of Marianne Celce-Murcia, consultant for the first edition of this project, and my friend. Finally, I wish to thank my family members, Elliott, Brent, and Gavin, for not once asking the (negative yes-no) question that must have occurred to them countless times: "Haven't you finished yet?" As we all have discovered, this project has a life of its own and is never really finished! And, for this, I am exceedingly grateful. Happy Grammaring all!

A Special Thanks

The series director, authors, and publisher would like to thank the following reviewers whose experienced observations and thoughtful suggestions have assisted us in creating and revising ***Grammar Dimensions***.

Michelle Alvarez
University of Miami
Coral Gables, Florida

Edina Pingleton Bagley
Nassau Community College
Garden City, New York

Jane Berger
Solano Community College,
California

Mary Bottega
San Jose State University

Mary Brooks
Eastern Washington University

Christina Broucqsault
California State Polytechnic University

José Carmona
Hudson Community College

Susan Carnell
University of Texas at Arlington

Susana Christie
San Diego State University

Diana Christopher
Georgetown University

Gwendolyn Cooper
Rutgers University

Julia Correia
Henderson State University
Arkadelphia, Arkansas

Sue Cozzarelli
EF International, San Diego

Catherine Crystal
Laney College, California

Kevin Ccross
University of San Francisco

Julie Damron
Interlink at Valparaiso University, Indiana

Glen Deckert
Eastern Michigan University

Eric Dwyer
University of Texas at Austin

Nikki Ellman
Laney College
Oakland, California

Ann Eubank
Jefferson Community College

Alice Fine
UCLA Extension

Alicia Going
The English Language Study Center, Oregon

Molly Gould
University of Delaware

Maren M. Hargis
San Diego Mesa College

Penny Harrold
Universidad de Monterrey
Monterrey, Mexico

Robin Hendrickson
Riverside City College
Riverside, California

Mary Herbert
University of California, Davis Extension

Jane Hilbert
ELS Language Center, Florida International University

Eli Hinkel
Xavier University

Kathy Hitchcox
International English Institute, Fresno

Abeer Hubi
Altarbia Alislamia Schools
Riyadh, Saudi Arabia

Joyce Hutchings
Georgetown University

Heather Jeddy
Northern Virginia Community College

Judi Keen
University of California, Davis, and *Sacramento City College*

Karli Kelber
American Language Institute, New York University

Anne Kornfield
LaGuardia Community College

Kay Longmire
Interlink at Valparaiso University, Indiana

Robin Longshaw
Rhode Island School of Design

Robert Ludwiczak
Texas A&M University
College Station, Texas

Bernadette McGlynn
ELS Language Center, St. Joseph's University

Billy McGowan
Aspect International, Boston

Margaret Mehran
Queens College

Richard Moore
University of Washington

Karen Moreno
Teikyo Post University, Connecticut

Gino Muzzetti
Santa Rosa Junior College, California

Mary Nance-Tager
LaGuardia Community College, City University of New York

So Nguyen
Orange Coast College
Costa Mesa, California

Karen O'Neill
San Jose State University

Mary O'Neal
Northern Virginia Community College

Nancy Pagliara
Northern Virginia Community College

Keith Pharis
Southern Illinois University

Amy Parker
ELS Language Center, San Francisco

Margene Petersen
ELS Language Center, Philadelphia

Nancy Pfingstag
University of North Carolina, Charlotte

Sally Prieto
Grand Rapids Community College

India Plough
Michigan State University

Mostafa Rahbar
University of Tennessee at Knoxville

Dudley Reynolds
Indiana University

Dzidra Rodins
DePaul University
Chicago, Illinois

Ann Salzman
University of Illinois at Urbana-Champaign

Jennifer Schmidt
San Francisco State University

Cynthia Schuemann
Miami-Dade Community College

Jennifer Schultz
Golden Gate University, California

Mary Beth Selbo
Wright College, City Colleges of Chicago

Mary Selseleh
American River College
Sacramento, California

Stephen Sheeran
Bishop's University, Lenoxville, Quebec

Kathy Sherak
San Francisco State University

Sandra E. Sklarew
Merritt Community College
Oakland, California

Keith Smith
ELS Language Center, San Francisco

Helen Solorzano
Northeastern University

Jorge Vazquez Solorzano
Bachillerato de la Reina de Mexico
S. C., Mexico, D. F., Mexico

Christina Valdez
Pasadena City College
Pasadena, California

Danielle Valentini
Oakland Community College
Farmington Hills, Michigan

Amelia Yongue
Howard Community College
Columbia, Maryland

UNIT 1

THE VERB *BE*

Affirmative Statements, Subject Pronouns

UNIT GOALS

- Use correct forms of the verb *be* in affirmative statements
- Use subject pronouns
- Use correct forms of contractions with subjects and the verb *be*
- Introduce, greet people, and say good-bye formally and informally

OPENING TASK

Introductions

STEP 1

Look at the pictures. Who are these people? Guess the information and fill in each box. Share your guesses with a partner.

An Phan

Nakiso Moyo

Jackie Veras

Young Min and Mi Jun Kim

NAME	AN PHAN	NAKISO MOYO	JACKIE VERAS	YOUNG MIN AND MI JUN KIM
Country		Zimbabwe		
Nationality	Vietnamese			
Age				
Single/Married/ Divorced			divorced	
Occupation				shopkeepers

STEP 2

Look at An's information card. Then complete the information card about yourself. Introduce yourself to the class.

INFORMATION CARD

Name: An Phan

Country: Vietnam

Nationality: Vietnamese

Age: 22 years old

Single/Married/Divorced: single

Occupation: student

INFORMATION CARD

Name: My name is ____________________.

Country: I am from ____________________.

Nationality: I'm ____________________.

Age: I'm ____________________.

Single/Married/Divorced: I'm ____________________.

Occupation: I'm ____________________.

* See Appendix 9 on page A-14 for answers to your guesses in Step 1.

form

FOCUS 1 *Be*: Affirmative Statements

SINGULAR

SUBJECT	VERB *BE*	
Jackie		from the Dominican Republic.
	is	
An		a student.

PLURAL

SUBJECT	VERB *BE*	
Young Min and Mi Jun	are	shopkeepers.
Shopkeepers		hard-working.

EXERCISE 1

Here are true statements about the people in the Opening Task. Fill in the correct form of *be* in each sentence.

1. An ________________ single.
2. Young Min and Mi Jun ________________ Korean.
3. Nakiso ________________ from Zimbabwe.
4. Jackie ________________ Dominican.
5. Young Min and Mi Jun ________________ shopkeepers.
6. An ________________ 22 years old.
7. Jackie ________________ a secretary.
8. Nakiso ________________ a Web designer.
9. Jackie ________________ 34 years old.
10. Young Min and Mi Jun ________________ both 50 years old.
11. An ________________ a student.
12. Jackie ________________ divorced.
13. Young Min and Mi Jun ________________ married.
14. Nakiso ________________ 28 years old.

EXERCISE 2

Use the world map to complete each sentence. Use the verb *be.* Write two sentences of your own. The first one has been done for you.

Continents/Regions

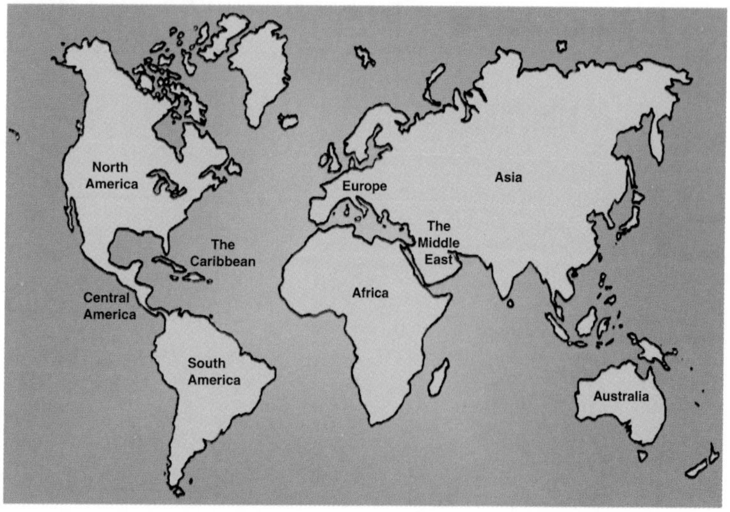

1. Japan ____is in Asia____.
2. The Dominican Republic and Haiti ________________.
3. Hungary, Slovakia, and the Czech Republic ________________.
4. Nicaragua ________________.
5. Portugal ________________.
6. Tunisia and Morocco ________________.
7. Canada ________________.
8. Bolivia, Paraguay, and Uruguay ________________.
9. Vietnam and Cambodia ________________.
10. Iran ________________.
11. Kenya and Tanzania ________________.
12. ________________.
13. ________________.

EXERCISE 3

Complete each sentence with the verb *be* and the name of a country. Write two sentences of your own.

Example: Tokyo ____is in Japan____.

1. Florence and Rome ________________.
2. Buenos Aires ________________.
3. London ________________.
4. Ho Chi Minh City ________________.
5. New Delhi ________________.
6. Melbourne and Sidney ________________.
7. ________________.
8. ________________.

form

FOCUS 2 Subject Pronouns with *Be*

SUBJECT PRONOUN	VERB *BE*	
I	am	single.
You	are	married.
He She It	is	Brazilian.
We You They	are	from Korea.

NOTE: Use subject pronouns only after you know the subject.

Chen is Chinese. He is from Shanghai.

EXERCISE 4

Read the dialogues. Fill in the blanks with a subject pronoun. The first one has been done for you.

1.

2.

3.

4.

5.

6.

EXERCISE 5

The subject pronouns in the sentences below are not correct. Circle the incorrect pronouns. Then write the correct sentences in the blanks or in your notebook.

1. Narong and Panya are from Thailand. — (You) are Southeast Asian. — They are Southeast Asian.
2. David is a teacher in the ESL program. — She is from Minnesota. — ________________.
3. You and Hamid are Algerian. — They are from Algeria. — ________________.
4. Tokyo is in Japan. — She is the capital city. — ________________.
5. Joel and I are from Montpellier. — They are from France. — ________________.
6. Ricardo and Jose Luis are from Lima. — You are Peruvian. — ________________.
7. Klara is from Prague. — He is Czech. — ________________.

form

FOCUS 3 Contraction with *Be*

SUBJECT PRONOUN + *BE*	*BE* CONTRACTIONS
I am	I'm
You are	You're
He is She is Korean. It is	He's She's from Korea. It's
We are You are They are	We're You're They're

EXERCISE 6

Information Gap. Here is a list of students in an ESL class. Work with a partner. Student A looks at List A and makes a statement about Student B on the list. Student B looks at List B on page A-15 and makes a second statement with a subject pronoun about Student 1.

Example: Student A says: *Mario is from Peru.* OR *Mario's from Peru.*

Student B says: *He is Peruvian.* OR *He's Peruvian.*

LIST A

MEN	COUNTRY	NATIONALITY
1. Mario	Peru	
2. Mohammed		Moroccan
3. Hideki and Yoshi	Japan	
4. Leonardo		Dominican
5. Oumar	Senegal	

MEN	COUNTRY	NATIONALITY
6. Lilik		Indonesian
7. Krystyna	Poland	
8. Liisa and Katja		Finnish
9. Belen	Spain	
10. Margarita and Dalia		Brazilian

11. I		
12. You		

EXERCISE 7

Make summary statements about the students in the ESL class in Exercise 6. Use the continents/regions and countries below. The first one has been done for you.

1. Africa Two students are from Africa. One is from Morocco, and one is from Senegal.
2. Asia ________________
3. Europe ________________
4. South America ________________
5. Dominican Republic ________________
6. Finland ________________

EXERCISE 8

Think about the people and places in this unit. Match the people and places on the left with the information on the right. Make two statements aloud. In the first statement, use the person's name. In the second statement, use the subject pronoun and a *be* contraction.

Example: 1. *Mi Jun is Korean.* *She's 50 years old.*

1. Mi Jun → c	a. in Vietnam/the capital
2. Dominican Republic	b. a shopkeeper/hard-working
3. Jackie	c. Korean/50 years old
4. Young Min and Mi Jun	d. an island/in the Caribbean
5. An Phan	e. Dominican/divorced
6. Seoul	f. Zimbabwean/28 years old
7. Hanoi	g. in Korea/the capital
8. Young Min	h. Vietnamese/from Ho Chi Minh City
9. Nakiso	i. married/from Korea

FOCUS 4 Using *Be* for Introductions

use

EXAMPLES	EXPLANATIONS
(a) Hello. My name's Gustavo. I'm from the Philippines.  (b) Hi! I'm Jennifer Brown. I'm from Florida. Please call me Jenny. 	Introducing yourself
(c) **Susan:** Hello, John. This is Mario Ortiz. He's from the Philippines. **John:** Hi, Mario. Nice to meet you.  **Mario:** Nice to meet you too, John.	Introducing another person
(d) **Jeff:** Hi, my name is Jeff Jones. I'm from California. What's your name?  **Alicia:** Alicia Torres. **Jeff:** Where are you from? **Alicia:** I'm from Chile. **Jeff:** Nice to meet you. **Alicia:** Pleased to meet you, too.	Meeting someone for the first time

EXERCISE 9

STEP 1 **Work in a group of four. Each person in the group introduces himself or herself to the group.**

Example: *Hello. I'm Yoshida Tokoyama. Please call me Yoshi. I'm from Japan.*

STEP 2 **Separate into two pairs. Each pair visits another pair in the class. Introduce your partner to the new pair.**

Example: A: *This is Yoshi. He's from Japan.*
B: *Nice to meet you, Yoshi.*

FOCUS 5 Greetings and Good-byes

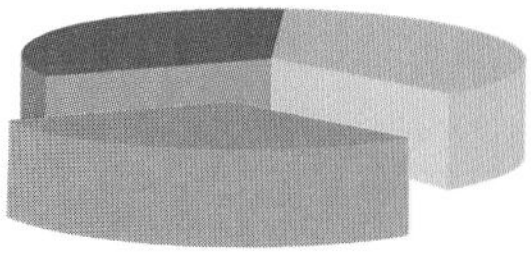

use

EXAMPLES	EXPLANATIONS
(a) **Ms. Chen:** Good morning, Mr. Silver. **Mr. Silver:** Good morning, Ms. Chen. How are you today? **Ms. Chen:** I'm fine, thank you. How are you? **Mr. Silver:** Just fine, thank you. Have a good day.  (b) **Bill:** Hello, Lautaro. How's everything? **Lautaro:** Fine, thanks. How are you? **Bill:** Great, thanks. **Lautaro:** Well, see you later. **Bill:** Take care.  (c) **Jake:** Hey, Yoshi. How're you doing? **Yoshi:** I'm OK. How about you? **Jake:** Not bad. **Yoshi:** I'm late for class. See you later. 	Greetings and good-byes can be formal or informal (very friendly). Formal ↕ Informal
(d) Hello, Ms. Smith. NOT: Hello, Ms. Susan Smith. NOT: Hello, Ms. Susan.	Use a title (*Mr., Mrs., Ms., Dr., Professor*) with a family name (last name), not with the full name, and rarely with the first name.

EXERCISE 10

STEP 1 Go back to Focus 5. Add the greetings, responses to greetings, and good-byes to the list.

GREETINGS	RESPONSES	GOOD-BYES
Good morning. How are you today?	I'm fine, thank you.	Have a good day.

STEP 2 Here are additional ways to greet, respond, and say good-bye. Add them to the correct list above.

Hi

Goodbye

Not Bad

Hey!

I'm OK.

What's up?

So Long

Bye

What's new?

I'm good

How's it going?

See you tomorrow.

Very well, thank you.

Pretty good

Take care.

STEP 3 Start a Learning Journal in a notebook. Section 1 is *Words and Expressions.* Listen to how people talk outside of class. Add the phrases from the chart above and add new phrases you hear to your Learning Journal. See Appendix 11 on page A-24 for more greetings.

EXERCISE 11

Form two parallel equal lines (A and B) in the middle of the room. Face your partner. Greet your partner and then say good-bye. Then, move to the left to face a new partner. Continue greeting and saying good-bye to your partners in new and different ways.

Example: Student A: *Hi. How are you?*
Student B: *Fine thanks. And you?*
Student A: *I'm great.*
Student B: *Take it easy!*
Student A: *Bye-bye.*

EXERCISE 12

Fill in the blanks in the conversation. Check *formal* or *informal.*

CONVERSATION 1	FORMAL	INFORMAL
Liz: Good morning, Professor Ramos.		
Prof. Ramos: ____________________, Liz. ____________________?		
Liz: I'm just fine, thank you. ____________________?		
Prof. Ramos: I'm very well, thank you. Nice to see you again.		
Liz: ____________________, too!		

CONVERSATION 2	FORMAL	INFORMAL
Peter: Hi there, Mandy. How are you doing?		
Mandy: ________________, thanks. How about you?		
Peter: ________________.		
Mandy: ________________, Pete.		
Pete: Bye-bye.		

CONVERSATION 3	FORMAL	INFORMAL
Sarah: Hey, Michele. ________________ my friend, Leo.		
Michele: ________________, Leo.		
Leo: Nice to meet you, too.		

Use Your English

ACTIVITY 1 writing/listening

On a piece of paper, write three sentences about yourself. Do not write your name on the paper. Give the paper to your teacher. Your teacher reads each paper and the class guesses who the person is.

Example: I am 22 years old. I'm from Indonesia. I'm Southeast Asian.

ACTIVITY 2 writing/speaking

STEP 1 Work in groups of 6. Make a chart like the chart below in your notebook.

NAME	COUNTRY	NATIONALITY	AGE	MALE/FEMALE	SINGLE/MARRIED/DIVORCED

STEP 2 Write summary statements about the students in your group. Report your findings to the class.

Example: Six students are Asian. One student is 18 years old.

ACTIVITY 3 speaking

Work with a partner. Choose a situation below and write a dialogue. Role-play in front of the class.

1. You are a student. Greet one of your teachers in school.
2. You are in the cafeteria at school. Greet your classmate.
3. Introduce yourself to a new person.
4. Introduce your friend to another classmate.
5. Greet a friend on the street. Say good-bye.

ACTIVITY 4 research on the web

Work with a partner. Find a picture of a person from a different country in an interesting occupation. Use the **images** search area in an Internet search engine such as Yahoo®, Google®, or Ask®. Print out the photo. Then write about the person.

Example: Enter the words *Russia* and *doctor* in a search engine. Click on the *Images* search for a photo.

This is Yuri Petrova. He's from Moscow. Moscow is in Russia. He is Russian. He's a doctor. He's 37 years old. He's married.

ACTIVITY 5 listening

CD Track 1

STEP 1 Listen to the conversations. Decide with your classmates if speakers in conversations 1, 2, and 3 use appropriate or inappropriate language.

STEP 2 Listen to the conversations again. Fill in the blanks.

1. **Paul:** Hey, Mike. ________ ________ ________?
   Mike: Not bad. ________ ________ ________, Paul?
   Paul: Oh, ________ ________. Listen, I have class right now. ________ ________ ________.
   Mike: ________ ________.
2. **Ms. Jones:** Good morning, Marie. I'm Ms. Jones. ________ ________ ________ ________.
   Marie: ________, Sally. ________ ________?
3. **Daughter:** Mom, Dad, this is my friend, Scott, from school . . .
   Parents: ________ ________ ________ ________, Scott.
   Scott: Yeah, thanks.

ACTIVITY 6 reflection

People often use gestures when they introduce themselves. In the United States, what gestures do people use? What gestures do people use in your country?

UNIT 2

THE VERB *BE*

Yes/No Questions, *Be* + Adjective, Negative Statements

UNIT GOALS

- Ask *yes/no* questions with the verb *be* and give short answers
- Use the verb *be* with adjectives
- Make negative statements and contractions with *be*

OPENING TASK

Asking Personal Questions

STEP 1

Here are some advertisements from the newspaper. Match each advertisement to the correct advertisers on the next page.

a.

b.

c.

d.

e.

f.

1. Dr. Sigmund, Psychologist ________
2. Success Employment Agency ________
3. Better Body Health Club ________
4. Fast Food Express ________
5. Cool School of English ________
6. Perfect Match Dating Service ________

STEP 2

Use the picture to create an advertisement for a cleaning company. Write the advertisement text and give the company a name.

____

____

____

____

____

____

____

____

form

FOCUS 1 *Be: Yes/No* Questions and Short Answers

YES/NO QUESTIONS	SHORT ANSWERS			
	Affirmative		Negative Contractions	
(a) Am I overweight?		you are.		you aren't. you're not.
(b) Are you worried?		I am.		I'm not.
(c) Is he/she lonely?		he/she is.		he/she isn't. he's/she's not.
(d) Is English hard?	Yes,	it is.	No,	it isn't. it's not.
(e) Are we out of shape?		you are.		you aren't. you're not.
(f) Are you single?		we are.		we aren't. we're not.
(g) Are verbs difficult?		they are.		they aren't. they're not.

Note: Do not use contractions in short answers with *yes*.

Yes, I am. NOT Yes, I'm.
Yes, he is. NOT Yes, he's.

EXERCISE 1

Ask your partner *yes/no* questions from the Opening Task on pages 14 and 15. Use short answers and contractions.

Example: **You:** *Are you single?*
Your Partner: *Yes, I am.* OR *No, I'm not.*

EXERCISE 2

Read the conversations. Fill in the blanks with a form of the verb *be* or a short answer.

1. **A:** Hello, this is the Better Body Health Club.

   B: Hello, ________________ you open on Sundays?

   A: Yes, ________________ ________________. We're open from seven in the morning until ten at night.

2. **Mitch:** Hello, my name is Mitch Brown. ________________ you Karen Jones?

   Karen: Yes, ________________ ________________.

   Mitch: I got your telephone number from the Perfect Match Dating Service. How are you, Karen?

   Karen: Fine, thanks. And you?

   Mitch: Not bad, thanks. ________________ ________________ free tonight?

   Karen: No, I'm sorry, ________________ ________________. How about tomorrow?

   Mitch: Great!

3. **A:** Hello, is this Dr. Sigmund's office?

   B: Yes, ________________ ________________.

   A: ________________ Dr. Sigmund busy? I need to speak to him.

   B: Just a minute, please.

4. **Secretary:** Cool School of English. May I help you?

   Hui Chen: Yes, I'd like some information about your classes, please.

   Secretary: What would you like to know?

   Hui Chen: ________________ the classes big?

   Secretary: No, ________________ ________________. We have only ten students in a class.

   Hui Chen: ________________ the teachers good?

   Secretary: Yes, ________________ ________________. All the teachers are excellent.

   Hui Chen: ________________ the tuition expensive?

   Secretary: No, ________________ ________________. It's only $800 for ten weeks.

   Hui Chen: O.K. Thank you very much.

   Secretary: You're welcome. Good-bye.

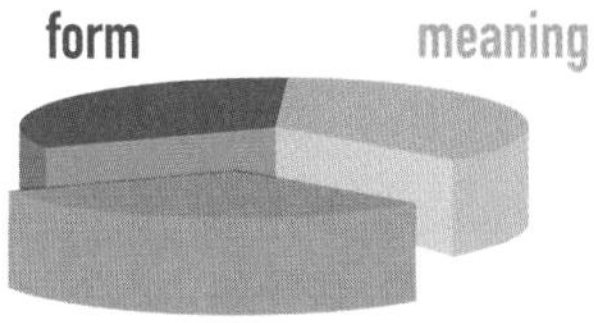

FOCUS 2 *Be* + Adjective

EXAMPLES	EXPLANATIONS
(a) Dr. Sigmund is **busy**. (b) The health club is **open**. (c) Verbs are **difficult**.	An adjective describes a person, place, or thing. Adjectives can come after a form of the verb *be*.
(d) They are **excellent**. (e) NOT: They are excellents.	Do not put "s" on the adjective when the subject is plural (more than one).
(f) The teachers are **very good**.	*Very* makes the adjective stronger. *Very* can come before most adjectives.

EXERCISE 3

Go back to the Opening Task on pages 14 and 15. Circle all the adjectives.

Example: Are you *single?*

EXERCISE 4

Information Gap. Work with a partner. Student 1 looks at two pictures: A and B on page 19. Student 2 has one picture on page A-16. Student 1 asks Student 2 a question about his/her picture using the adjective in parentheses. Which picture does your partner have: A or B? You circle the correct picture. Use the box of Opposites on this page to help you, if necessary.

Example: You look at pictures A and B. You look at the adjective.

Picture A	Picture B	Adjective
		(young)

You say: Is he young?
Your partner says: No, he isn't. He's old.
(You circle Picture A.)

OPPOSITES			
messy	sick	hardworking	happy
old ✔	strong	overweight	rich

	Picture A	Picture B	Adjective
1.			(thin)
2.	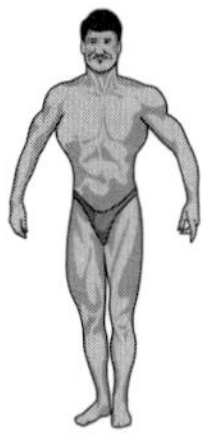		(weak)
3.			(neat)
4.			(healthy)
5.			(poor)
6.			(lazy)
7.			(sad)

EXERCISE 5

Stand up and walk around the room. Ask a classmate a question with the information in block #1. If the answer is *yes*, write the student's name in the square and move to another student. If the answer is *no*, ask a different question. Try to fill in the squares with different names.

Example: You: *Are you left-handed?*
Your classmate Carlos: *Yes, I am.*
(You write *Carlos* in block #1.)

1. ________________ is left-handed.	5. ________________ is energetic.	9. ________________ is serious.
2. ________________ is romantic.	6. ________________ is homesick.	10. ________________ is married.
3. ________________ is shy.	7. ________________ is healthy.	11. ________________ is athletic.
4. ________________ is talkative.	8. ________________ is stressed.	12. ________________ is nearsighted.

EXERCISE 6

Mark Heller is single and lonely. He wants a girlfriend. He puts this advertisement in the newspaper. Fill in the blanks with the subject pronoun and the correct form of the verb *be.* Use contractions where possible.

(1) I'm/I am 28 years old. (2) __________ 6' 2" tall. (3) __________ single. (4) __________ handsome and athletic. (5) __________ romantic. (6) __________ you under 30? (7) __________ you in good shape? (8) __________ you outgoing? (9) __________ you ready for a serious relationship? Then call me: (718) 555-7954.

EXERCISE 7

Ask a partner questions using the adjectives below.

funny	hardworking	neat
stubborn	messy	energetic
responsible	strong	serious
shy	optimistic	honest
outgoing	happy	friendly

Example: **You:** *Are you funny?*
Your Partner: *Yes, I am.* OR *No, I'm not.*

EXERCISE 8

What do you **like** about your partner? Write five statements.

Examples: My partner is great.
He's funny. He's energetic.

1. ______________________________
____

2. ______________________________
____

3. ______________________________
____

4. ______________________________
____

5. ______________________________
____

FOCUS 3 *Be*: Negative Statements and Contractions

NEGATIVE STATEMENT	CONTRACTION OF [SUBJECT + *BE*] + NOT	CONTRACTION OF [*BE* + NOT]
I am not shy.	I'm not shy.	—
You are not old.	You're not old.	You aren't old.
He / She / It } is not ready.	He's / She's / It's } not ready.	He / She / It } isn't ready.
We / You / They } are not nervous.	We're / You're / They're } not nervous.	We / You / They } aren't nervous.

Note: The contraction of [subject + *be*] followed by *not* (*he's not*) makes a negative statement stronger than a negative contraction of [*be* + not] (*he isn't*).

Example: **Teacher A:** Yoshi's very talkative in my class.
Teacher B: He's **not** talkative in my class. He's quiet.

EXERCISE 9

Read the statements below each identification card (ID card). If the information is correct, say, "That's right." If the information is not correct, make a negative statement with the *be* contraction + *not* and a correct affirmative statement. The first one is done for you.

Example: 1. *His last name is Yu-ho.*
You say: *His last name's not Yu-ho. It's Oh.*

Last Name:	Oh
First Name:	Yu-ho
Country:	Taiwan
Nationality:	Taiwanese
Age:	23
Marital Status:	single

1. His last name is Yu-ho.
2. He is Korean.
3. He's 25.
4. He's single.

Last Name:	*Ryperman*
First Name:	*Aline*
Country:	*Holland*
Nationality:	*Dutch*
Age:	*32*
Marital Status:	*married*

5. Her first name is Alice.
6. She's from Germany.
7. She is Dutch.
8. She's 52.

Last Name:	Mafegna
First Name:	Abiy
Country:	Ethiopia
Nationality:	Ethiopian
Age:	30
Marital Status:	single

9. His first name is Mafegna.
10. He's Indian.
11. He's 30.
12. He's married.

Last Name:	*Shram*
First Name:	*Jehad*
Country:	*Lebanon*
Nationality:	*Lebanese*
Age:	*27*
Marital Status:	*single*

13. Jehad is Jordanian.
14. He's from Lebanon.
15. He is 29.
16. He's single.

EXERCISE 10

Complete each dialogue with an affirmative or a negative statement and an adjective from the list below.

Adjectives:

delicious	lazy	ugly	beautiful	smart

1.

Ann: I'm short. I (a) ________________ fat.

I (b) ________________ ugly.

Marilyn: No, you (c) ________________.

You (d) ________________, Ann!

2.

Woman: This dinner is terrible! I'm sorry.

Guest: No, it (a) ________________.

It's (b) ________________!

3.

Mike: Sam, I (a) ________________ nervous about this test.

I (b) ________________ stupid, Sam!

Sam: No, you (c) ________________, Mike.

You (d) ________________! Your average is 98!

4.

Mother: My children are very hardworking.

Teacher: No, they ________________.

They're ________________.

5.

Salesperson: That dress is perfect on you.

Customer: Perfect? Oh no, it

(a) ________________.

It (b) ________________.

Use Your English

ACTIVITY 1 speaking

■ **STEP 1** Face reading is an old Chinese art. Faces tell about people's personalities. Read the descriptions of the five personalities. Circle all the adjectives.

Fire Water Earth Gold Wood

a. The **Fire** face is narrow at the forehead. The fire personality is outgoing, exciting, and interesting.

b. The **Water** face is round. Water people are smart, funny, and interesting.

c. The **Earth** face is square. The ears, mouth, and nose are large. The Earth person is strong, stubborn, active, and aggressive.

d. The **Gold** face is oblong. For the Chinese, the gold face is perfect. The eyes are beautiful. The people are very nice. They are lucky and successful.

e. The **Wood** face is a triangle. The forehead is high. The ears and nose are long. The wood personality is honest, curious, and wise.

■ **STEP 2** Work with a partner. Identify your face types. Are the descriptions true for your partner? Ask your partner questions. Then report your partner's answers to the class.

Example: *My partner's face type is FIRE. Fire people are outgoing. They are interesting. My partner is interesting. He's not outgoing. He's shy.*

ACTIVITY 2 speaking/writing

STEP 1 In Column A, check (✔) all the adjectives that describe you. Add more adjectives if you want to.

ADJECTIVE	COLUMN A: YOU	COLUMN B: YOUR PARTNER	ADJECTIVE	COLUMN A: YOU	COLUMN B: YOUR PARTNER
curious	❑	❑	funny	❑	❑
quiet	❑	❑	patient	❑	❑
talkative	❑	❑	messy	❑	❑
healthy	❑	❑	neat	❑	❑
athletic	❑	❑	romantic	❑	❑
lazy	❑	❑	affectionate	❑	❑
friendly	❑	❑	stubborn	❑	❑
serious	❑	❑	generous	❑	❑

STEP 2 Ask your partner *yes/no* questions with the adjectives in the box. Check the adjectives in Column B that describe your partner.

Example: **You ask:** *Are you curious?*
Your partner answers: *Yes, I am.* OR *No, I'm not.*

STEP 3 Write about how you and your partner are similar or how you are different.

Examples:

My partner and I are similar	My partner and I are different
1. We are both athletic.	1. My partner is serious. I'm funny.

ACTIVITY 3 speaking/writing

You're looking for a new roommate. Write five *yes/no* questions to interview your classmates. Some examples are: *Are you neat? Are you responsible?* Ask your questions to three classmates. Decide who is the best roommate for you.

ACTIVITY 4 writing

Write your own personal advertisement for the newspaper, or write one for a friend who is single.

My name is ____________________

I'm ____________________ (nationality).

I'm ____________________ years old.

I'm ____________________ (adjective).

I'm ____________________ (adjective).

And I'm ____________________ (adjective).

Are you ____________________ (adjective)?

Are you ____________________ (adjective)?

PLEASE E-MAIL ME!

ACTIVITY 5 research on the web

Work with a partner. Enter the name of a newspaper in the search area of an Internet search engine such as Yahoo®, Google®, or Ask®. Search for an advertisement in this online newspaper. Then share the advertisement with your class.

Hint: Use the words *classifieds* to search for the advertisement section of an online newspaper. Choose a category (e.g., *autos, personals*). Then choose an advertisement.

ACTIVITY 6 reflection

Are you a good student? Are you hardworking or are you lazy? Are you organized or are you forgetful? Think about how you can be a better student.

UNIT

3

THE VERB *BE*

Information Questions, *It* with Time and Weather, and Prepositions of Location

UNIT GOALS

- Ask information questions with the verb *be*
- Use *it* to talk about the weather and the time
- Use prepositions of location

OPENING TASK

World Knowledge Game

Test your world knowledge. Work in groups of five. One person reads each answer aloud. The group makes the question. Use the pictures to help you.

Example: The Taj Mahal

One student reads the answer aloud: *The answer is "in India."*

The group makes the question: *Where is the Taj Mahal?*

TOPIC	ANSWER	WHAT IS THE QUESTION?
 The Great Wall	in China	____________________?
 Bono	a rock star	____________________?
 The Amazon River	a river in South America	____________________?
 The Himalayas	in India, Nepal and China	____________________?
 Independence Day	on July 4th	____________________?
 The Pyramids in Egypt	about 4,700 years old	____________________?

FOCUS 1 Information Questions With *Be*

form meaning

We use *wh*-question words (such as *who, what, when, where, why* and *how*) to ask for specific information.

QUESTION WORD	*BE*	SUBJECT	ANSWER	MEANING
What	is 's	the Amazon?	a river	THING
Where	are	the Himalayas?	in India, Nepal, and China	PLACE
Who	is 's	the lead singer of U2?	Bono	PEOPLE
How	is 's	the weather in Argentina in June?	It's cold.	CONDITION
When	is 's	Thanksgiving in the United States?	on the fourth Thursday in November	TIME
It's 9:00 P.M.* in New York. What time	is	it in San Francisco?	It's 6:00 P.M.	CLOCK TIME
How old	are	the Pyramids in Egypt?	about 4,700 years old	AGE
Why	is 's	July 4th special in the United States?	because it's Independence Day	REASON

*P.M. = afternoon, evening, night

EXERCISE 1

Fill in the blanks with one of these *wh*-question words: *what, where, how, who, when, how old, what time,* and *why.* The first has been done for you.

Questions	Answers
1. ___How old___ is the Great Wall of China?	about 2,200 years old
2. ________ are the authors of *Grammar Dimensions, Book 1?*	Victoria Badalamenti and Carolyn Henner-Stanchina
3. ________ is Morocco?	in Africa
4. ________ is the weather in the summer in Washington, D.C.?	It's hot.

Questions	Answers
5. ______________ is the capital of Belgium?	Brussels
6. ______________ is the first day of summer?	June 21st
7. It's 10 A.M.* in Boston. ______________ is it in Barcelona?	It's 4:00 P.M.
8. ______________ is Independence Day in France?	July 14th
9. ______________ are you in this class?	to learn English
10. ______________ are the Nile and the Mississippi?	rivers

*A.M. = morning

EXERCISE 2

The questions and answers are about a Romanian woman named Sanda. Fill in the blanks with an information question word and the verb *be*.

Questions	Answers
1. ________ ________ your name?	Sanda
2. ________ ________ your last name?	Curticapean
3. ________ ________ you from?	Romania
4. ________ ________ Romania?	It's in Central Europe.
5. ________ ________ the capital of Romania?	Bucharest
6. ________ ________ ________ you?	I'm 25.
7. ________ ________ your birthday?	on October 10th
8. ________ ________ you here?	to study English
9. ________ ________ the food in your country?	It's delicious.
10. ________ ________ your favorite food?	Militei. They're small grilled sausages.
11. ________ ________ the people in your country?	They're very friendly.
12. ________ ________ the weather?	It's cold in the winter and hot in the summer.
13. ________ ________ your national holiday?	December 1st
14. ________ ________ this day important to Romanians?	because it's Unification Day (Romania and Transylvania)

EXERCISE 3

Work with a partner. Ask your partner the questions from Exercise 2. (Change the country name in Questions 4 and 5.) Report your partner's answers to the class.

EXERCISE 4

Test Your Knowledge of Your Classmates

Write five questions about your classmates with the question word *who*. Then ask your partner the questions.

Example: *Who's from Asia?*
Who is 25 years old?

FOCUS 2 How to Ask Questions about English

use

When you need to ask about a word in English, you say:
What is the meaning of *crowded?*
What is the spelling of *crowded?*
What is the pronunciation of *c-r-o-w-d-e-d?*

EXERCISE 5

Read the paragraph below. Underline the words you don't know or can't pronounce. Ask your teacher or classmates questions.

Example: *What is the meaning of <u>crowded</u>?*

<u>Vancouver</u>

Vancouver is a city in Western Canada. It's on the Pacific coast. The city is magnificent. It is clean and open. It isn't crowded. Almost three-quarters of the population are of British ancestry. Other ethnic groups are the Chinese, French, Japanese, and East Indians. As a result, the food is varied and delicious. It is a wonderful place for a vacation.

FOCUS 3 Using *It* to Talk about the Weather

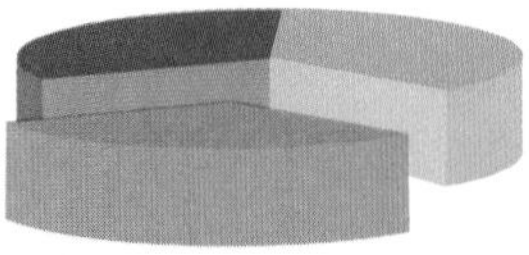

QUESTIONS	ANSWERS		
How's the weather in New York City?	It's sunny It's hot It's humid	in the	summer.
	It's cold It's snowy It's icy		winter.
	It's cloudy It's rainy It's mild		spring.
	It's windy It's cool It's damp		fall.
What's the temperature today?	It's 77 degrees Fahrenheit/25 degrees Celsius.		

EXERCISE 6

Work in groups of five. Take turns asking each other questions about the weather in each classmate's city/country in different seasons.

Examples: *When is summer in Quito? How's the weather in Quito in the summer? What is the temperature in summer? In winter?*

EXERCISE 7

Information Gap. Work with a partner. Student A looks at Map A, and Student B looks at Map B on page A-17. You each have some information about the weather in the different cities on the maps. You need more information. Ask each other questions to find out the missing information. Take turns asking questions.

Example: **You:** *How's the weather in San Francisco today?*

Your Partner: *It's sunny.*

You: *What's the temperature?*

Your Partner: *It's 65 degrees.*

MAP A

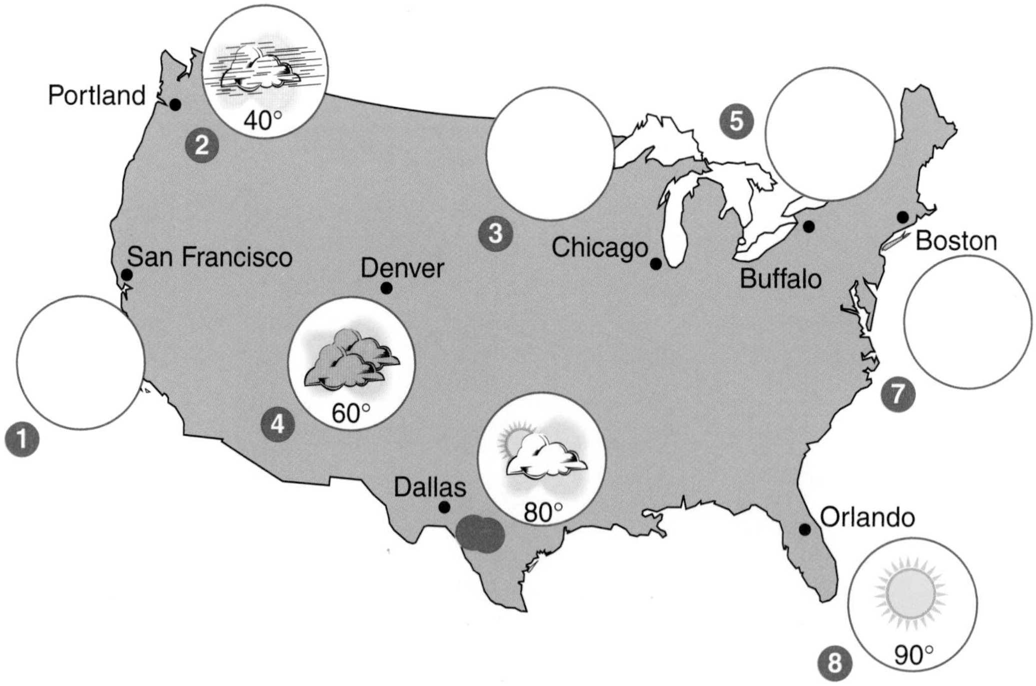

FOCUS 4 Using *It* to Talk about Time

use

WHAT TIME IS IT?		
3:00	It's three o'clock. It's three.	
3:05	It's three oh* five. It's five after three.	
3:15	It's three-fifteen. It's a quarter past three. It's a quarter after three.	
3:30	It's three-thirty. It's half past three.	
3:45	It's three forty-five. It's a quarter to four.	
3:50	It's three-fifty. It's ten to four.	
12:00	It's twelve o'clock. It's noon. (twelve P.M.) It's midnight. (twelve A.M.)	

*The word "oh" is often used to refer to the zero as in 3:05. This is spoken, not written.

EXERCISE 8

LISTEN AND DRAW

STEP 1 **Work with a partner. Student A looks at the times for numbers 1–4 on Chart B on page A-16. Student B asks, "What time is it?" Student A says the time in different ways. Student B draws the time on the clocks below.**

Example: Student B asks: *What time is it?*

Student A sees: *6:30.*

Student A says: *It's six-thirty.*

and *It's half past six.*

Student B writes:

Chart A

1. 

2. 

3. 

4. 

STEP 2 **Then switch roles with your partner. Student B looks at the times for numbers 5–8 on Chart B on page A-16. Student A asks, "What time is it?" Student B says the times. Student A draws the time on the clocks below.**

5. 

6. 

7. 

8. 

EXERCISE 9

Work with a partner. Look at the map of the time zones in the United States. Take turns asking the time and answering the questions. Make two questions of your own.

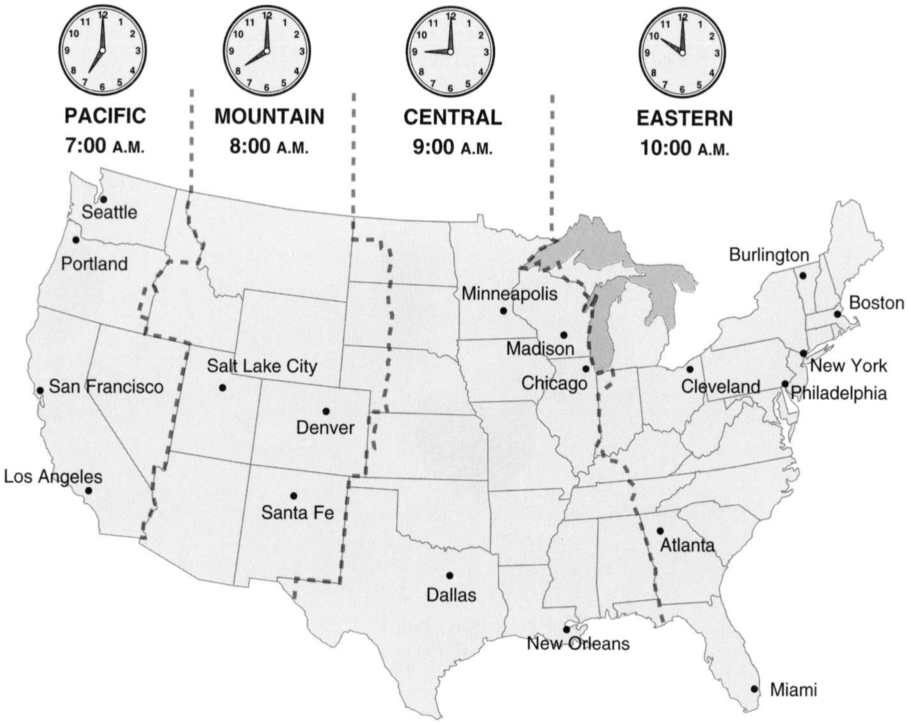

Example: It's 7:00 A.M. in San Francisco. What time is it in Philadelphia? *10 A.M.*

1. It's 10:45 P.M. in Miami. What time is it in Salt Lake City?
2. It's 6:50 P.M. in Minneapolis. What time is it in New Orleans?
3. It's 10:30 P.M. in Santa Fe. What time is it in Chicago?
4. It's 2:15 A.M. in Los Angeles. What time is it in Boston?
5. It's 9:10 A.M. in Dallas. What time is it in Portland?
6. It's 10:20 A.M. in Atlanta. What time is it in Denver?
7. It's 10:05 A.M. in Seattle. What time is it in Cleveland?
8. It's 6:00 P.M. in New York. What time is it in your hometown in your country?
9. ____?
10. ____?

FOCUS 5 Prepositions of Location

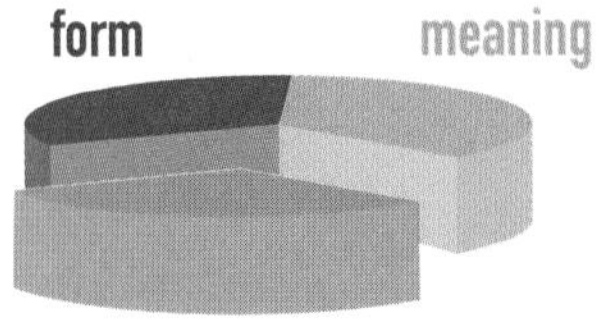

COMMON PREPOSITIONS OF LOCATION

Prepositions of location tell where something is.

(a) The ball is **on/on top of** the box.

(b) The ball is **under/underneath/ below** the box.

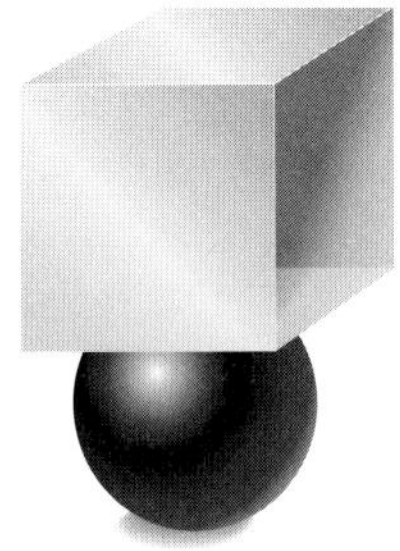

(c) The ball is **above** the box.

(d) The ball is **in front of** the box.

(e) The ball is **in back of/ behind** the box.

(f) The ball is **next to** the box.

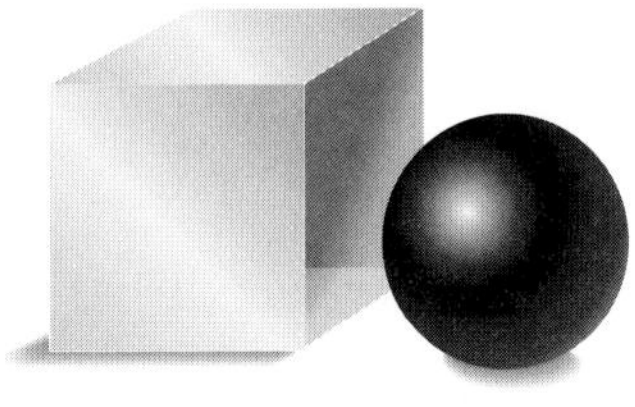

(g) The ball is **near** the box. It isn't next to the box.

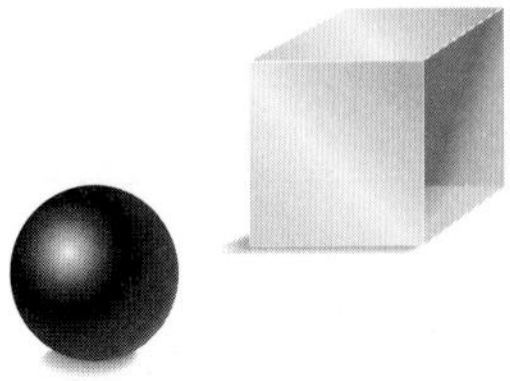

(h) The ball is **far from** the box.

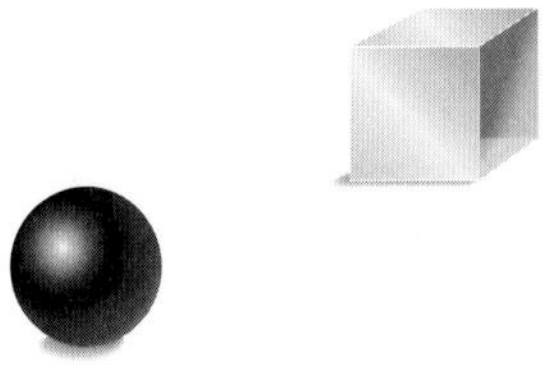

(i) The ball is **in/ inside** the box.

(j) The ball is **outside** the box.

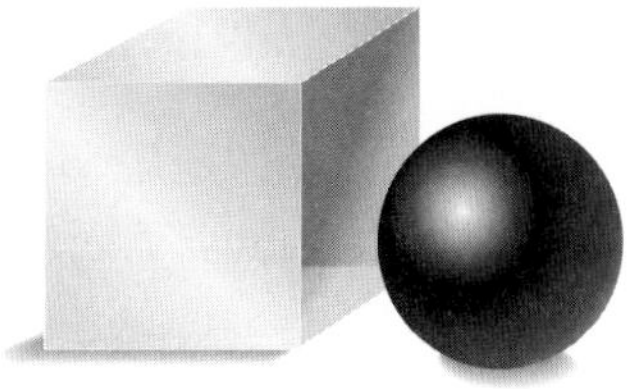

(k) The ball is **opposite/ across from** the box.

(l) The ball is **between** the two boxes.

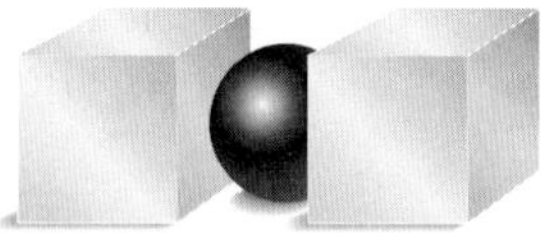

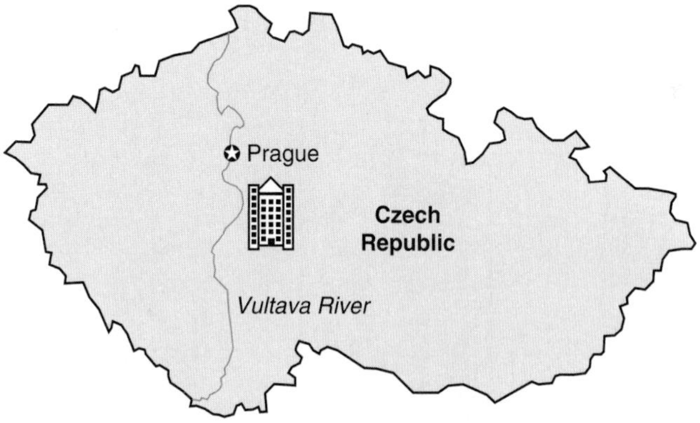

SUBJECT +	*BE* +	PREPOSITIONAL PHRASE (PREPOSITION + NOUN)
Prague	is	**in** the Czech Republic.
It	's	**on** the Vultava River.
The hotel	is	**near** the Vultava River.

EXERCISE 10

Information Gap. You are going on a trip tomorrow, but you cannot find the items 1–6 in Picture A. Your partner cannot find items 7–12 on page A-18. Ask each other questions with *where* to find the items.

Example: You ask: *Where are my sneakers?*
Your partner says: *They're under the bed.*

Picture A

1. 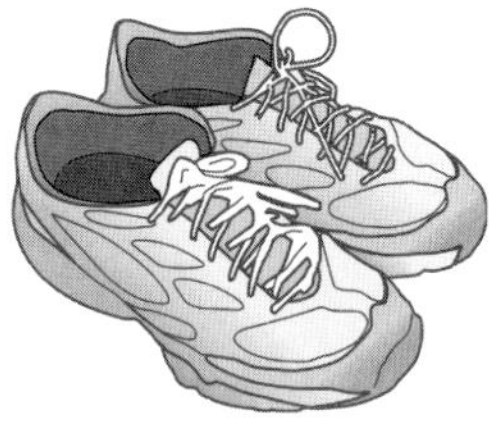
sneakers

2. 
cell phone

3. 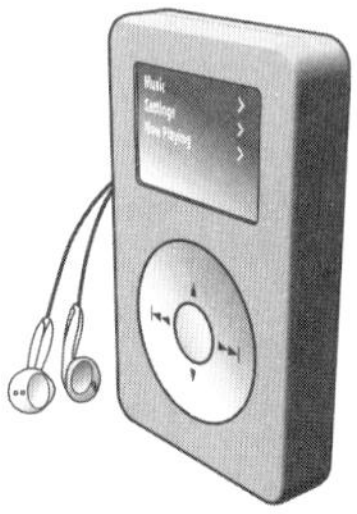
MP3 player

4. 

passports

5. 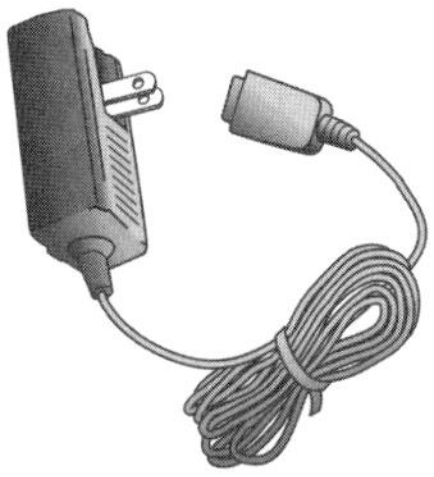
cell phone charger

6. 
digital camera

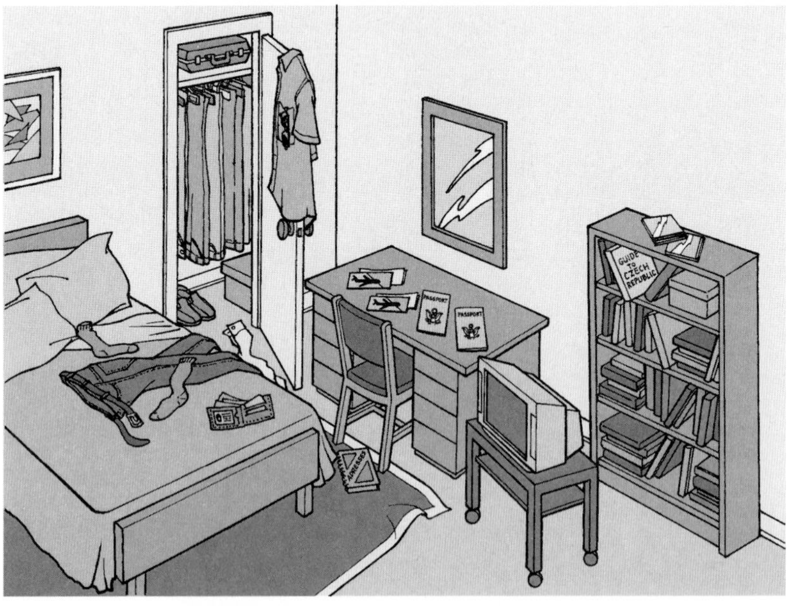

EXERCISE 11

This is a map of a neighborhood. The names of the places are missing. Read the sentences below, and write the letter of the places on the correct line. The first one has been done for you.

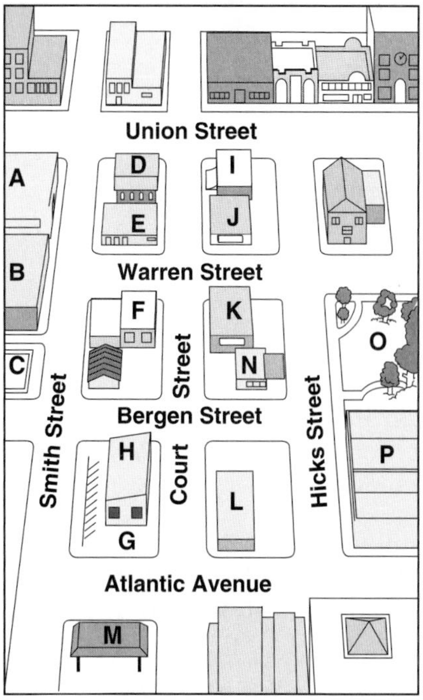

O 1. The park is on the corner of Hicks and Warren Street.

____ 2. The hospital is next to the park.

____ 3. The bank is on the southwest corner of Court Street and Union.

____ 4. The drugstore is next to the bank.

____ 5. The candy store is across the street from the drugstore on Court Street.

____ 6. The video store is near the candy store.

____ 7. The movie theater is on the west side of Court Street between Bergen and Atlantic.

____ 8. The parking lot is behind the movie theater.

____ 9. The bakery is across the street from the movie theater.

____ 10. The gas station is on the corner of Hicks and Bergen.

____ 11. The hardware store is on the southeast corner of Court Street and Warren.

____ 12. The bookstore is across from the hardware store.

____ 13. The newsstand is on the corner of Bergen and Smith Streets.

____ 14. The pet store is on the southwest corner of Union Street and Smith Street.

____ 15. The supermarket is between the pet store and the newsstand on Smith Street.

____ 16. The diner is on Atlantic Avenue.

Use Your English

ACTIVITY 1 speaking

"Test Your World Knowledge" Game
Make two teams.

STEP 1 Team 1 chooses a category and an amount of money. Team 2 asks a question with *where* or *what*. If Team 1 answers correctly, they get the money.

STEP 2 Team 2 chooses a category and an amount of money. Team 1 asks a question with *where* or *what*. If Team 2 answers correctly, they get the money. The team with the most money at the end wins.

Example: Team 1: *"Monuments" for $10.*
Team 2: *Where is the Forbidden City?*
Team 1: *It's in Beijing, the People's Republic of China.*

CATEGORIES

	Monuments	Famous Places	Countries	Rivers, Mts, Deserts	Capitals
Question	*Where is/are...?*	*Where is/ are...?*	*Where is...?*	*Where is/ are...?*	*What's the capital of...?*
$10	The Forbidden City	The Great Barrier Reef	Kabul	The Andes Mountains	The United States
$20	The Parthenon	Victoria Falls	Buenos Aires	The Gobi Desert	Chile
$30	The Kremlin	The Grand Canyon	Havana	The Ganges River	Myanmar
$40	The Eiffel Tower	The Pyramids	Athens	Mt. Everest	Finland
$50	The Statue of Liberty	Machu Picchu	New Delhi	The Mekong Delta	Morocco

*See Appendix 9 on page A-14 for answers.

ACTIVITY 2 speaking/writing

■ **STEP 1** Look at the images of people and places around the world. Identify these with a partner.

■ **STEP 2** You and your partner are researchers for a newspaper. Ask and answer questions about each photo with a partner.

Example: Who is he? *He's Bono, the lead singer of the band U2.*

Where is Kofi Anan from? *He's from Ghana.*

Note: Turn to Appendix 9, page A-15 for information on these people and places.

ACTIVITY 3 writing/speaking

Work in groups of four. Use your own world knowledge to create a quiz. Write five information questions. Each group asks their questions to the class.

Example: *Where are the Galapagos Islands?*

ACTIVITY 4 research/speaking

Find a weather map in your local newspaper. Work with a partner. Ask questions about the weather in different cities in the United States and around the world.

ACTIVITY 5 research on the web

STEP 1 Work in pairs. Choose a country that you want to visit. Use an Internet search engine such as Yahoo® or Google® or Ask® to search for information about a country.

Hint: Use the keywords *world* and *fact* to find a Web site with this information. Make a chart like this in your notebook.

COUNTRY:					
Location	Capital	Weather (Climate)	Language	Population	Currency

STEP 2 Join another pair and ask each other questions about your countries.

Example:

What is your country?	*Indonesia*
Where is Indonesia?	*In Southeast Asia*
What's the capital of Indonesia?	*Jakarta*

ACTIVITY 6 speaking

Work with a partner from another country. Teach your partner two expressions in your native language. Your partner asks you questions about the meaning, the spelling, and the pronunciation.

ACTIVITY 7 speaking/writing

Draw a map of your hometown or your home now. Describe your map to your partner. Then write down the description. Use prepositions of location.

Example: *This is my house. It's on Main Street. It's next to the drugstore. The drugstore is on the corner of Main and 1st Avenue. The supermarket is opposite the drugstore.*

ACTIVITY 8 listening

CD Track 2

Listen to the telephone conversation between Jenny and John. The phone connection is very bad. Fill in the blanks with the questions you hear.

Jenny: Hello?

John: Hi, Jenny!!! ____?

Jenny: I'm fine. ____?

John: It's John!!!

Jenny: John?? You sound so far away. ______________________________?

John: I'm in China!!

Jenny: What?? ____?

John: I'm here to study . . . in Beijing. It's really great . . . hello, hello??? Jenny, ____?

Jenny: Yes, John. I'm just really sleepy.

John: Sleepy? Why? ____?

Jenny: It's 3:00 in the morning here, John! Remember . . . the time difference!!??

John: Oh, I'm so sorry, Jenny. I'll call you back later.

Jenny: OK, good idea! Bye.

John: Bye!

ACTIVITY 9 reflection

When you study, it is helpful to have a study area. Ask a partner about his or her study area and study habits. Talk about your study area.

Example: Where is your study area? Is it quiet or noisy? What is in your study area? books? class notes? When is your study time?

UNIT 4

NOUNS

Count and Noncount Nouns, *Be* + Adjective + Noun

UNIT GOALS

- Understand the difference between count and noncount nouns
- Use the articles *a/an* with singular count nouns
- Know how to spell and pronounce regular plural nouns
- Know how to form the irregular plurals of nouns
- Ask questions with *how much*
- Make statements with *be* + adjective + noun

OPENING TASK

Supplies

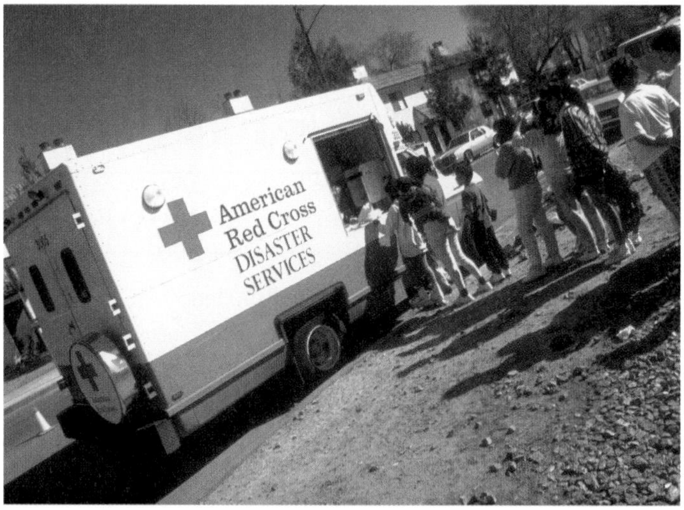

STEP 1

After a natural disaster, people give things to relief organizations such as the Red Cross. You are a relief worker. Your job is to put the items into the correct boxes. Write the name of the items on page 47 in the correct box or near the correct box below.

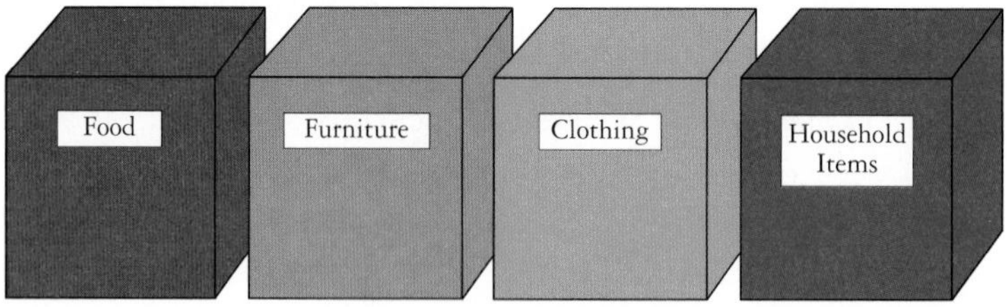

STEP 2

Now use the graphic organizer below. Study the words in each circle. Write a name for Category 1 and Category 2 on the lines inside the circle. Note: The categories are types of nouns. Add more words to the other circles.

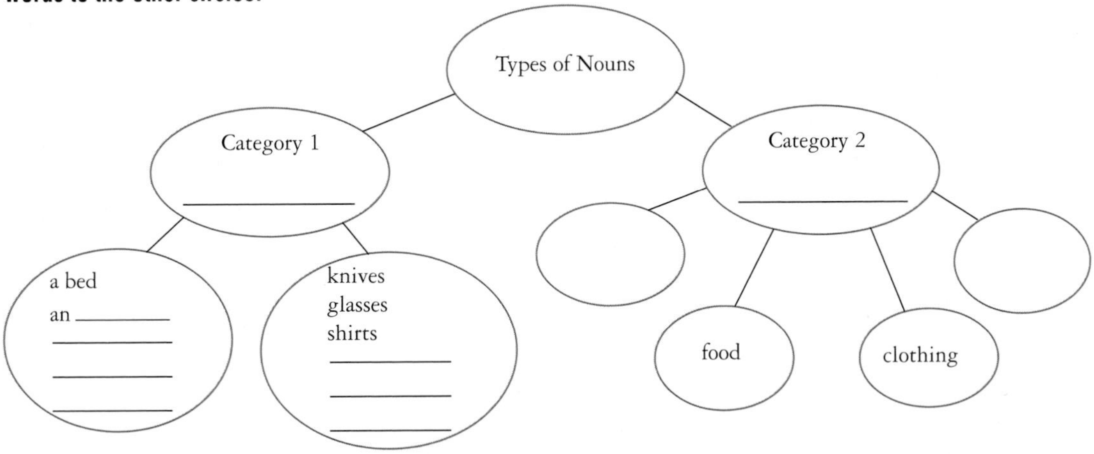

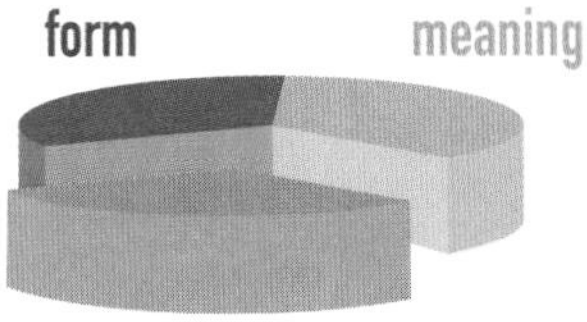

FOCUS 1 Count Nouns and Noncount Nouns

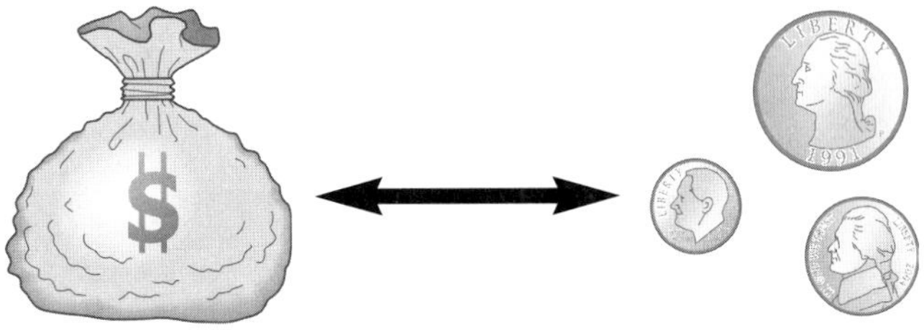
Money Coins

We can see things as whole or as separate things we can count. We use noncount nouns like *money* when we see something as whole. We use count nouns like *coins* when we refer to things we can count.

EXAMPLES			EXPLANATIONS
Count Nouns			**Things we can count**
SINGULAR	a dress	an egg	Count nouns take *a/an* in the singular. They take *–s* or *–es* in the plural.
PLURAL	dresses	eggs	
Noncount Nouns			**Things we don't count**
money clothing			Noncount nouns have one form. They are not singular or plural.

EXERCISE 1

Look at the list of words from the Opening Task. Check *count noun* or *noncount noun.*

	COUNT NOUN	NONCOUNT NOUN
jacket		
armchair		
water		
dishes		
table		
bread		
bed		
sandwiches		
furniture		
shoes		
undershirt		
glasses		
food		
clothing		
knives		

form

FOCUS 2 The Articles *a/an* with Singular Count Nouns

A/AN	EXAMPLE	EXPLANATION
A	a house a movie a uniform	Use *a* before a word beginning with a consonant sound. *Uniform* begins with a vowel but has the consonant sound of "y" as in *you*
An	an orange an egg an hour	Use *an* before a word beginning with a vowel sound. *Hour* begins with a consonant letter, but the letter is not pronounced. The first sound in this word is a vowel sound.

EXERCISE 2

Write the words from the box in the correct circle. Then, read your lists to your partner with *a* or *an.*

earring	bed	watch	necklace
screwdriver	table	apple	hammer
orange	ax	ring	desk
armchair	banana	pear	handsaw

FRUIT
orange

FURNITURE

JEWELRY

TOOLS

EXERCISE 3

For each photo, write a sentence to show the person's occupation. Use *a/an.*

Examples:

a waiter
He's a waiter.

an athlete
She's an athlete.

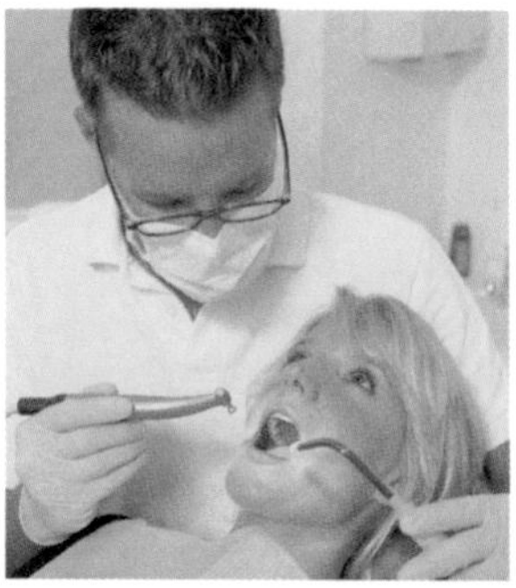

1. dentist
___

2. cashier
___

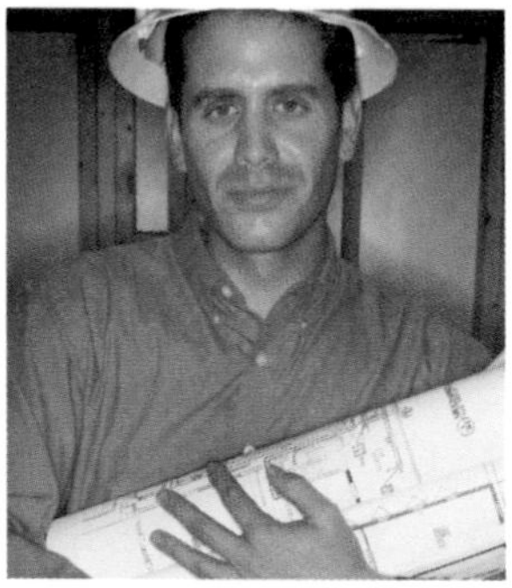

3. engineer
___

4. doctor
___

5. nurse
___

6. accountant
___

7. flight attendant ________

8. hairdresser ________

9. chef ________

10. teacher ________

EXERCISE 4

Test your knowledge. Work with a partner. Read the question on the left. One person finds the correct answer on the right and reads it using *a/an*. Take turns asking and answering questions.

Example: **You:** *What's Poland?* **Your Partner:** *(o) It's a country.*

1. What's Poland?	a. It's ______ continent.
2. What is Thanksgiving?	b. It's ______ car.
3. What is the Atlantic?	c. It's ______ hour.
4. What is Puerto Rico?	d. It's ______ clock.
5. What's the Sahara?	e. It's ______ river.
6. What is Africa?	f. It's ______ island.
7. What's New York?	g. It's ______ holiday in the United States.
8. What's the Concorde?	h. It's ______ museum.
9. What's Big Ben?	i. It's ______ university.
10. What is the Louvre?	j. It's ______ ocean.
11. What is Harvard?	k. It's ______ city.
12. What's sixty minutes?	l. It's ______ airplane.
13. What's a Mercedes?	m. It's ______language.
14. What's the Amazon?	n. It's ______ desert.
15. What's Portuguese?	o. It's ______ country.
16. What's a horse?	p. It's ______ animal.
17. What's *a* or *an*?	q. It's ______ article!

form

FOCUS 3 Spelling of Regular Plural Count Nouns

SINGULAR	PLURAL	EXPLANATIONS
(a) a car a book	two cars three books	To make the plural form of most count nouns, add *-s.*
(b) a boy a radio	our boys two radios	Nouns that end in: vowel + *y* vowel + *o* Plural form: add *-s.*
(c) a bus a class a sandwich a dish a box	two buses three classes four sandwiches five dishes six boxes	Nouns that end in: *s* *ss* *ch* *sh* *x* Plural form: add *-es.*
(d) a potato a tomato	six potatoes four tomatoes	Nouns that end in: consonant + *o* Plural form: add *-es.*
(e) a battery a city	batteries cities	Nouns that end in: consonant + *y* Plural form: change *y* to *i,* add *-es.*
(f) a knife a leaf	two knives seven leaves	Nouns that end in: *f* or *fe* Plural form: change *f* to *v,* add *-es.*
Exceptions: chief belief chef roof	 chiefs beliefs chefs roofs	

EXERCISE 5

Write the plural form of the words below.

1. party ____________
2. umbrella ____________
3. photo ____________
4. watch ____________
5. fax ____________
6. wife ____________
7. candle ____________
8. dictionary ____________
9. scarf ____________
10. glass ____________
11. month ____________
12. brush ____________
13. family ____________
14. gas ____________
15. story ____________
16. key ____________

EXERCISE 6

Complete the sentences with the verb *be* and the plural of one of the nouns in the box.

desert	city	story	gas	university	state	holiday
month	mountain	country	continent	company	ocean	river

1. Thanksgiving and Christmas ______are holidays______.
2. The Atlantic and the Pacific ____________.
3. Africa and Asia ____________.
4. Princeton and Yale ____________.
5. IBM and SONY ____________.
6. "Cinderella" and "Beauty and the Beast" ____________.
7. The Alps ____________.
8. Colombia and Venezuela ____________ in South America.
9. Colorado and Vermont ____________ in the United States.
10. Vienna and Oslo ____________ in Europe.
11. The Sahara and the Gobi ____________.
12. The Amazon and the Nile ____________.
13. Oxygen and hydrogen ____________.
14. April and October ____________.

form

FOCUS 4 Regular Plural Nouns:

Pronunciation of Final *-s* and *-es*

EXAMPLES	EXPLANATIONS
(a) beliefs, books, groups, students, months	/S/ Final *–s* is pronounced /s/ after voiceless sounds: /f/, /k/, /p/, /t/, and /th/ or /θ/
(b) cabs, beds, dogs, pills, rooms, pens, cars, leaves, radios	/Z/ Final *–s* is pronounced /z/ after voiced sounds: /b/, /d/, /g/, /l/, /m/, /n/, /r/, /v/ and vowels
(c) classes, faces exercises, quizzes dishes, wishes watches, sandwiches colleges, pages	/IZ/ Final *–es* is pronounced /iz/ after: "s" sounds "z" sounds "sh" or ʃ sounds "ch" or tʃ sounds "ge/dge" or dʒ sounds
(d) class-es college-s	The ending /IZ/ adds an extra syllable to the noun.

EXERCISE 7

Here are the "Tools of the Trade" for each occupation in Exercise 3. List the tools of the trade in the plural form under the correct occupation. Then, read your lists to your partner. Check the final pronunciation /s/, /z/, or /IZ/. One tool has done for you.

computer	dish	clip	razor	spoon
blackboard	message	bowl	~~book~~	pencil
comb	knife	brush	telephone	envelope
dictionary	oven	hairdryer	quiz	fax

	/s/	/z/	/IZ/
TEACHER			
books	✔		
SECRETARY			
CHEF			
HAIRDRESSER			

EXERCISE 8

Look at the list of common measurements. Make the measurement on the right plural. Then, read the statements aloud using the verb *equals*.

Example: 98.6 degrees Fahrenheit = 37 degree<u>s</u> Celsius.
You say: *Ninety-eight point six degrees Fahrenheit equals thirty-seven degrees Celsius.*

1. one foot = 12 inch ____
2. one pound = 16 ounce ____
3. one minute = 60 second ____
4. one hour = 60 minute ____
5. one day = 24 hour ____
6. one year = 365 day ____
7. one quart = 2 pint ____
8. one gallon = 4 quart ____
9. one inch = 2 ½ centimeter ____
10. one kilo = 2.2 pound ____

EXERCISE 9

Rhymes. Make the nouns in italics plural. Then read the rhymes aloud.

1. **On Education**

Word ____, *sentence* ____, *exercise* ____, *rule* ____,
Dictionary ____ *textbook* ____ *page* ____ , *school* ____,
Classroom ____, *teacher* ____, *student* ____, —*all jewel* ____
Of education, these are the *tool* ____

2. **On Age**

Day ____, *week* ____, *month* ____, *year* ____.

Getting old? Please, no *tear* ____!!!

3. **On Imports**

The *shoe* ____ are Brazilian,

The *glove* ____ are Italian,

The *chef* ____ are from France;

from South America—the salsa dance.

The *toy* ____ are Chinese,

The *camera* ____ are Japanese:

Tell me, what's American, please?

form

FOCUS 5 Irregular Plural Nouns

EXAMPLES		EXPLANATIONS
(a) child man woman foot tooth mouse person	children men women feet teeth mice people	Some nouns change spelling in the plural.
(b) a deer a sheep a fish	two deer three sheep four fish	Some nouns do not change in the plural. They have the same singular and plural form.
(c) scissors pajamas clothes pants/slacks/trousers/jeans/shorts glasses, eyeglasses, sunglasses		Some nouns are always plural. They have no singular form.
(d) The scissors **are** sharp. The jeans **are** expensive.		Use a plural verb with these nouns.

EXERCISE 10

STEP 1 **Work in pairs. Match each noun to the correct part of the picture by asking questions. Use *a/an* when necessary.**

Examples: *What's number 1?* *An eyebrow.*
What's number 2? *Toes.*

STEP 2 **Then label the parts of the picture, using *a/an* when necessary.**

eyebrow	sunglasses	teeth	lips	nose	ear
hand	fingers	arm	shirt	shorts	feet
toes	sandal	freckles	baseball cap	eye	hair

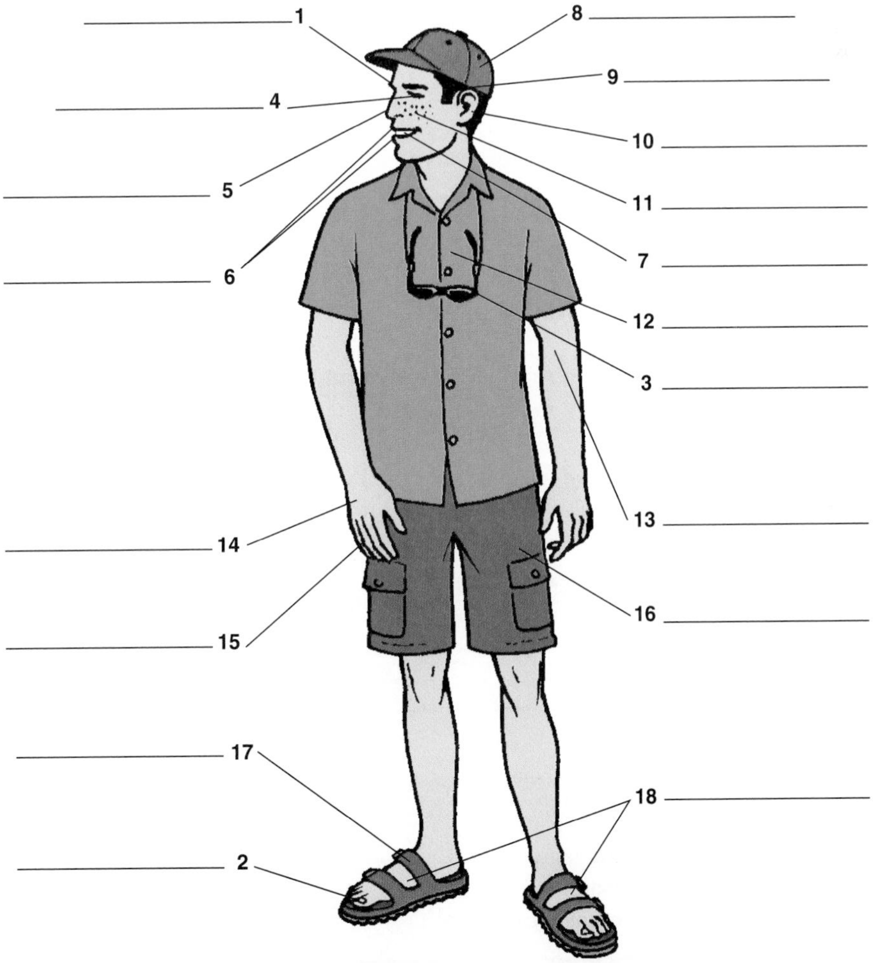

form

FOCUS 6 Count and Noncount Nouns

COUNT NOUNS . . .	NONCOUNT NOUNS . . .
Can take *a/an* or *one* in the singular. (a) It's a job. (b) I'm on vacation for one week.	Cannot take *a/an* or *one* in the singular. (c) It's work.
Can take *-s* or *-es* in the plural. (d) They are earrings. (e) They're watches.	Cannot take *-s* or *-es*. (f) It's jewelry.
Can take a singular or plural verb. (g) It **is** a table. (h) They **are** chairs.	Always takes a singular verb. (i) Furniture **is** expensive.
To ask about prices with count nouns, say (j) How much **is** a cell phone in Japan? (singular) (k) How much **are** newspapers in Russia? (plural)	To ask about prices with noncount nouns, say (l) How much **is** gas in Italy? Some noncount nouns end in *-s*, but they also take singular verbs. The **news is** important. **Mathematics is** an interesting subject.

Some Common Noncount Nouns

SUBSTANCES/ MATERIAL		FOOD		LIQUIDS	SCHOOL SUBJECTS	ACTIVITIES
cotton		bread	bacon	coffee	biology	aerobics
glass	air	cheese		juice	economics	baseball
gold	silver	chocolate		milk	history	chess
oxygen		fish		oil	mathematics	homework
paper		fruit		soup	music	housework
plastic		rice		tea	politics	soccer
wood		salt		water	psychology	work

WHOLE WITH INDIVIDUAL PARTS			ABSTRACT NOUNS				
clothing	garbage	luggage	advice	fun	help	love	pollution
food	traffic	mail	beauty	happiness	information	news	truth
furniture	jewelry	money (cash)	crime	health	knowledge	peace	

EXERCISE 11

Oswaldo is an international student arriving in Wisconsin with his wife. Read his conversations. Check *count* or *noncount* for each underlined noun.

	COUNT	NONCOUNT
1. Oswaldo is at the airport with his wife.		
Oswaldo: a. It's cold in Wisconsin. I need warm clothing.	a. ______	______
b. Where's my coat?	b. ______	______
Paola: c. It's in the black suitcase.	c. ______	______
Oswaldo: d. Where is the luggage?	d. ______	______
Paola: e. It's still on the plane!	e. ______	______
2. Oswaldo is at the University of Wisconsin.		
Secretary: a. Oswaldo, here are three letters for you.	a. ______	______
Oswaldo: b. Thanks. Mail from home is important to me.	b. ______	______
3. Oswaldo is with an American student.		
Oswaldo: a. How's the food in the cafeteria?	a. ______	______
Student: b. The vegetables are good.	b. ______	______
c. The fruit is fresh.	c. ______	______
d. The meat is terrible.	d. ______	______
4. Oswaldo is with his new American teacher.		
Oswaldo: a. This is a lot of homework for the first day.	a. ______	______
Teacher: b. The exercises are easy. Don't worry!	b. ______	______
5. Oswaldo is with his wife at home.		
Oswaldo: a. I need some cash.	a. ______	______
Wife: b. Here's twenty dollars.	b. ______	______

EXERCISE 12

Work with a partner. Use the words to ask questions about your partner's country. Change roles.

Example: hamburgers/popular/in....?
You: *Are hamburgers popular in Italy?*
Your partner: *Yes, they are.* OR *No, they aren't.*

1. pizza/popular/in....?
2. fruit/cheap/in...?
3. cars/big/in...?
4. electricity/cheap/in...?
5. American music/popular/in...?
6. college tuition/expensive/in...?
7. rent/expensive/in...?
8. families/big/in...?
9. taxes/high/in...?
10. public transportation/good/in...?

FOCUS 7 Questions with *How Much*

use

COUNT NOUNS		NONCOUNT NOUNS
To ask about prices with count nouns say,		To ask about prices with noncount nouns say,
(a) How much **is** a television set in Taiwan?	SINGULAR	(c) How much **is** gas in Italy?
(b) How much **are** jeans in Russia?	PLURAL	

EXERCISE 13

STEP 1 **Write the price of the following items in your country.**

STEP 2 **Work with a partner. Ask questions about the price of the items in your partner's country. Add two items of your own.**

Example: How much is gas in your country?

ITEMS	PRICE IN YOUR COUNTRY:	PRICE IN YOUR PARTNER'S COUNTRY:
gas	__________	__________
a bus/train ride	__________	__________
a movie ticket	__________	__________
coffee	__________	__________
a daily newspaper	__________	__________
a month's rent	__________	__________
eyeglasses	__________	__________
a cell phone	__________	__________
a CD (compact disc)	__________	__________
jeans	__________	__________
1. (other)	__________	__________
2. (other)	__________	__________

form

FOCUS 8 *Be* + Adjective + Noun

EXAMPLES	EXPLANATIONS
(a) Princeton and Yale are **private** universities.	An adjective can come before the noun.
(b) They are **excellent** colleges.	Do not put *-s* on the adjective when the noun is plural.
(c) It's **a** large university. (d) English is **a** universal language.	Use *a* before an adjective with a consonant or a consonant sound.
(e) He's **an** "A" student. (f) She's **an** honor student.	Use *an* before an adjective with a vowel sound.
(g) Psychology is a **very** interesting subject.	Put *very* before most adjectives to make the adjectives stronger.

EXERCISE 14

Tour the United States. Choose an adjective from the box. Make sentences using *be + adjective + noun*. You can also use *very*. Remember: you can use an adjective more than once.

beautiful	exciting	spectacular	famous
small	crowded	expensive	tall
huge	popular	long	important
historic	international		

Example: Disneyworld __is a very popular__ place in Florida.

1. The United Nations ________________ organization in New York City.
2. The Golden Gate ________________ bridge in San Francisco.
3. The Keys ________________ islands off the coast of Florida.
4. The Mississippi ________________ river flowing from Minnesota to the Gulf of Mexico.
5. Bryce and Zion ________________ national parks in Utah.
6. Niagara Falls ________________ waterfall between the United States and Canada.
7. The Lincoln Memorial ________________ monument in Washington, D.C.
8. Alaska and Hawaii ________________ vacation spots in the United States.
9. Philadelphia, Pennsylvania, ________________ place to visit.

Use Your English

ACTIVITY 1 writing/speaking

Categorizing Game

STEP 1 Get into two teams. Copy these categories as a chart in your notebook.

Part of the Body	Things You Put on Food	Things in a Big City	Things You Need When You Travel	Things in a Woman's Handbag

STEP 2 Write the words in the box under the correct category. Then, next to each word, write *C* for count nouns and *NC* for noncount nouns.

salt	ears	keys	skyscraper	luggage
money	traffic	passport	teeth	sugar
pickles	wallet	noise	toes	pen
makeup	nose	time	pollution	hair
matches	theater	map	cell phone	eyes
butter	crime	cheese	ketchup	ticket

STEP 3 Each correct answer is one point. The team with the most points wins. Find the winning team.

ACTIVITY 2 speaking

Plan a party for the class. Get into small groups. Each group plans what they are going to bring to the party under the following categories:

FOOD DRINKS PAPER GOODS ENTERTAINMENT

Compare your plans with the other groups' plans. Which one is the best plan?

ACTIVITY 3 research on web

Search the Internet for restaurant menus. Enter the name of a restaurant you know in the search area of an Internet search engine such as Yahoo®, Google®, or Ask®. OR enter the word "restaurant menu" and the name of your city. Print out the menu. Find ten count nouns and ten noncount nouns on the menu. In your *Learning Journal,* make a section called "Nouns: Count/Noncount." Organize the words in this section.

ACTIVITY 4 listening/speaking

CD Track 3

STEP 1 Listen to what kind of pizza the woman orders.

STEP 2 Check (✔) what the woman wants on the pizza. Then write *C* for count nouns and *NC* for noncount nouns.

☐ cheese ____	☐ pepperoni ____	☐ peppers ____	☐ tomatoes ____
☐ olives ____	☐ mushrooms ____	☐ onions ____	☐ anchovies ____

STEP 3 Role-play: Ask a classmate about his or her favorite pizza, then telephone the pizza store to order it.

ACTIVITY 5 reflection

It is difficult to remember new vocabulary words. In this Unit, you see different *strategies* to help you remember new words. For example:

1. Use *graphic organizers* to group new words in categories. The Opening Task, Step 2, Exercise 2, Exercise 7, and Activity 1use graphic organizers.
2. Draw pictures and label them with the new words as in Exercise 10.

In your Learning Journal, organize the new words in this Unit using one of these two strategies, or another strategy you use to remember new vocabulary. Discuss why you like that strategy with your classmates.

UNIT

5

THE VERB *HAVE*

Affirmative and Negative Statements, Questions and Short Answers, *Some/Any*

UNIT GOALS

- Make affirmative statements with the verb *have*
- Make negative statements with *do*
- Ask *yes/no* questions with *do* and give short answers
- Use *some/any*
- Ask for something politely
- Use the verb *have* to describe people

OPENING TASK

Modern and Traditional Lifestyles

STEP 1

Look at the photographs of two Inuit women in North Canada and at the chart on the next page. Check (✔) and say the things you think Mary has. Check and say the things you think Nilaulaq (Nila) and her husband have.

Mary

Nilaulaq

Mary's son

Napachee

	MARY	NILAULAQ (NILA) AND HER HUSBAND, NAPACHEE
1. a house		
2. an Inuit name		
3. Inuit clothing		
4. dogs		
5. furniture		
6. electricity		
7. fresh fish		
8. a bed		
9. a tent		
10. canned food		

STEP 2

Talk to your partner about the photographs. Who has a traditional lifestyle? Who has a modern lifestyle? Say why.

1. ______________________________ a traditional lifestyle.
2. ______________________________ a modern lifestyle.

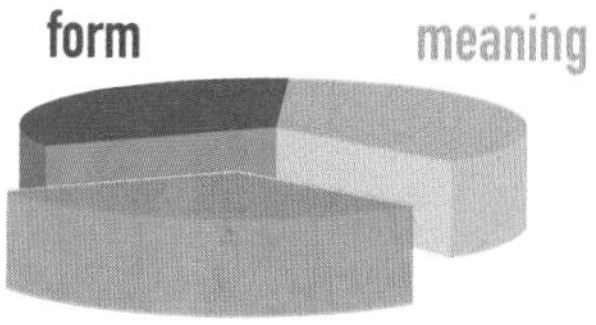

FOCUS 1 *Have* and *Has*: Affirmative Statements

The verb *have* means to own or possess.

SUBJECT	VERB	
I You	**have**	a telephone.
He She It Mary	**has**	a clock.
We You They Nila and Napachee	**have**	children.

EXERCISE 1

Fill in the blanks about Nilaulaq and Mary with *have* or *has*. Read the sentences aloud.

A. Nilaulaq _____has_____ an Inuit name. She is married. Her husband, Napachee, _______________ an Inuit name, too. They _______________ two children. They _______________ two dogs. Nilaulaq is proud. She says, "I _______________ a beautiful family."

B. Mary _______________ wallpaper in her house. Mary _______________ a clock. She _______________ photographs and a map. She _______________ furniture. She _______________ canned food on the shelf.

C. Modern Inuit people live in towns. The towns _______________ stores. Modern Inuit people _______________ jobs. They _______________ money.

form

FOCUS 2 *Have*: Negative Statements and Contractions

SUBJECT	*DO/DOES*	BASE FORM OF VERB	
I You We They Nilaulaq and her husband	do not (don't)	have	a telephone.
He She It Nilaulaq	does not (doesn't)		

EXERCISE 2

What are some differences between traditional and modern families? Write a paragraph about traditional families and a paragraph about modern families. Start each paragraph with the topic sentences below. Then write sentences with *has/have* or *doesn't have/don't have.* Add these sentences to the topic sentences to write a paragraph.

Topic Sentence 1: *Traditional* families are big.

1. They ________________ a mother and a father.
2. They ________________ many children.
3. They often ________________ grandparents living with them.
4. They sometimes ________________ other relatives living with them.
5. In a traditional family, only the father ________________ a job.
6. The mother ________________ a job outside the home.
7. The children ________________ a babysitter.

Topic Sentence 2: *Modern* families are different.

8. Sometimes they ________________ only two people.
9. Sometimes the parents ________________ one or two children.
10. Sometimes they ________________ children.
11. Sometimes the children ________________ only one parent.
12. Sometimes the father ________________ the main responsibility for the children.
13. Sometimes the children ________________ a babysitter.

Now make one sentence of your own about traditional families and one sentence about modern families.

14. ____
15. ____

form

FOCUS 3 *Have: Yes/No* Questions and Short Answers

YES/NO QUESTIONS

Do/Does	*Subject*	*Have*	
Do	I you we they Nilaulaq and Napachee	have	a television?
Does	he she it Mary		

AFFIRMATIVE SHORT ANSWERS

Yes,	I you we they	do.
	he she it	does.

NEGATIVE SHORT ANSWERS

No,	I you we they	do not. (don't)
	he she it	does not. (doesn't)

EXERCISE 3

STEP 1 **Work with a partner. Try to "predict" the answers to the questions in the chart on page 69 by looking at the pictures. Write questions with *have* using the information in the first column. Answer your own and your partner's questions.**

Horse and carriage in Lancaster, Pennsylvania

Daniel

An Amish family

John Lapp

INFORMATION	QUESTION	MY PREDICTION
Example: An Amish man/car	*Does an Amish man have a car?*	*No, he doesn't.*
1. Amish people/a simple way of life		
2. Amish women/jewelry		
3. An Amish home/electricity		
4. An Amish farmer/horses		
5. An Amish home/telephone		
6. Amish people/their own language		
7. An Amish child/computer		
8. Amish people/colorful clothing		
9. An Amish home/television		
10. Amish children/Amish teachers		
11. Amish children/classes after 8th grade		
12. Amish people/a modern lifestyle		

STEP 2 **Read the text below about the Amish. Check your answers to the questions you wrote.**

The Amish

The Amish are a special group of Americans. There are about 85,000 Amish people in the United States. Many of the Amish live on farmland in the state of Pennsylvania. They have a simple way of life. For religious reasons, their lifestyle is different from most Americans. They have their own language called Pennsylvania Dutch. It is like German.

The Amish are farmers, but they don't have machines on their farms. They have horses. They do not have electricity or telephones in their homes. They don't have photographs or musical instruments.

The Amish are called "the plain people." They wear dark clothing. The clothing doesn't have buttons. The men all have beards and wear hats. The women wear long dresses and hats.

Amish children have one-room schoolhouses. They have Amish teachers. They have no school after the eighth grade. Some children have a problem with this and leave the community.

The Amish have a very traditional lifestyle. Their community is very close.

EXERCISE 4

Work with a partner. Look back at the photographs in the Opening Task on pages 64 and 65. Take turns asking and answering questions about the Inuit people. Use short answers. You can also answer "I don't know."

Example: You: *Does Mary have a house?*
Your partner: *Yes, she does.*

1. Mary/children
2. Nila/bed
3. Napachee/boat
4. Mary/wallpaper in her house
5. Nila/furniture
6. Mary/an Inuit name
7. Nila's children/Inuit clothing
8. Nila/a television set
9. Mary/canned food
10. Nila/dogs

EXERCISE 5

Find someone who has. . .

Ask your classmates if they have the things on the list below. Write the names of the students who say *yes.*

Example: *Do you have a cell phone?*
Yes, I do. OR *No, I don't.*

Things	Students' Names
1. a cell phone	________________
2. a pet	________________
3. a car	________________
4. children	________________
5. relatives in this country	________________
6. a job	________________
7. English-speaking friends	________________
8. a bicycle	________________
9. a driver's license	________________
10. a DVD player	________________
11. an MP3 player	________________
12. a digital camera	________________

form

FOCUS 4 Some/Any

EXAMPLES		EXPLANATIONS
STATEMENT	(a) The children have **some** books. (b) They have **some** money.	Use *some* in statements to suggest a limited amount (with plural count nouns and noncount nouns).
NEGATIVE	(c) They don't have **any** books. (d) She doesn't have **any** money.	Use *any* in negative statements (with plural count nouns and noncount nouns).
QUESTION	(e) Do they have **any** books? (f) Does she have **any** money?	Use *any* in questions (with plural count nouns and noncount nouns).

EXERCISE 6

Complete the rhyme with *some* or *any.*

I don't have (1) ____________ time today.
I have (2) ____________ problems to solve.
I have (3) ____________ bills to pay.
Do you have (4) ____________ time to play?
I have (5) ____________ places to go.
I have (6) ____________ people to see.
Do you have (7) ____________ advice for me?
Yes, I do: "Slow down!"

EXERCISE 7

Read the sentences below. Say if each is true or false. If it's false, change it to make a true sentence. Base your answers on the information from the pictures and the reading in Exercise 3.

Example: John Lapp has some electrical machines on his farm.
False. He doesn't have any electrical machines on his farm.

1. Daniel has some colorful T-shirts.
2. John Lapp's wife has some expensive jewelry.
3. Amish people have different ideas about education.
4. The Amish have very big telephone bills.
5. Amish schools have some non-Amish teachers.
6. Amish people have strong religious beliefs.
7. Amish people have some very different habits.
8. Some Amish people have a problem with this traditional lifestyle.

FOCUS 5 Asking for Something Politely

use

EXAMPLES	EXPLANATION
Ask: (a) Excuse me, do you have an eraser? Answer: (b) Yes, I do. OR Sure. (c) No, I don't. OR Sorry, I don't.	Use *Do you have . . . ?* to ask for something politely.

EXERCISE 8

Work in pairs. You need to borrow five items from your partner. Keep asking questions until you get a total of five items. The words in the box may help you. Add other items you think of.

Examples: *Do you have an eraser?*
Yes, I do.

Do you have any gum?
No, I don't. OR *Sorry, I don't.*

eraser	gum	notebook
pen	whiteout	piece of paper
pencil	stapler	English-English dictionary
calculator	ruler	electronic dictionary
stamp	quarter (25 cents)	change
tissue	pencil sharpener	aspirin

FOCUS 6 Using *Have* To Describe People

use

This is an image of my older brother. He **has** short hair. He **has** a mustache. He **has** a thin face.

HAIR	FACE	EYES	OTHER
Type straight / wavy curly	**Shape** round / square / long thin /oval	**Shape** round / narrow almond-shaped	a mustache / a beard bangs / high cheek bones dimples / freckles / bald eyebrows / braids
Color dark / light / black brown / red / blond gray / white	**Complexion** light /dark / medium	**Color** brown / blue / green gray / hazel / dark light	
Length long /short medium-length			

EXERCISE 9

Look at the photographs of Mary and Nilaulaq and of the Amish on pages 64, 65, and 68. Fill in the blanks with *be* or *have* and the correct nouns.

1. John Lapp is Amish. (a) He ____is____ married. (b) He ________ long ________. (c) He ________ a long ________.
2. (a) Nilaulaq ________ an Inuit name. (b) She ________ long black ________. (c) She ________ a nice smile.
3. (a) Daniel ________ a young Amish boy. (b) He ________ long blond hair. (c) He ________ bangs.
4. (a) Mary ________ a modern Inuit woman. (b) Mary ________ a round face. (c) She ________ dark hair.

EXERCISE 10

You need to seat these guests at the dinner table on page 75. Write the letter of each description next to the correct photograph. Write the number of the photograph on the correct name card at the table.

Photographs:

1. ____________________

4. ____________________

2. ____________________

5. ____________________

3. ____________________

6. ____________________

Descriptions:

a. Rodrigo has a mustache and short, dark, curly hair. He wears glasses. He has an oval face and bushy eyebrows. He's at the head of the table on the left side.

b. Opposite Rodrigo is Chita. She has big, round, happy eyes. She has a tan hat. Her hair is dark, and she has two shoulder-length braids.

c. Min is to the left of Rodrigo. She has short, dark hair and bangs. She has brown almond-shaped eyes.

d. Next to Min is Gonzalo. Gonzalo has a kind face. He has a beard and mustache. His hair and beard are dark, but a little gray. He has big, bright, round eyes.

e. Across from Min is Karl. Karl is almost bald. He has a white mustache and beard. He has wrinkles in his forehead. He has a long, narrow face.

f. Across from Gonzalo and next to Karl is Dominique. Dominique is a very cute woman. She has short hair. It's light brown. She has thin eyebrows and high cheekbones. She has a nice smile.

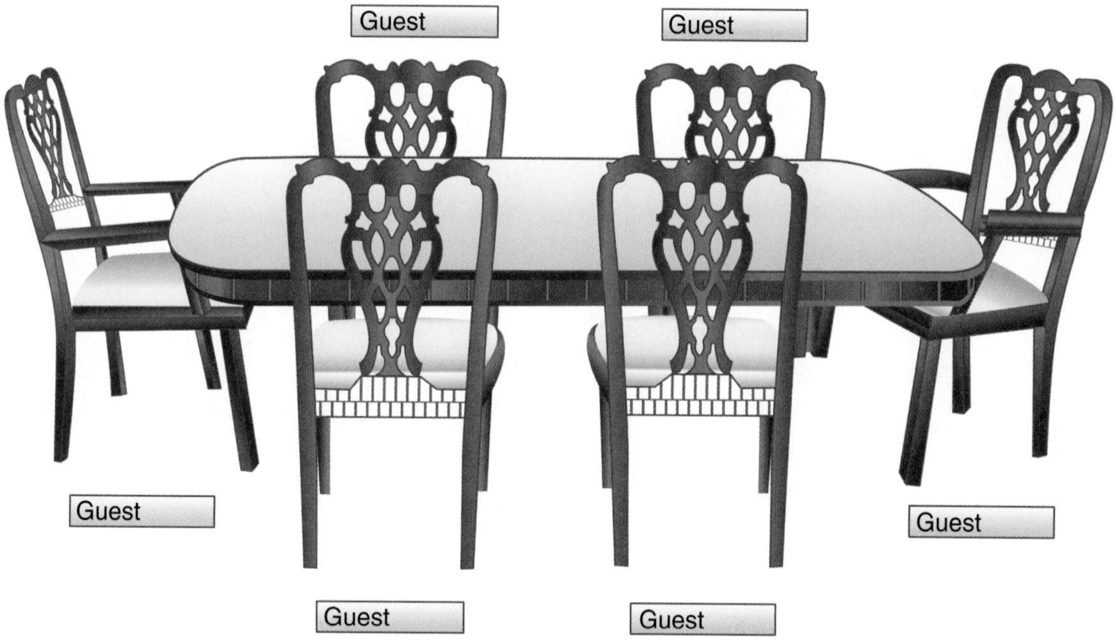

FOCUS 7 Using *Have* to Talk about Illnesses

USE

Use *have* to talk about or ask questions about illnesses.

Harry **has** a headache.

Harry **has** a cold.

He **has** a sore throat.

He **has** a stuffy nose.

He **has** an earache.

He **has** a fever.

He **has** a stomachache.

He **has** a toothache.

Does he **have** a good doctor?

EXERCISE 11

Write the sentence or question a nurse is saying to a doctor using the verb *have*.

1. Mary / stomachache
2. John / cold
3. I / toothache
4. Do / we / medicine
5. You / stuffy nose
6. Do / Nila and Napachee / good doctor
7. I / sore throat
8. She / fever

EXERCISE 12

Correct the errors in the sentences.

1. He have a car.
2. She have not a house.
3. He no have a TV set.
4. He doesn't is rich.
5. She doesn't has a stomachache.
6. Does he has a sister?
7. Does she is an Inuit?
8. Excuse me, have you change?
9. She does not plays tennis.
10. He don't have any money.

Use Your English

ACTIVITY 1 writing/speaking

WHO IS HE OR SHE?

Write a description of one of your classmates. Do not write the person's name. Read your description to the class. Your classmates guess who it is.

Example: *This student is tall. He has short black hair. He has brown eyes. He has a mustache. Who is he?*

ACTIVITY 2 research on the web

Search the Internet for information about a culture you know with traditional lifestyles. Enter keywords such as *Amish* or *Inuit* in the search area of an Internet search engine such as Yahoo®, Google®, or Ask®. Write about the culture. What do they look like? How are their lives different? What do they have? What do they not have? Share your findings with the class.

ACTIVITY 3 speaking

Work in groups. Look at the list of things that are part of United States culture. Do you have them in your country? What is your opinion of these things? Discuss this with your group.

Example: *In my country today, we have fast-food restaurants. I like them because the food is good, and it's not expensive.*

OR

I don't like them because the food is not healthy, and in these restaurants we have no time to talk.

- fast-food restaurants
- take-out restaurants
- 24-hour supermarkets
- daycare centers
- superstores
- nursing homes
- a free public school system

ACTIVITY 4 speaking

STEP 1

My Dream Life

Imagine your dream life. What do you have? Choose five items from the list below from your dream life. Add dream items of your own. Write your items in the first column in the chart below.

a beautiful house	a car	expensive jewelry
15 minutes of fame	freedom	an interesting job
a good knowledge of English	a great spouse	money
some good friends	a good education	free time
some excitement in my life	good luck	good health
a big family	world peace	a swimming pool

MY DREAM LIST	CLASSMATE 1 LIST	CLASSMATE 2 LIST	CLASSMATE 3 LIST
1.			
2.			
3.			
4.			
5.			
6.			
7.			

STEP 2

Talk to three other students, and write their items in the remaining columns. Compare your dream items. Are they the same or different?

Example:

You: *What do you have on your dream list?*

Classmate 1: *I have free time. I also have good friends.*

ACTIVITY 5 listening/speaking

CD Track 4

Listen to the information about Bhutan. Then listen again, and check *True* or *False* for each statement. If the statement is false, make the statement correct.

Example: *1. False: Bhutan doesn't have a modern culture. It has a traditional culture.*

	TRUE	FALSE	
1. Bhutan has a modern culture.		✔	
2. Bhutan has a president.			
3. The government has a rule about clothing.			
4. The people have religious festivals.			
5. People don't have Internet.			
6. People have television.			
7. People have electricity.			
8. Every village has schools.			

ACTIVITY 6 reflection

Read the statements about learning English. Check the statements that are true for you. Then explain your answers to a partner.

	TRUE	FALSE
1. I have confidence in my ability to learn English.		
2. I have a good "ear" for language.		
3. I have good pronunciation.		
4. I have good ideas about how to learn English.		
5. I have a good memory.		
6. I have the motivation to learn English.		
7. I have experience with different languages.		
8. I have opportunities to practice English outside of class.		

UNIT 6

THIS/THAT/THESE/THOSE AND POSSESSIVES

UNIT GOALS

- Use *this, that, these, those* correctly
- Ask what things are
- Use possessive nouns, adjectives, and pronouns
- Ask questions with *whose*

OPENING TASK

We Are What We Wear

STEP 1

Work in small groups. Look quickly at the photos of Liberty and Catherine. Discuss your first impressions of each woman.

LIBERTY

CATHERINE

STEP 2

Now look at the five pairs of items below. Which items belong to Liberty and which belong to Catherine? Write their names on the lines.

dress

 ______________  ______________

handbag

 ______________  ______________

shoes

 ______________  ______________

necklace

 ______________  ______________

earrings

 ______________ 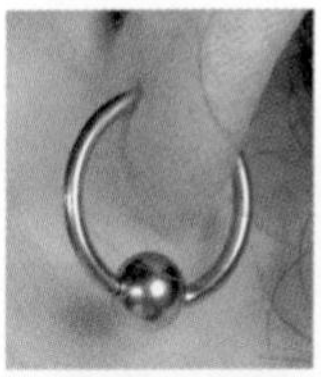 ______________

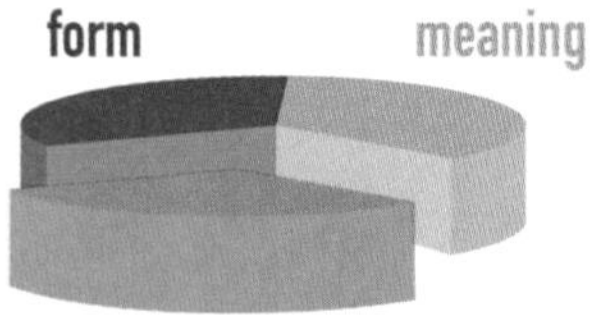

FOCUS 1 *This, These, That, Those*

NEAR SPEAKER		FAR FROM SPEAKER
Singular		
(a) **This** is a **short** dress.	Pronoun*	(c) **That** is a **long** dress.
(b) **This** dress is **short**.	Adjective*	(d) **That** dress is **long**.
Plural		
(e) **These** are **pearl** earrings.	Pronoun	(g) **Those** are **trendy** earrings.
(f) **These** earrings are **gold**.	Adjective	(h) **Those** earrings are **silver**.
Noncount		
(i) **This** is **traditional** jewelry.	Pronoun	(k) **That** is **modern** jewelry.
(j) **This** jewelry is **traditional**.	Adjective	(l) **That** jewelry is **modern**.
	*NOTE: A pronoun takes the place of a noun. An adjective describes a noun.	

EXERCISE 1

Are the following items singular, plural, or noncount? Fill in the blanks with *this, that, these, those* and the correct form of the verb *be*.

1. ___That___ ___is___ a sweater. (FAR)
2. __________ __________ high-heeled shoes. (NEAR)
3. __________ __________ a belt. (FAR)
4. __________ __________ shorts. (NEAR)
5. __________ __________ a dress. (NEAR)
6. __________ __________ sunglasses. (NEAR)
7. __________ __________ jewelry. (FAR)
8. __________ __________ a skirt. (NEAR)
9. __________ __________ blouses. (FAR)
10. __________ __________ women's clothing. (FAR)

EXERCISE 2

We Are What We Eat

Kim is a healthy person. She eats only healthy food. Complete each statement with *this, that, these, or those*. Then circle the things you think Kim eats/drinks.

NEAR	FAR
1. a. ________ chips are baked.	b. ________ chips are fried.
2. a. ________ nuts are salty.	b. ________ nuts are salt-free.
3. a. ________ coffee is decaffeinated.	b. ________ coffee has caffeine.
4. a. ________ potatoes are fried.	b. ________ potatoes are boiled.
5. a. ________ ice cream is fattening.	b. ________ ice cream is low-fat.
6. a. ________ vegetables are fried.	b. ________ vegetables are raw.
7. a. ________ meat is fatty.	b. ________ meat is lean.
8. a. ________ salad dressing is oily.	b. ________ salad dressing is light.
9. a. ________ candy is sugar-free.	b. ________ candy has sugar.
10. a. ________ bread is white.	b. ________ bread is whole wheat.

FOCUS 2 Asking What Things Are

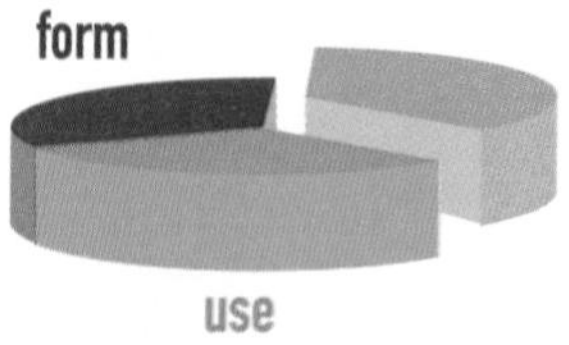

QUESTIONS	ANSWERS
(a) What's **this?** **that?**	Singular **It's a** sandwich. **It's an** egg.
(b) What are **these?** **those?**	Plural **They are** french fries. **They're** cookies.
(c) What's **this** dish? **that** dish?	Noncount **It's** soup. **It's** rice.

EXERCISE 3

This is Nuria's first American party. She doesn't know what Americans eat. She asks her American friend, Chris, about the food on the table.

For each item, match the letter for the picture with the word. Ask a question with *what* about each item. Fill in the subject, verb, and *a/an* where necessary.

Letter in the Picture

1.	What's this?	It's a	hamburger.	d
2.			hot dog.	
3.			french fries.	
4.			ketchup.	
5.			pizza.	
6.			sandwich.	
7.			doughnuts.	
8.			cookies.	
9.			muffin.	
10.			ice cream.	
11.			mustard.	
12.			candy.	

form

FOCUS 3 Possessive Nouns

EXAMPLES	EXPLANATIONS
(a) The boy has a dog. **The boy's dog** is small. (b) Carol has a cat. **Carol's cat** is cute.	Add an apostrophe (') and *s* to a singular noun.
(c) My boss has a nice suit. My **boss's suit is expensive**. My **boss' suit is gray**. (d) James has a sister. **James's** sister is pretty. **James'** sister is happy.	Add an apostrophe (') and *s* or just an apostrophe (') to singular nouns and names that end in *-s*
(e) The neighbors have a dog. The **neighbors' dog** is beautiful.	Add only an apostrophe (') at the end of a plural noun.
(f) The **children's dog is gentle**. (g) This store has **women's clothing**.	Add apostrophe (') and *s* to irregular plural nouns.
(h) Paul and **Mary's dog** is friendly. (i) My mother-in-**law's cookies** are delicious.	For two or more subjects or a subject with hyphens (-), add apostrophe (') and *s* at the end of last noun.

EXERCISE 4

We Are What We Do

A hobby is an activity we do in our free time. Look at the pictures. Match each person to a hobby. Write two statements about the person's hobby. Use possessive nouns. Use the person's name in the first statement. Use another subject (*man, woman,* etc.) in the second statement.

Example:

Helen (photography)

a. Helen's hobby is photography.

b. The woman's hobby is photography.

HOBBIES			
photography	playing the piano	hiking	reading
gardening	dancing	astronomy	collecting stamps
traveling	surfing the Internet		

Karla and Julio

1. a. ______________________
   b. ______________________

Chris

2. a. ______________________
   b. ______________________

Carol

3. a. ______________________
   b. ______________________

Joel and Eugene

4. a. ______________________
   b. ______________________

Alexis

5. a. ______________________
   b. ______________________

6. a. ______________________
   b. ______________________

Donald

Judy, Ellen and Gina

7. a. ______________________
   b. ______________________

8. a. ______________________
   b. ______________________

Alice

Sonia and Tommy

9. a. ______________________
   b. ______________________

EXERCISE 5

We Are Our Family

Think back to Liberty and Catherine in the Opening Task. Liberty and Catherine are sisters.

This is their family tree. Write true statements about the family using possessive nouns. Read each statement aloud.

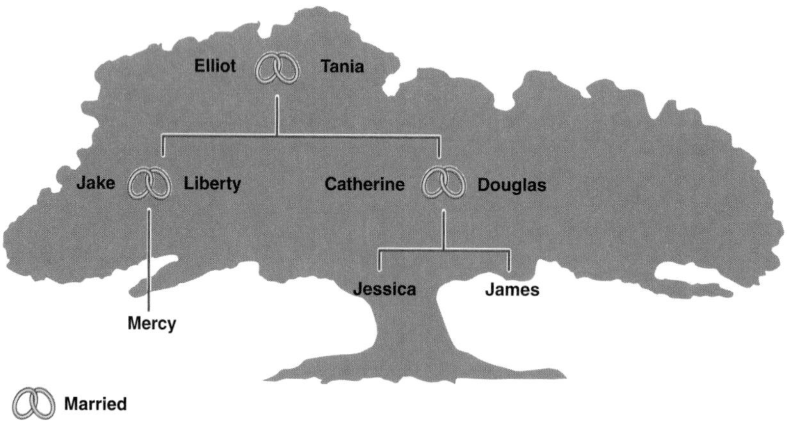

1. Elliot and Tania are ______________________ parents.
2. Jake is ______________________ husband.
3. Catherine is ______________________ wife.
4. Liberty is ______________________ sister-in-law.
5. Jake is ______________________ brother-in-law.
6. Douglas is ______________________ husband.
7. Mercy is ______________________ niece.
8. Jessica is ______________________ sister.
9. Mercy is ______________________ cousin.
10. Jake is ______________________ uncle.
11. Liberty is ______________________ mother.
12. Liberty is ______________________ sister.
13. Jake is ______________________ father.
14. Elliot is ______________________ husband.
15. Tania is ______________________ mother-in-law.
16. Tania is ______________________ grandmother.
17. James is ______________________ son.

EXERCISE 6

Look carefully at the apostrophes in the phrases below. How many people are there in each phrase? How many dogs? Check *one* or *more than one* for each sentence.

	HOW MANY PEOPLE?		HOW MANY DOGS?	
	ONE	MORE THAN ONE	ONE	MORE THAN ONE
1. my daughter's dog	✔	______	✔	______
2. my daughters' dogs	______	______	______	______
3. my son's dog	______	______	______	______
4. my sons' dogs	______	______	______	______
5. my sons' dog	______	______	______	______
6. my son's dogs	______	______	______	______
7. my children's dog	______	______	______	______
8. my children's dogs	______	______	______	______

form

FOCUS 4 Possessive Adjectives and Possessive Pronouns

POSSESSIVE ADJECTIVES		POSSESSIVE PRONOUNS	
My	car is new.	The car is	**mine.**
Your	house is beautiful.	The house is	**yours.**
His	dog is old.	The dog is	**his.**
Its	fur is white.	(**Its** cannot be a possessive pronoun.)	
Her	jewelry is expensive.	The jewelry is	**hers.**
Our	children are cute.	The children are	**ours.**
Their	television is big.	The television is	**theirs.**

NOTES:

- Do not confuse a possessive adjective (*its*) with the contraction of *it's* (*it* + *is*).

  Example: I have a Siamese cat. **It's** a pure breed. **Its** eyes are deep blue.

- Use possessive adjectives with parts of the body.

  Example: **My** hair is black. **Your** eyes are blue.

EXERCISE 7

Fill in each blank with a possessive adjective or possessive pronoun.

1.

Man: Excuse me, miss. Is this ________________ scarf?

Woman: No, it's not ________________. I have ________________ scarf, thanks.

Man: Oh, I'm sorry. By the way, what's ________________ name?

Woman: Anna. What's ________________?

2.

Couple 1: Pardon me, but these are ________________ seats.

Couple 2: I don't think so. These are ________________ seats.
Here are ________________ tickets.

Couple 1: We're very sorry. It's ________________ mistake.

3.

Girl 1: Are these ________________ glasses?

Girl 2: No, I have ________________. They're ________________, and she really needs ________________ glasses.

Girls 1 and 2: Here are ________________ glasses.

Girl 3: Thank you so much. These are ________________ favorite glasses!

4.

Police Officer: Is this ________________ car, young man?

Young Man: Yes, it is, Sir.

Police Officer: Where is ________________ registration?

Young Man: It's right here, Sir, in ________________ wallet, Sir, with ________________ license, Sir.

5.

Boy 1: Who's ________________ new friend?

Boy 2: That's Zack. He's a real computer wiz. He has ________________ own Web site. Zack's parents have ________________ own computer company. Maybe computers are in ________________ genes!

EXERCISE 8

We Are Our Pets

DOG A.

DOG B.

Fill in each blank with a possessive word (a possessive adjective or a possessive pronoun). Then look at the two dogs. Whose dog is A? Whose dog is B?

Many people have pets. (1) ________________ pets are very important to them. They are very close to (2) ________________ pets. Liberty and Catherine's families love pets. "Pets are part of ________________ family," says Liberty. Jake has a dog. (3) ________________ dog is strong. (4) ________________ nose is flat. (5) ________________ legs are short. (6) ________________ dog has a big neck and small ears.

Jessica also has a dog. Her brother James says the dog is (7) ________________, but Jessica says it's really (8) ________________. (9) ________________ dog is beautiful. (10) ________________ fur is a red-brown color. (11) ________________ ears are very long, with curly fur.

Sometimes, people look like their dogs. Can you match each dog to (12) ________________ owner?

Jake says: "Dog ________________ is ________________."

Jessica says: "Dog ________________ is ________________."

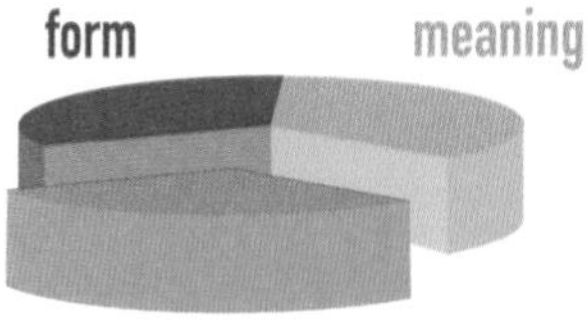

FOCUS 5 Questions with *Whose*

Use *whose* to ask who owns or possesses something.

WHOSE	NOUN	VERB		ANSWERS
Whose	dog	is	this?	It's Jessica's dog. It's her dog. It's hers. Jessica's.
Whose	glasses	are	these?	They're Peter's glasses. They're his glasses. They're his. Peter's.

EXAMPLES	EXPLANATIONS
(a) **Who's** she? My sister. (b) **Whose** car is that? Mine.	Do not confuse *who*'s and *whose*. *Who*'s and *whose* have the same pronunciation. *Who*'s = *who is*. *Whose* asks about who owns something.

EXERCISE 9

We Are What We Do: Jobs

Ask questions with *whose* to find out who owns each object. Answer in two ways, as in the example.

Example: *Whose hammer is this?*
It's Jackie's hammer. It's hers.

a. John is a hairdresser.

b. Jackie is a carpenter.

c. Jim is a secretary.

d. Pierre and Daniel are cooks.

1. spoon

2. pencil sharpener

3. shampoo

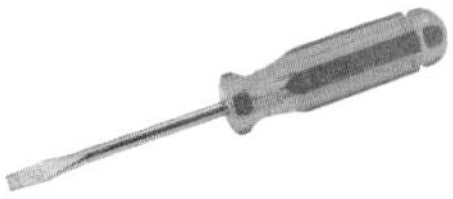
4. screwdriver

5. computer

6. comb

7. hammer

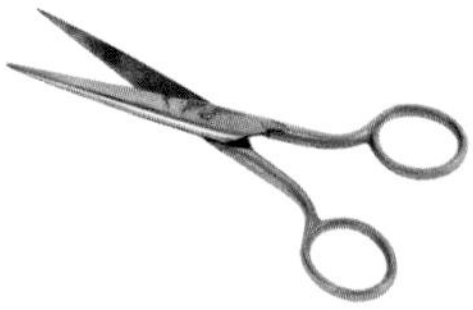
8. scissors

9. saucepan

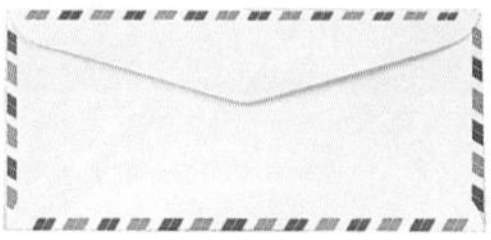
10. envelope

11. can opener

12. nails

EXERCISE 10

Correct the errors in the following sentences.

1. This is Jake dog.
2. Catherine is married. Douglas is her wife.
3. That computer is her's.
4. Is Liberty the sister of Catherine?
5. Who's son-in-law is Douglas?
6. Douglas and Catherine have two children. Jessica and James are theirs children.
7. What's that name's dog?
8. The Jake's dog is small.
9. Whose hungry?
10. This dogs are cute.
11. A: Is this the dog's food?
    B: Yes, that's its.
12. The dog has food on the face.

Use Your English

ACTIVITY 1 writing

Draw your family tree. Exchange family trees with a partner. Write five statements about your classmate's family.

ACTIVITY 2 speaking

Each student puts a personal object into a bag. One student picks an object and asks, "Whose is this?" The class guesses who the owner is. If the class is not correct, the owner says, "It's mine."

ACTIVITY 3 speaking/writing

STEP 1 Bring something to class that you feel is special from your country or another country you know (for example, something you eat, something you wear, or something people use). Tell the class about the special thing. Tell why it is special.

Examples: *This is a special dress. It's for a wedding.*
These are ankle bracelets from India. They're made of silver.

STEP 2 Choose one of the objects from the class presentations. Write what you know about it.

ACTIVITY 4 research on the Web

Find photos of different kinds of foods on the Internet, including foods from your country. Print out the photos. Work with a partner. Ask each other about the photos.

Example: You: *What's this?*
Your partner: *It's Japanese food. It's sushi.*

ACTIVITY 5 listening

CD Track 5

STEP 1 Listen to the conversation. What are the people talking about?

STEP 2 Listen again. In the chart, write *this, that, these,* or *those* next to each thing. Then check (✔) if each thing is near or far from the speaker.

THIS/THAT/THESE/THOSE?		NEAR	FAR FROM
1. these	chairs	✔	
2.	table		
3.	lamp		
4.	pictures		
5.	statue		
6.	sofa		
7.	cushions		

ACTIVITY 6 reflection

Bring in pictures of ten objects you <u>don't</u> know the English word for. Work with a partner. Ask questions about what the objects are. Your partner tries to identify the object or uses other language to describe the object.

Example: You: *What's that?*
Your partner: *It's a thing for exercise.*
It's a machine to walk on.

UNIT

7

THERE IS/THERE ARE, A/AN VERSUS *THE*

UNIT GOALS

- Understand the meaning of *there + be*
- Know when to use *there + be* to focus on new information
- Make affirmative and negative statements, and *yes/no* questions with *there + be*
- Choose between *a/an* and *the*

OPENING TASK

Whose Apartment Is This?

STEP 1

Read the statements on the next page. Then fill in the circle for the type of person you think lives in this apartment.

1. The person
   - ○ is a man. ○ is a woman.
2. The person
   - ○ has a baby. ○ doesn't have a baby.
3. The person
   - ○ has a pet. ○ doesn't have a pet.
4. The person
   - ○ is athletic. ○ isn't athletic.
5. The person
   - ○ drinks coffee. ○ doesn't drink coffee.
6. The person
   - ○ is well educated. ○ isn't well educated.
7. The person
   - ○ likes music. ○ doesn't like music.
8. The person
   - ○ is on a diet. ○ isn't on a diet.
9. The person
   - ○ is neat. ○ isn't neat.
10. The person
    - ○ is computer-literate. ○ isn't computer-literate.

STEP 2

List reasons for your choices.

I think this person is a man/woman because . . . . (Add your reason)

FOCUS 1 *There + Be*

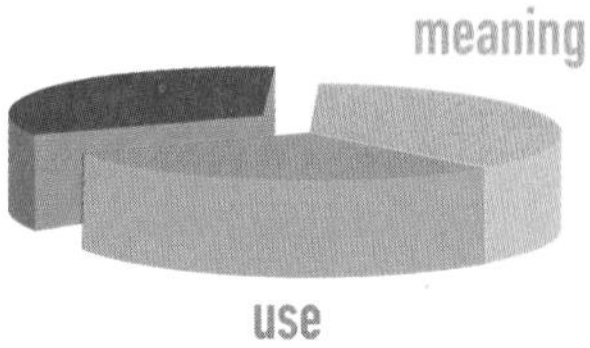

EXAMPLES	EXPLANATIONS
	Use *there* + *be:*
(a) **There are** a lot of things in the apartment.	to show something or somebody exists.
(b) **There is** a cat under the bed.	to show something or somebody's location.
(c) **There is** a mouse in the house. NOT: A mouse is in the house.	when you talk about something or somebody for the first time.
(d) **There are** two men in the picture below. **They are** not happy.	Do not confuse *there are* and *they are.*

EXERCISE 1

Circle the letter for the correct sentence.

Example: a. Two men are in this picture.
(b.) There are two men in this picture.

1. An angry restaurant customer says,
   a. "Waiter, a fly is in my soup."
   b. "Waiter, there's a fly in my soup."
2. The waiter answers,
   a. "Sorry, sir. There's more soup in the kitchen."
   b. "Sorry, sir. More soup is in the kitchen."
3. The customer gets the check. He says,
   a. "Waiter, a mistake is on the check."
   b. "Waiter, there's a mistake on the check."
4. The waiter answers,
   a. "Sorry, sir. There's a new manager here today."
   b. "Sorry, sir. A new manager is here today."

form

FOCUS 2 There Is/There Are

The form of the *be* verb depends on the noun phrase that follows it.

THERE + BE	NOUN PHRASE		EXPLANATIONS
(a) There is There's	an angry man	at the table.	singular count noun
(b) There are	two people	in the restaurant.	plural count noun
(c) There is There's	soup	in his dish.	noncount noun
(d) There is There's	a dining room, a kitchen, and two restrooms	in this restaurant.	When there is more than one noun, *be* agrees with the first noun.

EXERCISE 2

Go back to the Opening Task on page 98. Write sentences about the picture with *there is/are* and the words below.

Example: one bed in the apartment
There's one bed in the apartment.

1. a tennis racquet in the closet
2. high-heeled shoes in the closet
3. women's clothing in the closet
4. sneakers in the closet
5. a coat in the closet
6. CDs on the shelf
7. a CD player on the shelf
8. books on the bookcase
9. women's jewelry in the box on the table
10. coffee in the coffee pot
11. a big cake on the counter
12. an exercise bicycle in the apartment
13. an expensive rug on the floor
14. two pillows on the bed
15. a guitar against the wall

EXERCISE 3

STEP 1 **Get into groups. Choose one student to read the following sentences. Listen to the description and draw the picture.**

1. There's a table in the center of the room.
2. There are two chairs at the table—one at each end.
3. There's a tablecloth on the table.
4. There's a plate on each end of the table. On one plate, there's a steak and potatoes.
5. The other plate is empty. There's only a napkin next to the plate.
6. Next to the empty plate, there's an empty glass.
7. Next to the plate with food, there's a glass with water in it.
8. There's a bottle of water on the right side of the table. The bottle is half full.
9. There is a vase in the center of the table.
10. There are eight flowers on the floor next to the table.

STEP 2 **Compare your drawings. Whose is correct? Who is a good artist?**

STEP 3 **Choose the best title for your picture.**

a. A Wonderful Dinner
b. Disappointed Again!
c. Always Eat Your Vegetables

form

FOCUS 3 *There Isn't/There Aren't/There's No/There Are No*

THERE	*BE + NOT*		TYPE OF NOUN
There	isn't	a vase on the table.	singular count noun
There	aren't	any children in this restaurant.	plural count noun
There	isn't	any water on the table.	noncount noun

THERE	*BE*	*NO*	
There	is	no	vase on the table.
There	are	no	children in the restaurant.
There	's	no	water on the table.

EXERCISE 4

Go back to the Opening Task on page 98. Make sentences with *there is/there are*, *there isn't/there aren't,* or *there's no/there are no* with the words below.

Example: armchair *There isn't an armchair in the apartment.*
OR *There's no armchair in the apartment.*

1. television
2. rug
3. men's clothing
4. crib
5. window
6. desk
7. books
8. toys
9. exercise bicycle
10. plants
11. coffee pot
12. ties

EXERCISE 5

Use the information in the chart below about the city "Utopia." Write sentences with *there is/there are, there isn't/there aren't,* or *there's no/there are no.*

Example: *In Utopia, there aren't any guns.*
In Utopia, there are no guns.

The City of Utopia

	YES	NO		YES	NO
1. guns		✔	7. universities	✔	
2. public transportation	✔		8. noise		✔
3. crime		✔	9. jobs	✔	
4. museums	✔		10. parks	✔	
5. traffic problems		✔	11. poor people		✔
6. unemployment		✔	12. hospitals	✔	

EXERCISE 6

Read the politician's speech about the city of Utopia. Fill in the blanks with *there is/there are*, *there isn't/there aren't,* or *there's no/there are no.*

Good evening, Ladies and Gentlemen. I am the Mayor of Utopia. I am here tonight to talk about our wonderful city.

Today, (1) ___there are___ 75,000 people in our city. We are all happy. (2) _______________ problems in our city.

(3) _______________ jobs for all our people.
(4) _______________ good schools for the children.
(5) _______________ beautiful houses for all our families. The houses are comfortable. They aren't expensive.

(6) _______________ homeless people on our streets. Our neighborhoods are safe. (7) _______________ crime here.
(8) _______________ drugs. Our streets are clean.
(9) _______________ garbage on the streets.
(10) _______________ pollution.

(11) _______________ many museums, theaters, and parks in our city. (12) _______________ entertainment for all.
(13) _______________ good, cheap public transportation for everyone.

(14) _______________ many reasons why Utopia is a great city! (15) _______________ an excellent quality of life here in Utopia. And don't forget: (16) _______________ an election this year. I want to be your Mayor for four more years. Are you happy in Utopia? Then (17) _______________ only one thing to do: VOTE FOR ME, your Mayor Lucas Lime, on November sixth!

form

FOCUS 4 *Yes/No* Questions with *There Is/There Are*

Yes/No Questions	Short Answers	Type of Noun
(a) **Is there** a computer in the room?	Yes, there is. No, there isn't.	singular count noun
(b) **Are there** any books on the shelves?	Yes, there are. No, there aren't.	plural count noun
(c) **Is there** any jewelry in the box?	Yes, there is. No, there isn't.	noncount noun

EXERCISE 7

Complete the questions for each picture.

1. ___Are there___ any messages for me?

2. ________________ any food in here, Mom?

3. ________________ a doctor in the house?

4. Excuse me, ________________ a post office near here?

5. ________________ any tickets available for the 10:00 show?

6. ________________ any room for me?

7. ________________ a seat for me?

8. ________________ any small sizes?

9. ________________ any more instructions in the box?

10. ________________ a bathroom on this floor?

EXERCISE 8

Test your knowledge. Ask your partner *yes/no* questions with *Is there/Are there* and the words below.

Example: eggs in an eggplant
Are there any eggs in an eggplant?
No, there aren't.

1. rain in a desert
2. two billion people in China
3. fifty-two states in the United States
4. earthquakes in Japan
5. billions of stars in the sky
6. life on the moon
7. trees at the North Pole
8. cure for the common cold
9. months with 28 days
10. female world leaders

FOCUS 5 Choosing *A/An* or *The*

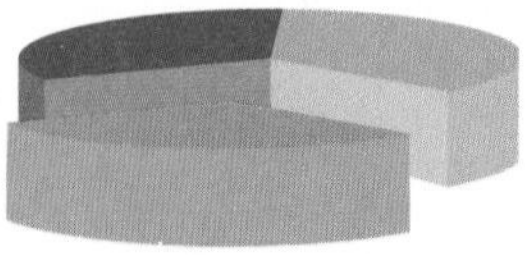

A/An and *the* are articles. *A/An* are indefinite articles (see Unit 4). *The* is the definite article.

A/AN	*THE*
Use only with singular count nouns. (a) Susan has **a** bicycle.	Use with all nouns. (b) **The** bicycle is new. (*singular count*) (c) **The** books are on the shelf. (*plural count*) (d) **The** jewelry is in the box. (*noncount*)
Use to talk about a person or thing for the first time. (e) Susan has **a** necklace.	Use the second time you talk about a person or thing. (f) Susan has a necklace. **The** necklace is beautiful.
Use to classify people, animals, and things. (g) She is **an** actress.	Use when both speakers know which noun they are talking about. (h) When's **the** party? It's at 8:00. Use when the noun is the only one. (i) **The** sun is hot.

EXERCISE 9

Look at the pictures. Fill in the blanks with *a/an* or *the*.

1. **Passenger:** Boy, it's hot. Do you have . . . air conditioner in this car?

   Driver: Yes, but . . . air conditioner doesn't work. Sorry about that!

2. **Husband:** What's in . . . box?

   Wife: I have . . . surprise for you.

   Husband: What's . . . surprise?

   Wife: Open it!

3. **Jeff:** Do you have . . . key or do I?

   Matt: I think . . . key's in the car.

4. **Man:** Who's that?

   Woman: Oh, that's Linda Adams. She's . . . investment banker. She's . . . number one person in the bank.

5. **Teenage girl:** . . . sun is burning hot! Let's move into . . . shade.

   Friend: That's . . . great idea!

6. **Pedestrian 1:** Excuse me, do you have . . . time?

   Pedestrian 2: Sorry, I don't have . . . watch.

7. **Friend 1:** There's . . . new restaurant in my neighborhood.

   Friend 2: Really? What is it?

   Friend 1: It's . . . Vietnamese place. . . . food is great!

EXERCISE 10

Read the paragraph. Fill in *a/an* or *the.*

Maria lives in (1) ______________ exciting, multicultural neighborhood. There are people from all different countries in (2) ______________ neighborhood. There are many shops. There's (3) ______________ Italian bakery, (4) ______________ international wine store, (5) ______________ jewelry shop, (6) ______________ bookstore, (7) ______________ Asian cafe and food market, and many restaurants. (8) ______________ main street is always busy.

Maria owns (9) ______________ small restaurant on (10) ______________ side street. (11) ______________ restaurant has only ten tables. It is (12) ______________ very popular place. There is always (13) ______________ line to get in. Maria has (14) ______________ cook from France, (15) ______________ waiter from Argentina, and (16) ______________ receptionist from Brazil. (17) ______________ menu is varied and (18) ______________ food is delicious.

Maria is (19) ______________ good boss. Everyone is happy in (20) ______________ restaurant.

EXERCISE 11

Correct the errors in the following sentences.

1. It's a picture on a wall.
2. There are a bathroom, a kitchen, and a living room in my house.
3. There have three bedrooms and two bathrooms in the apartment.
4. Is a good restaurant in my neighborhood.
5. There aren't milk in the refrigerator.
6. In my picture, have one woman and two men.
7. Are homeless people in your city?
8. Is there a jewelry in the box?
9. a. *Is there a foreign student advisor in the college?*

   b. Yes, a foreign student advisor is in room 418.
10. a. *Are there any museums in your town?*

    b. Yes, they are.
11. Excuse me, is there the men's room in this restaurant?
12. a. *Do you have any children?*

    b. Yes, I have the daughter.
13. Are there pollution in your city?
14. There no are women in the government.
15. There are no any poor people in Utopia.
16. Is a student here to see you.

Use Your English

ACTIVITY 1 writing/speaking

STEP 1 Work with a partner. Look at the two pictures. Find ten differences and write sentences with *there is/isn't* or *there are/aren't*. Compare your sentences with those of another pair of students.

Example: *In Picture A, there is a round mirror above the bed. In Picture B, there's a rectangular mirror above the bed. It's broken.*

STEP 2 Which bedroom would you rather live in? Explain why.

ACTIVITY 2 speaking

STEP 1 Find out about your partner's neighborhood. Ask questions with *Is there . . .? Are there . . .?* Check *Yes* or *No* in the chart.

Example: You: *Is there a hospital in your neighborhood?*
Your partner: *Yes, there is.* OR *No, there isn't.*

	YES	NO
supermarkets		
banks or ATM machines		
fast-food restaurants		
gas station		
post office		
public library		
schools		
crime		
coffee shops		
public transportation		
police station		
pharmacy		

STEP 2 Tell the class or group about your classmate's neighborhood.

ACTIVITY 3 writing

Write a letter to the mayor of your city. Write about the problems in your city or neighborhood.

Example: Dear Mr. Mayor,
I live in ________________. There are many problems in my neighborhood.

ACTIVITY 4 speaking/writing

STEP 1 Use the categories below to find out about your classmates. Fill in the blanks with numbers of students.

Students in your class: ________________

Male: ________________ /Female: ________________

Number of nationalities: ________________

Married: ________________ /Single: ________________

Short hair: ________________ /Long hair: ________________

Brown eyes: ______________ /Blue or Green eyes: ______________

Shy: ________________ /Outgoing: ________________

Add your own categories.

STEP 2 Write sentences about your classmates.

Example: *There are five nationalities in my class. There are ten Mexicans, two Japanese, three Koreans, one Vietnamese, and one Brazilian in my class.*

ACTIVITY 5 research on the web

STEP 1 Think of a place that you love or want to visit. Use a search engine such as Google® or Ask® or Yahoo® to search the Internet for a photograph of the place. Print out the photograph, and on a separate piece of paper write a short description of this place.

STEP 2 The class posts all the photographs on the blackboard. Then, post all the descriptions around the room. Go around the room and read about the different places. Match the photographs with the correct descriptions. Tell the class which photo you found for each description.

ACTIVITY 6 listening

CD Track 6

■ **STEP 1** Listen to the story about Sharon's life and about Paul's life.

■ **STEP 2** In your opinion, who has a better life? Which do you like better? Explain your answer in a short paragraph.

ACTIVITY 7 reflection

Work in a small group of three. Is English similar to your native language, or is it different? Read the statements below about English. Then make statements about your native language. Review the units in the book to help you, if necessary.

IN ENGLISH	IN MY NATIVE LANGUAGE
1. There is a form using *there is* and *there are*. (This unit.)	
2. There is a singular and plural form of the verb *be*. (*He is a student. They are students.*) (Unit 1)	
3. There is a subject pronoun *he* for males and *she* for females. (Unit 1)	
4. There are no plural forms of adjectives. (*He is young. They are young.*) (Unit 2)	
5. There are singular and plural count nouns and also noncount nouns. (*pen, pens, money*) (Unit 4)	
6. There are different spelling rules for plural nouns. (*book-books*; *party-parties*) (Unit 4)	
7. There are possessive nouns. (*the boy's mother*) (Unit 6)	
8. There are possessive adjectives. (*My car is new.*) (Unit 6)	
9. There are possessive pronouns. (*The car is mine.*) (Unit 6)	
10. There are definite and indefinite articles. (*a/an; the*) (This unit)	

UNIT

8

SIMPLE PRESENT TENSE

Affirmative and Negative Statements, Time Expressions: *In/On/At, Like/Need/Want*

UNIT GOALS

- Make affirmative and negative statements using the simple present tense
- Know how to spell and pronounce the third person singular form of verbs in the simple present tense
- Use frequency and time expressions
- Use the simple present tense to:
  - talk about habits and routines
  - talk about things that are always true
  - talk about what you like, want, or need

OPENING TASK

Looking at Healthy and Unhealthy Lifestyles

MICHAEL

SAM

STEP 1

Look at the photos of Michael and Sam. Michael has a very healthy lifestyle. Sam has an unhealthy lifestyle. Use your own knowledge of healthy and unhealthy habits. Imagine what Michael's and Sam's habits are. Discuss their habits with your partner.

STEP 2

For each habit, write one statement about Michael and one statement about Sam.

HABITS	MICHAEL'S HABITS	SAM'S HABITS
1. FOOD		
2. DRINK		
3. EXERCISE		
4. CIGARETTES		
5. SLEEP		
6. HOBBIES or ACTIVITIES		

form

FOCUS 1 Simple Present Tense: Affirmative Statements

SUBJECT	VERB
I You* We They	work.
He She It *Both singular and plural	works.

EXERCISE 1

Read the true statements about Michael and Sam. Circle the correct form of the verb in each statement.

1. Michael and Sam are friends. They (work/works) at the same computer company.
2. Michael (love/loves) his job.
3. Sam (feel/feels) stressed at work.
4. They (share/shares) an office.
5. They (work/works) hard.
6. Michael (eat/eats) three healthy meals every day.
7. He (drink/drinks) a lot of water.
8. Sam (skip/skips) breakfast.
9. He (order/orders) take-out food from nearby restaurants.
10. Michael and Sam both (like/likes) sports.
11. Michael (get/gets) a good night's sleep.
12. Sam has trouble sleeping at night. He (take/takes) sleeping pills to help him sleep.
13. Michael and Sam (watch/watches) football on TV together on weekends.
14. Sam (smoke/smokes) half a pack of cigarettes a day.
15. Michael and Sam (go/goes) out for dinner together on Friday nights.
16. Michael (exercise/exercises) three times a week.
17. Sam (spend/spends) his free time in front of the TV.
18. Michael and Sam (buy/buys) season tickets to baseball games.

EXERCISE 2

Work with a partner. For each habit, find one thing about you and your partner that is the same. Write a sentence in the **WE** column. Then write two more sentences. Look at item 3 for an example.

HABIT	WE	YOU	YOUR PARTNER
1. FOOD			
2. DRINK			
3. EXERCISE	We both like sports.	I play tennis.	He plays soccer.
4. CIGARETTES			
5. SLEEP			
6. HOBBIES or ACTIVITIES			

FOCUS 2 Talking About Habits and Routines

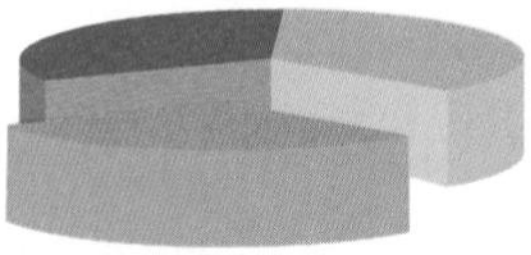
use

EXAMPLES	EXPLANATION
(a) Michael exercises several times a week. (b) Michael and Sam eat dinner together on Friday nights.	Use the simple present tense to talk about habits or routines (things that happen again and again).

EXERCISE 3

Match each occupation with what the people do. Use the correct verb forms and make statements aloud.

Example: *A doctor takes care of sick people.*

1. a doctor	a. repair cars
2. construction workers	b. enforce the law
3. a mechanic	c. greet people
4. air traffic controllers	d. take care of sick people
5. a receptionist	e. build houses
6. taxi drivers	f. direct airplanes
7. police officers	g. work in emergencies
8. a firefighter	h. take passengers to different places

Which of these jobs are the most stressful? Explain why.

FOCUS 3 Third Person Singular: Spelling and Pronunciation

form

BASE FORM OF VERB	SPELLING	PRONUNCIATION
1. The final sound of the verb is "voiceless" (for example: *f/k/p/t/s/th*): **sleep**	Add *s*. Michael **sleeps** eight hours a night.	/s/
2. The final sound of the verb is "voiced" (for example: *b/d/g/l/m/n/r/v* or a vowel): **feel**	Add *s*. He **feels** stressed.	/z/
3. The verb ends in **sh**, **ch**, **x**, **z**, or **ss**: **watch**	Add *es*. Sam **watches** TV.	This adds another syllable to the verb. /iz/
4. The verb ends in a consonant + **y**: **worry**	Change *y* to *i* and add *es*. Sam **worries** about his job.	/z/
5. The verb ends in a vowel + **y**: **play**	Add *s*. Michael **plays** tennis on Sunday.	/z/
6. Irregular Forms: **have** **go** **do**	 Michael **has** a healthy lifestyle. He **goes** to the gym twice a week. Michael **does** the cooking.	 /z/ /z/ /z/

EXERCISE 4

The pictures of Lazy Louie and his wife Hannah are not in the correct order. Number the pictures in the correct order. Then write the number of the picture next to the sentences below. Finally, circle all the simple present tense verbs.

☐ 

☐ 

☐ 

☐ 

☐ 

☐ 

______ a. Poor lazy Louie leaves the house and goes jogging.

______ b. He lies down on the bench and says, "Finally, I am free!" Then he goes to sleep.

______ c. Lazy Louie hates exercise. He wants to sleep, but he gets up. He puts on his clothes and sneakers with his eyes closed. Hannah pushes him out of the house.

______ d. Lazy Louie loves to sleep. He dreams about sleeping! But he snores all the time, and his wife gets no sleep. Hannah is tired and needs to do something.

______ e. He runs to the park and finds his favorite bench.

______ f. Hannah finds a way to get Louie out of bed. She wakes him at 6:45 every morning. He continues to sleep. She shakes him. She shouts in his ear, "Time to get up! You need your exercise, dear!"

EXERCISE 5

Here is a list of third-person singular verbs from the story about Lazy Louie. Read the verbs aloud. Then check (✓) the sound you say at the end of the verb. Compare your answers with a partner.

VERB	/s/	/z/	/iz/
1. loves		✓	
2. dreams			
3. snores			
4. gets			
5. needs			
6. finds			
7. wakes			
8. continues			
9. shakes			
10. shouts			
11. hates			
12. wants			
13. puts			
14. pushes			
15. leaves			
16. goes			
17. runs			
18. lies			
19. says			

EXERCISE 6

Work in groups of five. Sit in a circle. The first person in the circle starts to tell the story of Louie and Hannah and the next continues, and so on all around the circle. The pictures in Exercise 4 and the verb list in Exercise 5 will help you.

FOCUS 4 Frequency and Time Expressions

EXAMPLES	EXPLANATIONS
every morning/afternoon/evening/night every day/week/year every summer/winter/spring/fall all the time once a week twice a month three times a year	*Frequency expressions* tell how often we do something.
in + the morning / the afternoon / the evening (more general) in + 1986 / the summer / June on + Wednesday(s) / March 17 / the weekend at + 7:30 / night / noon (more specific)	*Time expressions* tell when we do something.

EXERCISE 7

Lifestyle of a College Student. Fill in the blanks with a frequency or time expression.

Jay is a nursing student at a college. Jay gets up (1) ________________ 7:00 (2) ________________ day of the week. He leaves home (3) ________________ 8:00 and gets to work (4) ________________ 8:45. He finishes work (5) ________________ 1:00. He attends classes at the college (6) ________________ the afternoon three days a week. He works at a local hospital two afternoons (7) ________________. (8) ________________ the evening, he cooks dinner and studies. He reviews his work and his experiences at the hospital (9) ________________ night. He goes to bed late (10) ________________ weekdays.

(11) ________________ Saturday, Jay works at his second job. Jay is busy almost all the time, but (12) ________________ Saturday nights, he goes out with friends. (13) ________________ Sunday mornings, Jay sleeps late. (14) ________________ the afternoon, he does the laundry and food shopping. (15) ________________ the evening, he studies. Jay is typical of many working students at colleges in the United States.

form

FOCUS 5 Frequency and Time Expressions

EXAMPLES	EXPLANATIONS
(a) They cook dinner **every night.** (b) Jay plays soccer **twice a week.**	Frequency and time expressions usually come at the end of a sentence.
(c) They cook dinner **every night at 7:00.** (d) They cook dinner **at 7:00 every night.**	When there is both a frequency and a time expression in one sentence, the frequency expression can come before or after the time expression.
(e) **Once a week,** they go out to eat. (f) **On weekends,** they stay in.	Frequency and time expressions can sometimes come at the beginning of a sentence. Use a comma (,) after the expressions at the beginning of a sentence.
(g) I work **on Saturdays.** (h) I work **Saturdays.** (i) I work **on July 4th.** (j) I work **July 4th.**	With days and dates, *on* is not necessary.

EXERCISE 8

Make true statements about your habits or routines using the time and frequency expressions below and the simple present tense.

Example: once a week
You say: *I go to the movies once a week.*

1. once a week ______________________________
2. every weekend ______________________________
3. twice a week ______________________________
4. on my birthday ______________________________
5. once a year ______________________________
6. at 7:30 in the morning ______________________________
7. on Friday nights ______________________________
8. in September ______________________________
9. in the summer ______________________________
10. all the time ______________________________
11. on December 31 ______________________________
12. at 6:00 in the evening ______________________________

EXERCISE 9

Erika is a teacher at a community college. Look at Erika's weekly schedule. Then fill in the blanks in the exercise with the simple present tense or a frequency or time expression.

	MONDAY	TUESDAY	WEDNESDAY	THURSDAY	FRIDAY
7:00	wake up				
7:30	eat breakfast at home				go out for breakfast
9:30	teach French	go jogging	teach French	do aerobics	teach French
12:00	eat lunch at school	eat lunch at home	eat lunch at school	eat lunch at home	attend meetings
3:00	play tennis	prepare lessons	play tennis	go food shopping	clean apartment
6:00	meet a friend for dinner	go to cooking class	go to the movies	take dancing lessons	go out with friends
8:00	do the laundry	spend time on the Internet	read students' papers	prepare lessons	
10:30	go to bed early				
12:00					go to bed

1. Erika ______ *goes food shopping* ______ on Thursday afternoon.
2. Erika cleans her apartment ______ *on Friday afternoon* ______.
3. Erika ______________________ every day at 7:00.
4. She eats breakfast at home ______________________.
5. Once a week, on Friday mornings, she ______________________.
6. She ______________________ three times a week.
7. She does aerobics ______________________.
8. She eats lunch at school ______________________.
9. She attends meetings ______________________.
10. She eats lunch at home ______________________.
11. She goes to cooking class ______________________.
12. She reads students' papers ______________________.
13. On Friday evening, she ______________________.
14. She goes to bed early ______________________.
15. She ______________________ at midnight on Friday.
16. She does the laundry ______________________.
17. She ______________________ at 8:00 on Thursday night.

Now make three more statements about Erika's schedule.

form

FOCUS 6 Simple Present: Negative Statements

SUBJECT	*DO/DOES NOT*	BASE FORM OF VERB
I You* We They Michael and Sam	do not don't	work.
He She It Erika	does not doesn't	

*Both singular and plural.

EXERCISE 10

Refer to the Opening Task on pages 116 and 117. For each verb below, make a true negative statement about Michael or Sam.

Example: smoke
Michael doesn't smoke.

1. drink soda
2. exercise a lot
3. skip breakfast
4. eat healthy food
5. order take-out food from restaurants
6. get a good night's sleep
7. sit home and watch TV
8. drink a lot of water
9. feel stressed
10. take sleeping pills

EXERCISE 11

Go back to the statements you wrote for the Opening Task on page 117 and correct them, if necessary.

EXERCISE 12

STEP 1 **Do you have a healthy lifestyle? Check (✔) *Yes* or *No.***

	Yes	No
1. I smoke.	______	______
2. I exercise three times a week.	______	______
3. I eat fruit and vegetables.	______	______
4. I eat junk food.	______	______
5. I sleep 8 hours a night.	______	______
6. I skip meals.	______	______
7. I eat red meat almost every day.	______	______
8. I find time to relax.	______	______
9. I worry all the time.	______	______
10. I use sunscreen.	______	______
11. I overeat.	______	______
12. I drink 3–4 glasses of water a day.	______	______

STEP 2 **Work with a partner. Look at your partner's *Yes* and *No* checks. Tell the class why your partner has a healthy or an unhealthy lifestyle.**

Example: *My partner has a very healthy life. He doesn't smoke. He exercises almost every day.*

FOCUS 7 Useful Expressions with Common Verbs

Try to remember these useful expressions:

DO	GO	HAVE	MAKE	TAKE
homework	home	breakfast	decisions	a vacation
the housework	to school	lunch	money	a test
the dishes	to the doctor	dinner	breakfast	a nap
the shopping	to the beach	a snack	lunch	a rest
the cleaning	shopping/dancing	a drink	dinner	a break
the cooking	skiing/swimming/fishing	a party	plans	a trip
the laundry	hiking			

EXERCISE 13

Work in groups of five. Write each of the expressions in Focus 7 on separate pieces of paper. Put the papers in a hat. Each student takes a piece of paper and makes a true statement with that expression.

Example: Student chooses "a party": *I have a party on my birthday every year.*
"the shopping": *In my family, my father does the shopping.*

FOCUS 8 Talking About Things That Are Always True

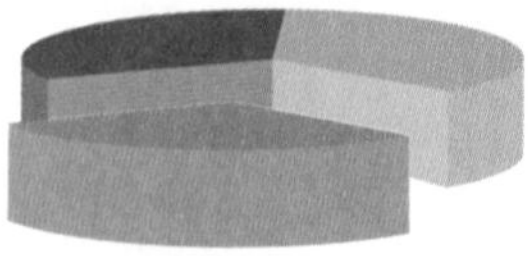

use

EXAMPLES	EXPLANATION
(a) The sun **rises** in the East and **sets** in the West. (b) Exercise **makes** our bodies strong and healthy. (c) A healthy person **doesn't smoke.**	Use the simple present to make generalizations or statements about things that always happen or things that are always true.

EXERCISE 14

Fill in the blanks with the simple present affirmative or negative form of the verb.

1. Workaholics (work) ____work____ all the time.
2. Vegetarians (eat) ______________ meat.
3. Couch potatoes (sit) ______________ in front of the TV all the time.
4. An alcoholic (drink) ______________ a lot of wine, beer, or liquor every day.
5. An insomniac (sleep) ______________ at night.
6. A stressed person (worry) ______________ a lot.
7. An unhealthy person (exercise) ______________ a lot.
8. An optimist (see) ______________ the glass half full.
9. A pessimist (see) ______________ the glass half empty.
10. A carnivore (love) ______________ meat.
11. Busy people (have) ______________ a lot of free time.
12. A healthy person (go) ______________ to a doctor once a year.
13. Lazy people (do) ______________ a lot of activities.
14. Liars (tell) ______________ the truth.

EXERCISE 15

Fill in the blanks. Use the simple present affirmative or negative of the verbs in parentheses.

Today, many Americans are under stress. They (move) (1) ___move___ at a fast pace. They (work) (2) ________________ long hours. They often (work) (3) ________________ overtime. Some Americans (need) (4) ________________ two or three jobs to pay their bills. People (have) (5) ________________ time for themselves or their families. An average worker (have) (6) ________________ too much work and (have) (7) ________________ enough time to finish it. As a result, many Americans (take) (8) ________________ vacations.

Why are Americans so busy all the time? One reason is that they (want) (9) ________________ many things. They (believe) (10) ________________ that money brings happiness. Another reason is modern technology. Modern technology (keep) (11) ________________ us busy and (give) (12) ________________ us stress. Technology (let) (13) ________________ us relax. We (wear) (14) ________________ beepers. We (carry) ________________ cell phones. We (use) (15) ________________ fax machines to send messages fast. We even (check) (16) ________________ our e-mail on vacation! We (take) (17) ________________ time to rest. Even on Sundays, many stores (stay) (18) ________________ open and people (go) (19) ________________ shopping. Today, stress is one of the top reasons why Americans (get) (20) ________________ sick.

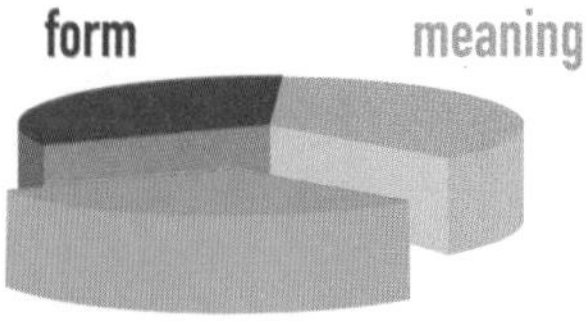

FOCUS 9 *Like, Want, Need*

EXAMPLES	EXPLANATIONS
I **like** / **want** / **need** coffee.	Subject + Verb + Noun
I **like** / **want** / **need** to drink coffee.	Subject + Verb + Infinitive
(a) I **like** jazz. (b) I love animals. I **want** a cat.	*Like* refers to something we enjoy. *Want* expresses desire.
(c) I have a headache. I **need** medicine.	*Need* refers to something that is necessary.

EXERCISE 16

Use the verbs *like, want,* and *need.* Write three sentences for each picture.

Example:

1. She likes to play tennis. She wants to win. She needs a good tennis racket.

PICTURE	*LIKE*	*WANT*	*NEED*
1. 	a. play tennis	b. win	c. a good tennis racket
2. 	a. cook	b. be a good cook	c. a cookbook

PICTURE	*LIKE*	*WANT*	*NEED*
3. 	a. sleep late in the morning	b. get up early today	c. a cup of strong coffee
4. 	a. the sun	b. protect their skin	c. sunscreen
5. 	a. write	b. write a book	c. peace and quiet
6. 	a. travel	b. stay in touch with friends at all times	c. a cell phone

EXERCISE 17

Correct the mistakes in the following sentences.

1. She is smile every day
2. He every day takes a walk.
3. He wash the dishes every night.
4. He don't cook dinner on Sundays.
5. We are study in the library on Saturdays.
6. They no work on Tuesdays.
7. English classes begin at September.
8. She need a pen to write.
9. He wants make a sandwich.
10. Erika plays tennis on 3:00.

Use Your English

ACTIVITY 1 speaking

STEP 1 Think of a person you admire. Tell your partner about this person. Then answer any questions your partner may have.

Example: *I admire my mother. She loves our family. She enjoys her work. She cooks great food. She doesn't get angry.*

STEP 2 Tell your partner about a person you are worried about. Then answer any questions your partner may have.

Example: *I am worried about my roommate. He works 12 hours a day. He doesn't eat healthy food. He doesn't exercise. He doesn't sleep. He only goes to work, then comes home and goes to bed. He doesn't have any fun.*

ACTIVITY 2 writing/speaking

What do you and your partner have in common? Write two affirmative statements and two negative statements with *like* for each category below.

- music
- books
- food
- movies
- cars

Example: *I like to listen to classical music. I also like rock. I don't like rap. I don't like to listen to opera.*

Share your sentences with your partner and find out what you both have in common. Report your results to the class.

Example: *I listen to classical music, but my partner likes hip-hop.*

ACTIVITY 3 writing/speaking

STEP 1

Fill out your own daily schedule using only the base form of the verb.

My schedule: (Name) ______________________________

	MON.	TUES.	WED.	THURS.	FRI.	SAT.	SUN.
Morning		6:00 go jogging					
Afternoon				3:00 go to the library			
Evening					8:00 go bowling		

STEP 2

Read your schedule to a partner. Take notes about his/her schedule. Write sentences about your partner's habits and routines. How are your habits different? Report to the class.

Example: *My partner wakes up at 10:00 on Sundays.*

My partner's schedule: (Name) ______________________________

	MON.	TUES.	WED.	THURS.	FRI.	SAT.	SUN.
Morning							10:00 wake up
Afternoon							
Evening							

ACTIVITY 4 writing/speaking

Write ten statements about the habits of people in the country you come from. Share your information with your classmates. Compare the habits of people in different countries.

Examples: 1. *In Korea, women don't change their names when they get married. People eat rice every day.*

2. *In Italy, people eat pasta.*

ACTIVITY 5 listening

People in different countries have different lifestyles.

CD Track 7

STEP 1

Listen to the descriptions of the lifestyles of people in the United States and in France. Use the chart and listen for specific information. Take notes on what you hear.

	THE UNITED STATES	FRANCE
Work Week		
Vacation Time		
Eating Habits		
% Obese		
Health Insurance		
Education		

STEP 2

Which lifestyle is similar to the lifestyle in your native country?

ACTIVITY 6 writing/speaking

Switching Lifestyles

STEP 1 Work in groups of six. Each person chooses to be one of the people below. Write five sentences about your lifestyle.

1. Hollywood actress

2. firefighter

3. homeless person

4. dancer

5. farmer

6. millionaire

STEP 2 Talk to different people in your group, and describe your lifestyle. Try to get another person to switch lifestyles with you.

Example: "Hollywood actress": *I have a fantastic lifestyle. I make a movie every year. I make a lot of money. I own three homes. I travel all the time.*

ACTIVITY 7 research on the web

STEP 1 Use a search engine such as Google® or Yahoo® or Ask® to search the Internet for healthy habits to improve your life. Use the keywords *healthy habit improve life.*

STEP 2 Then create a survey on healthy habits in the chart on the next page. List a habit. Ask students if they do or don't do the habit.

HEALTHY HABIT SURVEY	YES	NO
1. I wash my hands during the day.		
2.		
3.		
4.		
5.		

STEP 3 Form a group. Survey your group members about their healthy habits. Count up the responses and share your findings with the class.

ACTIVITY 8 reflection

Look at the list of activities for practicing English outside of class. Use frequency and time expressions to say how frequently you do each activity.

1. I watch television.	I watch television two hours a night.
2. I listen to the radio.	
3. I read a newspaper.	
4. I try to speak to people in my neighborhood.	
5. I go to the movies.	
6. I use the Internet.	
7. I chat online.	
8. I review my lessons after class.	
9. I write in a journal.	
10. Add one of your own.	

Do you think you practice English enough outside of school? Discuss this in a group.

UNIT 9

SIMPLE PRESENT TENSE

Yes/No Questions, Adverbs of Frequency, *Wh*-Questions

UNIT GOALS

- Ask *yes/no* and *Wh*-questions in the simple present tense
- Understand the meaning and correct position of adverbs of frequency
- Ask questions with *who* and *whom*
- Ask for information about English

OPENING TASK

What Do Good Language Learners Do?

You are all "language learners" in this class. Are you *good* language learners? What do good language learners do?

STEP 1

Work in small groups. Read and discuss the "learning strategies" below. Cross out the learning strategies that are not helpful for good language learning.

Good language learners . . .

1. think about how to learn.
2. speak their native language a lot.
3. ask questions about the new language.
4. are afraid to make mistakes.
5. practice the new language.
6. stop listening when they don't understand.
7. guess the meanings of new words and expressions.
8. give up when they can't say things correctly.
9. think about how to be better language learners.
10. study the grammar of the new language.

STEP 2

Are your classmates good language learners? To find out, prepare a questionnaire using five strategies from Step 1. Add one question of your own.

Questionnaire: Learning Strategies

1.
2.
3.
4.
5.
6.

form

FOCUS 1 Simple Present: *Yes/No* Questions

DO/DOES	SUBJECT	BASE FORM OF VERB	SHORT ANSWERS *AFFIRMATIVE*			SHORT ANSWERS *NEGATIVE*		
Do	I you we they	work?	Yes,	I you we they	do.	No,	I you we they	do not. don't.
Does	he she it		Yes,	he she it	does.	No,	he she it	does not. doesn't.

EXERCISE 1

Go back to the questions on your questionnaire in the Opening Task on page 139 and correct them, if necessary.

EXERCISE 2

Are your classmates good language learners? Use your questionnaire to interview a new partner. Share something about your partner with the class.

EXERCISE 3

Information gap. Adriana and Sang-Woo are two different types of language learners. Work with a partner to find out how they are different. Student A looks at the chart on the next page. Student B looks at the chart on page A-19. Ask and answer questions to complete your chart.

Example: Student A: *Does Adriana want to meet English-speaking people?*
Student B: *Yes, she does.*

Example: Student B: *Does Sang-Woo want to meet English-speaking people?*
Student A: *No, he doesn't.*

Student A

	ADRIANA		SANG-WOO	
	YES	NO	YES	NO
1. like to learn English	✔			
2. want to meet English-speaking people				✔
3. feel nervous when speaking English		✔		
4. like to work in groups			✔	
5. need grammar rules to learn English	✔			
6. learn by speaking and listening to English				✔
7. learn by reading and writing English		✔		
8. learn slowly, step by step			✔	
9. try new ways of learning	✔			

EXERCISE 4

What kind of language learner are you? Look at Exercise 3 and write statements about yourself.

Example: *I like to learn English. I want to meet English-speaking people. I don't feel nervous when speaking English.*

EXERCISE 5

STEP 1 **Read the following paragraphs about students in the United States.**

(1) In the United States, a child usually starts kindergarten at age 5. (2) In public schools, boys and girls study together. (3) Children go to school five days a week. (4) They don't go to school on Saturdays. (5) They go to school from 8:30 A.M. to 3:00 P.M. (6) They don't wear uniforms. (7) In public schools, children do not study religion.

(8) In high school, some students take difficult exams to enter college. (9) A private college costs a lot of money. (10) The government doesn't pay for private colleges. (11) Many parents pay for their children's education. (12) Many students work after school to help pay for college.

STEP 2 Write 12 *yes/no* questions from the sentences marked 1–12 in the reading.

Questions

1. Does a child usually start kindergarten at age 5 in your country?
2. Do boys and girls usually study together?
3. ________________?
4. ________________?
5. ________________?
6. ________________?
7. ________________?
8. ________________?
9. ________________?
10. ________________?
11. ________________?
12. ________________?

STEP 3 Interview a classmate about his or her country with the questions you wrote. Write five sentences about school in your partner's home country.

Question 1

Example: In Korea, a child usually starts kindergarten at age 4 or 5.

1. ________________
2. ________________
3. ________________
4. ________________
5. ________________

STEP 4 Compare students in the United States to students in your home country.

FOCUS 2 Adverbs of Frequency

Question: How often does Nahal watch television?			
	always		100%
	almost always		↑
	usually		
Nahal	often/frequently	watches television.	
	sometimes		
	seldom/rarely		↓
	never		0%

EXERCISE 6

Read the questions and answers below. Circle the correct adverbs of frequency.

Example: Q: *Does Belinda read English/American newspapers?*
A: *She (always/seldom) reads an English or American newspaper. She buys one every morning.*

1. Q: Does Hamid ever use his hands when he speaks English?
   A: He (never/always) uses his hands. His hands help him explain things.
2. Q: Does Belinda ever guess the meanings of words?
   A: She (never/always) guesses the meanings of new words. She uses her dictionary all the time.
3. Q: Does Hamid ever think in English?
   A: He (never/usually) thinks in his own language first. Then he translates his words into English.
4. Q: Does Belinda ever sing in English?
   A: She (often/seldom) sings in English. She doesn't like to sing.
5. Q: Does Hamid ever write letters in English?
   A: He has an American friend in Boston. He misses him. He (rarely/often) writes letters to him in English.
6. Q: Does Belinda ever make telephone calls in English?
   A: She lives with her aunt. Her aunt speaks English. Her aunt makes the phone calls. Belinda (never/always) makes phone calls in English.
7. Q: Does Belinda ever talk to herself in English?
   A: She likes English. She (sometimes/rarely) talks to herself in English.
8. Q: Does Hamid ever think about how English works?
   A: He thinks grammar is very interesting. He (never/always) tries to understand how English works.

EXERCISE 7

The chart below shows learning habits and adverbs of frequency. Check the box that is true for you.

LEARNING HABITS	ADVERBS OF FREQUENCY						
	always	almost always	usually	often/ frequently	sometimes	seldom/ rarely	never
1. use a dictionary when reading							
2. speak English outside of class							
3. give up when you can't express yourself							
4. discuss learning problems with classmates							
5. practice English pronunciation							
6. review new vocabulary							
7. read books or newspapers in English							
8. ask questions about English							
9. think in English							
10. dream in English							

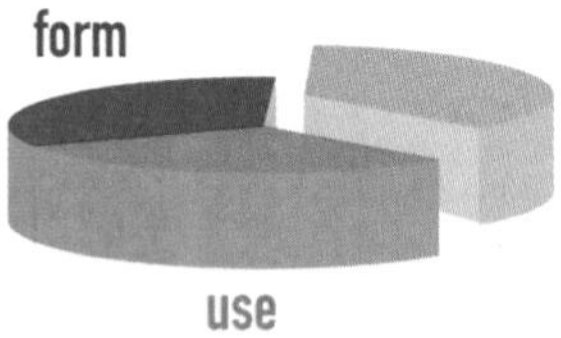

FOCUS 3 Position of Adverbs of Frequency

EXAMPLES	EXPLANATIONS
(a) They **always** come to class. (b) He **sometimes** asks questions in class. (c) He **never** asks questions.	Adverbs of frequency usually come between the subject and the verb.
(d) **Sometimes** I ask questions in class. (e) That's not true. He asks questions **often.**	Some adverbs of frequency can come at the beginning or at the end of a sentence for emphasis.
(f) They **are always** in class. (g) I **am never** late to class.	Adverbs of frequency come after the verb *be.*

EXERCISE 8

Go back to the chart in Exercise 7. Exchange books with a partner. Write statements about your partner's learning habits using adverbs of frequency.

Examples: *He always uses a dictionary.*
She rarely speaks to native speakers.

EXERCISE 9

STEP 1 **Make true statements about your home country by adding an adverb of frequency.**

Name of country: ____________________

In schools in my home country:

1. The students are of the same nationality.
   The students are usually of the same nationality.
2. The teachers are women.
   ____
3. Teachers hit students.
   ____

4. Teachers are young.

____

5. Teachers give homework.

____

6. Teachers are relaxed and friendly.

____

7. Students work together to learn.

____

8. The classrooms are noisy.

____

9. Students take tests.

____

10. Students help each other on tests.

____

STEP 2 **Discuss what you think is true for the United States.**

FOCUS 4 Simple Present: *Wh*-Questions

***WH*-QUESTION WORD**	***DO/DOES***	**SUBJECT**	**BASE FORM OF VERB**	
(a) **What**	**do**	I	**say**	in class?
(b) **When**	**do**	you	**review**	new vocabulary?
(c) **What time**	**do**	we	**take**	a break ?
(d) **Where**	**do**	they	**study**	English?
(e) **Why**	**does**	he	**need**	English?
(f) **How**	**does**	she	**practice**	pronunciation?
(g) **How often**	**does**	Maria	**use**	her electronic dictionary?
(h) **Who(m)***	**does**	George	**meet**	after school?

*Note: Refer to Focus 5, page 150 for an explanation of who(m).

EXERCISE 10

Immigrants to the United States learn English. But these days, many immigrants to the United States also learn languages **other than** English.

Match each question to its answer. Write the letter next to each question on the left.

___ 1. **Why** do they learn other languages?

___ 2. **What** (languages) do they learn?

___ 3. **Where** do they learn the other languages?

___ 4. **How** do they learn them?

___ 5. **How often** do they use these other languages?

___ 6. **What** do they think about (learning) English?

___ 7. **When** do they study English?

___ 8. **What time** do their English classes end?

___ 9. **Why** do language researchers want to study these immigrants?

a. They don't go to school. They learn these other languages at work.

b. They use these other languages every day.

c. Because they need these languages to do business in their neighborhoods.

d. They know they need to learn English.

e. They take English classes after work.

f. Because the researchers want to understand how people learn third and fourth languages.

g. They learn them by talking to different people in their neighborhoods when they do business.

h. They learn Spanish, Hindi, Korean, Chinese, etc.

i. Sometimes they end as late as 10 P.M.

EXERCISE 11

STEP 1 **Read the story of a student named Denise. Write *Wh*-questions with the words in parentheses. Ask two questions of your own about the story.**

Denise is a Haitian student in Washington, D.C. She speaks three languages—Creole, French, and English. She wants to be a bilingual teacher. Her English is very good, but she speaks with an accent. Sometimes people don't understand her when she speaks. She often meets her Haitian friends to talk about her problem. Denise feels embarrassed and seldom speaks English. She feels angry at Americans. She says Americans only speak English. They don't understand the problems people have when they learn a new language.

Example: (Denise/live) *Where does Denise live?*

1. (Denise/come from) ______________________________?
2. (Denise/want to be) ______________________________?
3. (Denise/speak English)? ______________________________?
4. (Denise/feel when she speaks English) ______________________________

   ______________________________?
5. (Denise/feel this way) ______________________________?
6. (Denise/feel angry) ______________________________?
7. ______________________________?
8. ______________________________?

STEP 2 **Read the story again. Take turns asking a partner the questions and answering them aloud.**

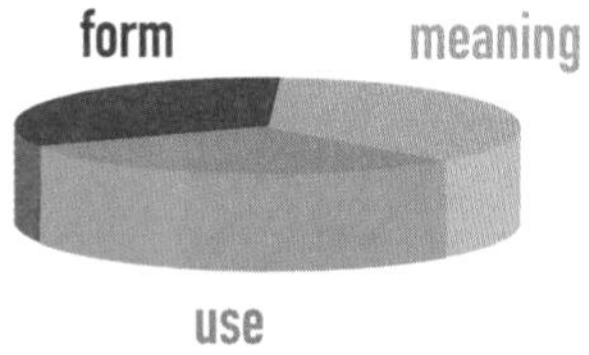

FOCUS 5 *Wh*-Questions with *Who/Whom*

EXAMPLES	EXPLANATIONS
(a) **Q: Who** usually meets her friends? **A:** Denise. (b) **Q: Who** speaks Creole? **A:** Denise and her Haitian friends.	*Who* asks a question about the **subject** (Denise) of the sentence. Do not use *do/does.*
(c) **Q: Who(m)** does Denise meet? **A:** Denise meets her friends.	*Who(m)* asks a question about the **object** (her friends) of the sentence.
(d) **Whom** does Denise call on Sundays?	Formal written English
(e) **Who** does Denise call on Sundays?	Informal or spoken English
(f) **Q: What** goes up but never comes down? **A:** Your age!	*What* can also be the subject of a question. Do not use *do/does* in this case.

EXERCISE 12

Fill in the blanks with *who* or *whom.*

Example: ___Who___ speaks English?
___Who(m)___ do you see every week?

1. ________________ likes English?
2. ________________ avoids English?
3. ________________ bites his or her nails before a test?
4. ________________ do you practice English with?
5. ________________ do you usually visit on weekends?
6. ________________ makes mistakes in English?
7. ________________ do you like in your ESL class?
8. ________________ understands the difference between *who* and *whom?*
9. ________________ do you help with English?

EXERCISE 13

STEP 1 **Read about immigrant families in the United States.**

Many families immigrate to the United States. At the beginning, the parents often have problems. They don't speak English. They don't learn English fast. The children usually learn English before the parents, so they translate for their parents. The children always help their parents. Sometimes, the children pay the rent to the landlords. They often talk with doctors about their parents' health. The children take their parents to job interviews. They solve the family's problems. This is a big responsibility for the children, and they feel important. But their parents sometimes feel sad and helpless. Life is often difficult for new immigrant families.

STEP 2 **Fill in the blanks with *who* (subject) or *whom* (object). Then answer the questions.**

Examples: Q: *Who learns English before the parents do?*
A: *The children (learn English before the parents).*
Q: *Whom do the children help?*
A: *(The children help) their parents.*

1. ______________ translates for the parents?
2. ______________ helps the parents?
3. ______________ do the children pay the rent to?
4. ______________ do the children often talk to about their parents' health?
5. ______________ do the children take to job interviews?
6. ______________ solves the family's problems?
7. ______________ feels important?
8. ______________ feels sad and helpless?

FOCUS 6 Getting Information About English

use

In a new language, you do not always know the words to say what you want. When you have a problem, ask for help.

EXAMPLES	EXPLANATIONS
You say:	When you:
(a) What does the word *decision* mean? (b) What does *strategy* mean?	want to know the **meaning** of a word
(c) How do you spell *remember?*	want to know the **spelling** of a word
(d) How do you pronounce *communicate?*	want to know the **pronunciation** of a word
(e) How do you say *a machine to clean floors?* (f) How do you say *the opposite of happy?*	don't know the word for something, and you want to communicate your meaning and learn new words

EXERCISE 14

Ask *Wh*-questions for the answers below.

Example: Q: *How do you say* ***special shoes you wear in the house?***
A: *You say* ***slippers.***

1. Q: ______________________________?
   A: You pronounce it laéŋ?-gwIdʒ.
2. Q: ______________________________?
   A: The word *guess* means you don't know the answer, but you try to find the answer in your head.
3. Q: ______________________________?
   A: You say *thin.*
4. Q: ______________________________?
   A: You spell it: c-o-m-m-u-n-i-c-a-t-e.
5. Q: ______________________________?
   A: *Strategy* means an action or actions you take to achieve a goal; for example, to learn English.

EXERCISE 15

Correct the errors in the following sentences.

1. Is he read books?
2. Do they good students?
3. What means *routines?*
4. I watch sometimes TV.
5. How often you listen to native speakers of English?
6. Does he studies in the library?
7. What does the class on Mondays?
8. How you say *not correct?*
9. I am never make mistakes.
10. Why you feel embarrassed to speak English?

Use Your English

ACTIVITY 1 writing/speaking

STEP 1 Work with a partner. Make a chart like the one below. Write at least ten questions you want to ask your classmates to compare their lives in their home countries and their lives here.

STEP 2 Ask each other your questions. Report the differences in your lives to the class.

QUESTION	IN YOUR HOME COUNTRY . . .	IN THE UNITED STATES . . .
1. Whom do you live with?		
2. Who cooks for you?		
3.		

ACTIVITY 2 writing/speaking

To learn English faster, you want to find an English-speaking roommate. Write ten questions to ask your classmates about their habits. Find a good "roommate" in your class.

Examples: *What language do you speak? Do you smoke? What time do you get up?*

ACTIVITY 3 writing/speaking

STEP 1 What do you know about the countries your classmates come from? Write ten questions about customs, habits, weather, schools, politics, and so on. Some examples are: *What do people usually do on weekends? How do people usually celebrate their birthdays?*

STEP 2 Find a classmate who comes from a different country and ask the questions. Then report to the class.

ACTIVITY 4 listening/speaking

CD Track 8

Listen to a researcher interviewing two students, Tereza and Rodrigo, about their language learning strategies. Decide if the person is saying yes or no. Write *Yes* or *No*. Decide who is a better language learner. Why? Discuss with your class.

	QUESTION				
	1	2	3	4	5
Tereza:					
Rodrigo:					

ACTIVITY 5 research on the web

Create your own questionnaire about good language learning. Use a search engine such as Google® or Ask® or Yahoo® to search the Internet for language learning tips. Use the key words *English learning tips.* Then create a questionnaire with five to ten questions. Ask a partner the questions. Is your partner a good language learner?

Example: Tip: Practice speaking English every day.
Question: *Do you practice speaking English every day?*

ACTIVITY 6 reflection

STEP 1 You want to write a letter to a friend in your country. Tell your friend about your language learning. First, think about the questions your friend wants to ask you. Write down five questions.

Examples: *How often do you speak English? Whom do you practice English with? What do you do in class?*

STEP 2 Write the letter to your friend. Include answers to the questions from Step 1.

Example: *Dear Sang,*
Learning English in the U.S. is very different. In class, we practice conversation and listening . . .

UNIT 10

IMPERATIVES AND PREPOSITIONS OF DIRECTION

UNIT GOALS

- Make affirmative and negative imperatives
- Understand the many functions of imperatives
- Use prepositions of direction
- Give directions

OPENING TASK

Exploring Your Community

When students go to college, there are many things they don't know. Imagine you are writing a *Handbook for New Students.* One of the chapters in the handbook is "Tips for Exploring Your Community."

STEP 1

Write five helpful ideas for getting to know your community.

Example: *Buy a map of your community.*

Tips for Exploring Your Community

Tip 1: ______________________________

Tip 2: ______________________________

Tip 3: ______________________________

Tip 4: ______________________________

Tip 5: ______________________________

STEP 2

Write two tips about what *not* to do when you want to explore your community.

Tip 6: ______________________________

Tip 7: ______________________________

form

FOCUS 1 Imperatives: Affirmative and Negative

Affirmative

BASE FORM OF VERB	
(a) Read	the local newspaper.
(b) Buy	a good guidebook.

EXAMPLE	EXPLANATION
(c) Use your student ID card. NOT: You use your student ID card.	The subject of the imperative is *you* (singular or plural), but we don't usually say or write the subject.

Negative

DO NOT/ DON'T	BASE FORM OF VERB	
(d) Do not	be	shy.
(e) Don't	stay	at home every weekend.

EXAMPLE	EXPLANATION
(f) **Do not walk** in the park after dark!	We usually use ***don't*** + **base form of verb** in spoken English. To make the negative imperative stronger, you can use ***do not*** + **base form of verb.**

EXERCISE 1

Go back to the ideas you wrote in the Opening Task on page 157. Rewrite your ideas. Check the affirmative and negative imperatives and correct any errors, if necessary. Share your list with a partner.

EXERCISE 2

Imagine you are writing three new chapters in the *Handbook for New Students.* Here are some tips for those chapters.

Tips:

a. Read a book.
b. E-mail your family.
c. Don't go to class.
d. Make new friends.
e. Listen to music.
f. Drink water and juice.
g. Rest a lot.
h. Don't drink coffee at night.
i. Don't eat alone.

STEP 1 **Match each tip to the correct chapter. Write each tip under its chapter title.**

Chapter 1 When you get a cold Or When you are sick	Chapter 2 When you can't sleep	Chapter 3 When you are homesick Or When you are lonely
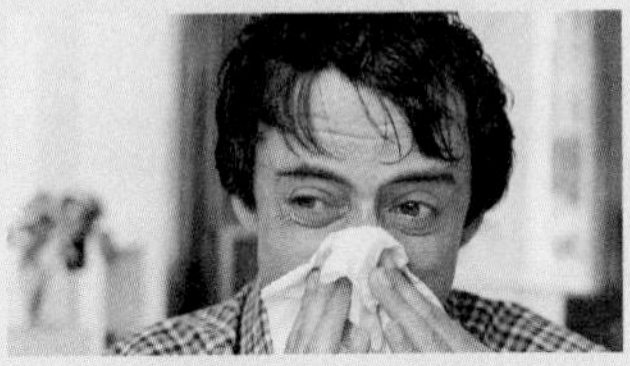		

STEP 2 **Work with a partner. Add two more tips to each chapter.**

Chapter 1 When you get a cold Or When you are sick	Chapter 2 When you can't sleep	Chapter 3 When you are homesick Or When you are lonely

STEP 3 **Underline the affirmative imperatives, and circle the negative imperatives in Step 1 and Step 2.**

FOCUS 2 Uses of Imperatives

use

Imperatives have different uses or functions. Look at the pictures and notice the functions of the imperatives in each situation.

a. Function: Offer something politely

b. Function: Give instruction

c. Function: Give directions

d. Function: Make a polite request

e. Function: Give a warning

f. Function: Give an order

g. Function: Apologize

h. Function: Give advice

EXERCISE 3

Refer to the pictures in Focus 2. Read each new sentence, and match it to the correct picture. Match its use or function.

IMPERATIVE	USE OR FUNCTION
1. Please be quiet!	
2. Please accept my apology and don't be angry at me.	
3. Get a broom!	
4. Be patient. Give her time.	
5. Please turn out the lights on your way out.	
6. For the post office, make a left at the corner.	
7. Have some iced coffee and a cookie.	
8. Be careful!	

EXERCISE 4

Imagine a situation with a roommate. You can use one of the situations from page 160, or come up with one of your own. Write a dialogue about the situation using imperatives. Then role-play the dialogue with a partner for the class.

EXERCISE 5

Another chapter in the *Handbook for New Students* is "How to Be Safe in Your Community." Fill in each blank with an affirmative or negative imperative from the verbs in the box below. You may use a verb more than once.

keep	know	wear	use
be	walk	leave	take

1. ______________ aware of people around you.
2. ______________ common sense.
3. ______________ the subway very late at night.
4. ______________ careful, especially at night.
5. ______________ your wallet in your front pocket.
6. ______________ expensive jewelry.
7. ______________ your valuables at home.
8. ______________ with a friend late at night.
9. ______________ afraid to ask people for help.
10. ______________ your neighborhood.

EXERCISE 6

Fill in each blank below with an affirmative or a negative imperative form of these verbs.

talk	keep	drink	be	drive
wear	obey	leave	look	use

To be a good driver, remember these rules:

1. ____________________ prepared to stop.

2. ____________________ at the road ahead.

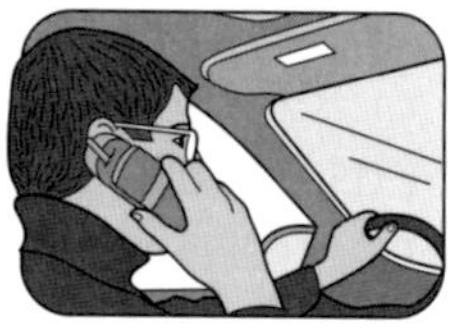

3. ____________________ on your cell phone while driving.

4. ____________________ the speed limit.

5. ____________________ space between your car and the car in front of you.

6. ____________________ your seat belt.

7. ____________________ if you are very tired or are on medication.

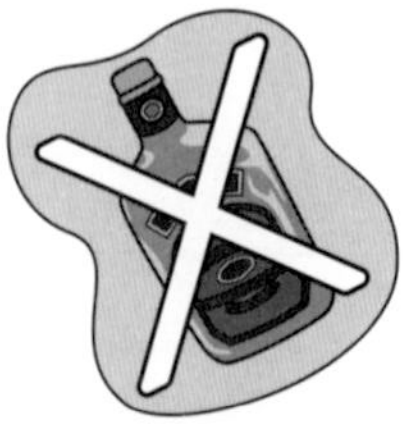

8. ____________________ and drive.

9. ________________ your horn only to warn others of danger.

10. ________________ your car in good condition.

EXERCISE 7

Quick Fix! Work in groups of four. Student A states a problem from the list below. The other three students offer advice. Student A chooses the advice he or she thinks is the best. The student who offers the best advice gets a point. Then Student B says a problem, and three other students give advice. The person with the most points wins.

Example: Student A says: *I feel homesick.*
Student B says: *Call a friend back home.*
Student C says: *E-mail your family.*
Student D says: *See a movie with a friend.*

Problems:

1. I don't like the food here.
2. My best friend is angry at me.
3. I have a problem with my roommate.
4. I have a really bad headache.
5. I can't sleep at night.
6. I have the hiccups.
7. I don't speak English very well.
8. I don't have any friends here.
9. There's nothing to do here; I feel bored on the weekends.
10. I have too much homework.
11. I don't have money.
12. I was sick. I missed class yesterday.

Add two problems of your own.

13. ____

14. ____

FOCUS 3 Using Imperatives Appropriately

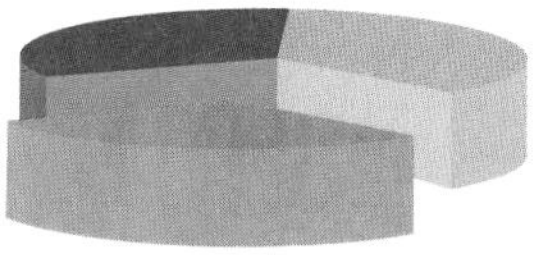
use

EXAMPLES	EXPLANATIONS
(a) Police officer to driver: Let me see your license. (b) One police officer to another: Follow that car!	Use an imperative when: the speaker has the right or authority to tell the listener to do something. the speaker and the listener are equals.
(c) **Please be** careful. (d) **Please don't stay** out late.	Use *please* to make the imperative more polite.
(e) **Don't stay** out late, **please.**	*Please* comes at the beginning or at the end of an imperative. In writing, put a comma before *please* at the end of a sentence.

EXERCISE 8

Check (✔) *Yes* if the imperative is appropriate in each situation. Check (✔) *No* if the imperative is not appropriate.

SITUATION	IMPERATIVE	YES	NO
1. A doctor says to a patient with a bad cold:	"Take two aspirin and call me in the morning."		
2. A policeman says to a driver:	"Give me your license."		
3. A teenager stops a man on the street and says:	"Hey, Mister. Tell me the time."		
4. You get on a very crowded bus. You say to the other people:	"Get out of my way."		
5. You tell your best friend that you are bored. Your friend says:	"Come to the show with me!"		
6. A student says to a staff person in the Admissions Office:	"Give me an application."		
7. Your roommate says: "Thanks so much for your help." You say:	"Sure, any time."		
8. Your friend calls you at 2:00 A.M. and wakes your roommate. Your roommate says:	"Please tell him not to call so late!"		

EXERCISE 9

Go back to Exercise 8. Correct the imperatives that are inappropriate and role-play the situation with a partner.

EXERCISE 10

Look at the cartoons below. Write an appropriate imperative for each situation.

1.

2.

3.

4.

5.

6.

meaning

FOCUS 4 Prepositions of Direction: *To, Away from, On (to), Off (of), In (to), Out of*

to

away from

in(to)

off (of)

on(to)

out of

EXAMPLES	EXPLANATIONS
(a) He gets **in (to)** a car. (b) He gets **on (to)** a bus. (c) He gets **out of** a taxi. (d) He gets **off (of)** a train.	Prepositions of direction show movement. For cars, taxis, and vans, use *in (to)* and *out of*. For buses, trains, ferries, boats, and planes, use *on (to)* and *off (of)*.

EXERCISE 11

Read about Tuyet's daily commute to college. Fill in the blanks with an appropriate preposition of direction.

In the morning, Tuyet gets (1) ________________ her car. She parks near the train station. She gets (2) ________________ her car. She gets (3) ________________ a train. The train goes (4) ________________ her college. She gets (5) ________________ the train. Then she goes to class. After class, she gets (6) ________________ the train again. The train goes (7) ________________ Tuyet's college. She gets (8) ________________ the train again. She gets (9) ________________ her car again. Then she drives home. Tuyet gets (10) ________________ her car again. She goes (11) ________________ her home. Her commute is finally over!

meaning

FOCUS 5 More Prepositions of Direction: *Up, Down, Across, Along, Around, Over, Through, Past*

up

down

across

along

around

over

through

past

EXERCISE 12

Read about Tapiwa's walk around his college campus. Fill in the blanks with an appropriate preposition of direction.

1. Tapiwa walked ________________ the Brookstone Bridge.
2. He went ________________ to the top of Green Tower.
3. From the top of the Green Tower, he looked ________________ at the campus.
4. Then, he walked all the way ________________ College Lake.
5. Next, he walked ________________ the Alumni Tunnel.
6. Tapiwa walked ________________ the Blue River.
7. Lastly, he walked ________________ the Science Center, but he didn't go inside. He walked to the dining hall. Then, he ate dinner.

FOCUS 6 Giving Directions

use

Look at the map and read the conversation below.

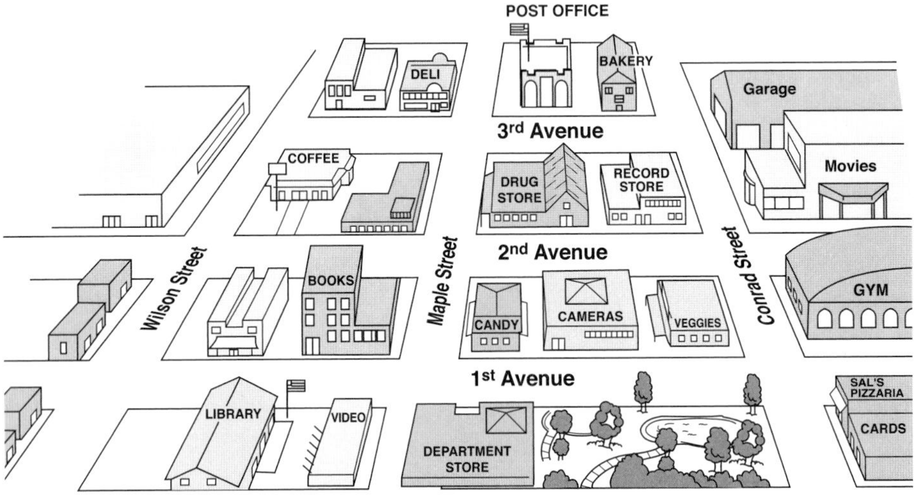

A: (at the bakery) Excuse me, how do I get to the department store?
B: Walk **down** Conrad Street until you get to First Avenue. Then turn **right** at the corner. Go **straight**. Walk one block. The department store is on the corner on the left.

EXERCISE 13

Look at the map above. Follow the directions below. Then answer the questions.

Example: You are at the record store on the corner of Second Avenue and Conrad Street. Walk down Conrad Street until you get to Third Avenue. Turn left at the corner. Walk one block. Cross Third Avenue. This place is on the right. Where are you?
Answer: *At the Post Office.*

1. You are at the bakery. Walk down Conrad Street and make a right on Second Avenue. Go straight and make a left on Maple Street. Walk across the street. Where are you? ____________________
2. You come out of the coffee shop on Second Avenue. Walk down Second Avenue and go two blocks. Turn right on Conrad Street. Go straight until you get to First Avenue. Make a left. Walk into the building on your right. Where are you?

   ____
3. You are at the library on First Avenue. Walk up Wilson Street. Make a right on Third Avenue. Go straight for two blocks. Then make a left on Conrad Street. Go across the street from the bakery. Where are you? ____________________

Now write two sets of directions and questions of your own.

Use Your English

ACTIVITY 1 writing/speaking

STEP 1 Make a list of cultural *do's* and *don'ts* for someone who will visit your region or country. Example: Korea/Greetings and farewells **Do's:** *Bow to say good-bye.* **Dont's:** *Don't touch or pat a man on the back—only if you are very good friends.*

STEP 2 Present the *do's* and *don'ts* to your class.

	DO'S	DON'TS
Greetings and farewells		
Eating		
Tipping (in a restaurant, at a hotel, a taxi driver)		
Visiting someone's home		
Giving and receiving gifts		
Gestures		
Other		

ACTIVITY 2 writing

Many people write to advice columns in the newspaper when they have a problem.

STEP 1 Write a letter to "Dear Dolores" on a piece of paper. Write about a problem a student may have. Ask for advice.

STEP 2 Exchange papers with a partner. Write a letter to answer your partner. Give your partner advice on his or her problem. For example:

You write: Dear Dolores,
I'm an international student. I'm here alone. I want to meet people. I want to make friends. I want to practice my English. Please help me!

Lonely Leo

Your partner writes: Dear Lonely Leo,
It's hard to be alone in a new place. Join a club at school. Talk to people in the cafeteria. Spend time with your classmates during breaks. Don't be discouraged. Good luck!

Dolores

ACTIVITY 3 writing

Work in groups. Write a short note to someone. Choose a purpose for the note from the list below:

- To offer something politely
- To give instructions
- To give directions
- To make a polite request
- To apologize for something you did

ACTIVITY 4 writing

Work in groups. Choose an interesting place in your own community for other students to visit. Using a map, write directions to get to that place from school.

ACTIVITY 5 research

Look around your neighborhood. Find imperatives in public signs or notices. Write them in your notebook. Bring the list to class, and discuss the meaning of the notices with your classmates.

ACTIVITY 6 writing

■ **STEP 1** **Directions Game:** Work in groups of two or three. Write directions for someone to go to different parts of the building you are in (the cafeteria, restroom, lost and found office, etc.).

Example: *Go out of the room. Turn left. Go to the end of the hallway. It's on the right.*

STEP 2 Give your directions to another student in class. The student follows the directions and then comes back to class with the name of the place where he or she ended up.

ACTIVITY 7 research on the web

Search the Internet for useful ideas or suggestions for college students. Use a search engine such as Google® or Yahoo® or Ask® and enter the keywords: *college survival tips.* Make a list of five tips. Share your list with the class.

ACTIVITY 8 listening

Listen to the following short conversations. For each conversation, write the correct function of the imperative in the chart.

CD Track 9

Give directions	Offer an apology
Make a polite request	Give advice

	FUNCTION OF THE IMPERATIVE
Conversation 1	
Conversation 2	
Conversation 3	
Conversation 4	
Conversation 5	

ACTIVITY 9 reflection

Brainstorm five to ten useful tips for new students coming to North America to study English. Write a list of tips and share them with the class. Explain how you use these tips in your life.

UNIT 11

QUANTIFIERS

UNIT GOALS

- Understand the meaning of quantifiers
- Know the difference between *a few* and *few, a little* and *little*
- Use the correct form of quantifiers with count/noncount nouns
- Ask questions with *How many . . ., How much . . .*
- Understand the meaning of measure words

OPENING TASK

Who Eats a Healthy Breakfast?

The chart on page 173 shows the number of calories and the amount of fat and cholesterol in the foods Billy, Brad, and Bobby eat for breakfast every day.

Calories are the amount of energy a food produces in the body. To lose weight, we need to reduce our calories.

There is **fat** in foods like butter, cheese, and meat. A lot of fat may be bad for your health.

There is **cholesterol** in foods like eggs, butter, and cheese. A lot of cholesterol may give you heart disease.

STEP 1

Look at the chart on the next page and answer the questions.

1. Is there a lot of fat in Bobby's breakfast?
2. Whose breakfast has only a little fat?
3. Whose breakfast has a lot of calories?
4. Are there any calories in Brad's breakfast?
5. How much cholesterol is there in each breakfast?
6. Which foods don't have any cholesterol?
7. Which foods have little fat?
8. Which food has a lot of cholesterol?

	CALORIES	FAT (GRAMS)	CHOLESTEROL (MILLIGRAMS)
Billy's Breakfast 			
eggs (2)	160	12	540
sausages (2)	310	27	67
blueberry muffin	135	5	19
whole milk	150	8	33
Brad's Breakfast 			
oatmeal	145	2	0
orange juice	80	0	0
nonfat milk	85	0	0
banana (1)	105	less than 1	0
Bobby's Breakfast 			
pancakes (2)	180	6	48
vanilla milkshake	250	7	26
doughnuts (2)	420	20	13

STEP 2

Whose breakfast is healthy? Write three sentences to explain why.

____________________ has a healthy breakfast.

1. ____ calories.
2. ____ fat.
3. ____ cholesterol.

form

FOCUS 1 Review of Count and Noncount Nouns

EXAMPLES	EXPLANATIONS
	Count nouns:
(a) Billy eats **a muffin** and **an egg.**	can have *a/an* in front of them.
(b) Brad likes **pancakes.**	can have plural forms.
(c) Billy eats **two eggs.**	can have a number in front of them.
(d) There **is** a **fast-food restaurant** near here.	can take singular or plural verbs.
(e) There **are** a lot of **calories** in a **milkshake.**	
(f) **How many eggs** does Billy eat?	can be in questions with *how many.*
	Noncount nouns:
(g) **Cereal** is healthy.	can't have *a/an* in front of them.
(h) He eats **bread** and **butter.**	can't have plural forms.
(i) It has a little **cholesterol.**	can't have a number in front of them.
(j) Nonfat **milk** is good for you.	can't take plural verbs.
(k) **How much cholesterol** does an egg have?	can be in questions with *how much.*

EXERCISE 1

Go back to the Opening Task chart on page 173. Make a list of the count and noncount nouns. Then add the kinds of foods you eat for breakfast to the count or noncount lists.

COUNT NOUNS	NONCOUNT NOUNS
eggs	milk

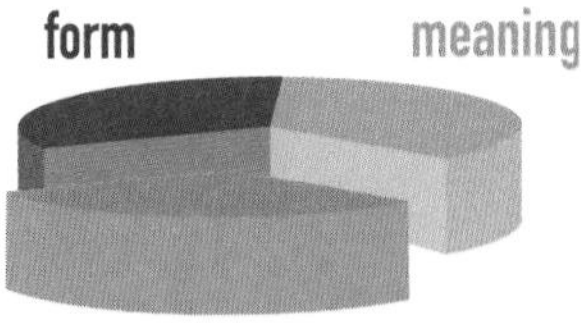

FOCUS 2 Quantifiers

Quantifiers are words or phrases that show how many things or how much of something we have.

Positive Meaning

COUNT NOUNS

		Quantifiers		
(a)	There are	many	eggs	
(b)	There are	a lot of lots of*	apples	in the refrigerator.
(c)	There are	some	carrots	
(d)	There are	a few	oranges	

*In informal speech, we often use *lots of* instead of *a lot of*.

NONCOUNT NOUNS

		Quantifiers		
(e)	There is	a lot of lots of	milk	
(f)	There is	some	juice	in the refrigerator.
(g)	There is	a little	cake	

NOT: *There is much milk in the refrigerator*. Do not use *much* in affirmative statements.

Negative Meaning

COUNT NOUNS

		Quantifiers		
(h)	There aren't	many	oranges	in the refrigerator.
(i)	There aren't	a lot of	oranges	
(j)	There are (very)	few	things	in the refrigerator that I like to eat.
(k)	There aren't	any	cookies	in the refrigerator.
(l)	There are	no	cookies	

*You can use *very* in front of *few* or *little* for emphasis.

NONCOUNT NOUNS

		Quantifiers		
(m)	There isn't	much**	fruit	
(n)	There isn't	a lot of	fruit	
(o)	There is (very)	little	cheese	in the refrigerator.
(p)	There isn't	any	butter	
(q)	There is	no	butter	

**Use *much* in negative statements.

EXERCISE 2

Test your knowledge about food. Check *True* or *False*. Then compare your answers to your partner's answers.

	TRUE	FALSE
1. There are no calories in water.	✔	
2. There's a lot of salt in fast food.		
3. There are no calories in soda.		
4. There's a lot of fat in cheese.		
5. There are very few calories in a small baked potato.		
6. There's very little cholesterol in fish.		
7. There are few vitamins in orange juice.		
8. There's some fat in low-fat yogurt.		
9. There isn't any sugar in fruit.		
10. There's a little caffeine in herbal tea.		

EXERCISE 3

Cross out the incorrect quantifier in each sentence.

Example: Bobby drinks ~~many~~ / a lot of / a little coffee.

1. This recipe has a lot of / a little / a few ingredients.
2. I try to eat a few / lots of / a little vegetables every day.
3. Fresh fruit and vegetables cost a lot of / a few / a little money.
4. My father has a little / a few / many health problems.
5. My mother has much / some / a few good recipes.
6. The doctor says to drink a lot of / many / lots of water.
7. There are a few / few / a little fast-food restaurants in this neighborhood.
8. There's no / some / many salt in this recipe.

EXERCISE 4

Use the chart in the Opening Task on page 173 to complete the statements by adding quantifiers.

1. Doughnuts have ___a lot of___ calories.
2. A banana doesn't have __________ calories.
3. There is __________ cholesterol in eggs.
4. There is __________ cholesterol in a muffin.
5. There is __________ fat in bananas.
6. Orange juice has __________ calories.
7. Sausages have __________ fat.
8. Eggs and pancakes have __________ fat.
9. There are __________ calories in cereal.
10. There is __________ cholesterol in orange juice.
11. There is __________ fat in oatmeal.
12. There is __________ fat in whole milk.

meaning

FOCUS 3 *A Few/Few, A Little/Little*

EXAMPLES	EXPLANATIONS
(a) She has **a few** books. = She has *some* books. (b) I have **a little** time. = I have *some* time.	*A few* and *a little* have a positive meaning for the speaker. The speaker means: *some,* or more than zero (a sufficient quantity).
(c) They have **few** books. = They don't have many books. (d) They have **little** time. = They don't have much time.	*Few* and *little* have a negative meaning for the speaker. The speaker means: *not much, not many,* almost zero (an insufficient quantity).

EXERCISE 5

Linda and Kathy are both Americans living in Europe for a year. Their experiences are very different. Fill in the blanks with *few/a few* or *little/a little.*

Linda is very lonely. She doesn't have a full-time job. She has (1) ____few____ friends and (2) ________ money. She works part-time as a baby sitter. She doesn't like this kind of work. She has (3) ________ patience for children. She speaks very (4) ________ Spanish.

Kathy loves to live in different countries. She speaks (5) ________ languages. She goes to a language school in Spain and she has (6) ________ very close friends. Kathy learns (7) ________ Spanish every day. She also works as a baby sitter and makes (8) ________ extra money. Kathy works hard, but she always has (9) ________ time to go out and have fun. She has (10) ________ problems in Spain.

EXERCISE 6

What does the speaker mean? Circle (a) or (b).

1. I have a little time to cook.	a. I don't usually cook. b. I sometimes cook.
2. I have little time to cook.	a. I don't usually cook. b. I always cook.
3. I have few job offers.	a. I expect to find a job. b. I don't expect to find a job.
4. I have a few job offers.	a. I expect to find a job. b. I don't expect to find a job.
5. This diet gives you a few choices of things to eat.	a. It's easy to follow this diet. b. It's not easy to follow this diet.
6. This diet gives you few choices of things to eat.	a. It's easy to follow this diet. b. It's not easy to follow this diet.
7. I have little money to spend on eating out.	a. I eat out. b. I don't eat out.
8. I have a little money to spend on eating out.	a. I eat out. b. I don't eat out.

form

FOCUS 4 Information Questions with *How Many* and *How Much*

INFORMATION QUESTION			ANSWER	EXPLANATIONS
	Count Noun			
(a) **How many**	universities	are there?	A lot.*	Use *how many* with **count nouns.**
(b) **How many**	brothers	do you have?	Two.	
(c) **How many**	oranges	do you eat every week?	A few.	
			**A lot of* shortens to *a lot* when we use it without a noun.	
	Noncount Noun			
(d) **How much**	money	do you have in your account?	$200	Use *how much* with **noncount nouns.**
(e) **How much**	time	do you have?	Not much.	
(f) **How much**	gas	do you need?	Five gallons.	

EXERCISE 7

Make questions with *how much* or *how many.* Then go back to the Opening Task on pages 172–173 and answer the questions.

1. How many pancakes does Bobby usually eat for breakfast?
2. How much juice does Brad drink?
3. ________ eggs does Billy have?
4. ________ cholesterol is there in two eggs?
5. ________ calories are there in a vanilla milkshake?
6. ________ cholesterol is there in a bowl of oatmeal?
7. ________ fat is there in two doughnuts?
8. ________ calories are there in two pancakes?
9. ________ sausages does Billy eat?
10. ________ cholesterol does Brad's breakfast have?

EXERCISE 8

Fill in the blanks with *how much* or *how many* or a quantifier (*a lot, a little, some, any, much, many*). Then read the conversations aloud.

1. **Mom:** How was school today, dear?

   Child: O.K., Mom . . .

   Mom: (a) ______________ homework do you have tonight?

   Child: I have (b) ______________ homework—three compositions plus I have a spelling test tomorrow!

   Mom: Don't worry, I have (c) ______________ time to help you tonight.

2. **Doctor:** Please remember to take this medicine, Mr. Josephson.

   Patient: (a) ______________ medicine do I need to take every day?

   Doctor: You need three red pills a day, one after every meal. And you need two blue pills a day, one in the morning and one before bed.

   Patient: Say that again, please . . . (b) ______________ red pills? (c) ______________ blue pills? And (d) ______________ pills do I need to take in all?

   Doctor: Three red pills and two blue pills. Five pills a day in all. Take these for a week. Then call me.

   Patient: O.K. Thanks, Doctor.

EXERCISE 9

Ask your partner questions about a city he or she knows. First ask a *yes/no* question with *there*. Then ask a question with *how many* or *how much*.

Examples: skyscrapers *Are there any skyscrapers in your city?*
How many skyscrapers are there?

crime *Is there any crime in your city?*
How much crime is there?

1. noise
2. universities
3. pollution
4. trash on the streets
5. parks
6. poor people
7. traffic

8. museums
9. beaches
10. American fast-food restaurants
11. public transportation
12. shopping malls
13. hospitals

EXERCISE 10

Information Gap. What does the average American eat?
Work with a partner. One student looks at Chart A, and the other students looks at Chart B on page A-19.

For each category on the left, ask a question using *how much* or *how many,* and answer using the correct information.

Yearly Consumption per Person in the United States in 2000

Chart A

CATEGORY	QUESTION
1. Meat (beef, pork, veal, lamb)	a.
2. Chicken	b. 66 pounds
3. Fish	c.
4. Milk	d. 23 gallons
5. Cheese	e. 30 pounds
6. Eggs	f.
7. Fats and Oils (vegetable oils, butter, margarine)	g.
8. Grain Products (bread, bakery items, etc.)	h. 200 pounds
9. Sugar	i.
Source: USDA	

FOCUS 5 Measure Words

Measure words change the way we see a thing. A measure word before a noncount noun tells us about the specific quantity.

Examples: *I drink a lot of coffee.* (coffee = noncount noun)
I drink four cups of coffee a day. (specific quantity)

a **can** of tuna a **jar** of jam a **tube** of toothpaste a **pitcher** of milk	a **box** of cereal a **bottle** of juice a **bag** of sugar a **bowl** of soup	Containers
a **slice** of pizza a **piece** of pie	a **glass** of milk a **cup** of coffee	Portions
a **cup** of flour a **pint** of ice cream a **teaspoon** of salt	a **quart**/a **liter** of milk a **pound** of sugar a **gallon** of water	Specific quantities
a **head** of lettuce a **sheet** of paper a **roll** of toilet paper	a **loaf** of bread a **bar** of soap	Other
a **bag** of apples a **pound** of onions BUT: a **dozen** eggs NOT: a dozen of eggs	a **can** of beans a **box** of chocolates BUT: **five thousand** people NOT: five thousand of people	Measure words can also be used with count nouns.

EXERCISE 11

Here is Maggie at the checkout counter. Write down her shopping list on the next page. Use measure words in the list.

Shopping List			
a pound of	coffee	______	oil
______	orange juice	______	soda
______	rice	______	bread
______	soup	______	soap
______	toothpaste	______	cabbage
______	candy	______	paper towels
______	eggs	______	beef
______	butter	______	peanut butter

EXERCISE 12

Work in a group of four.

STEP 1 **How much food do you have in your refrigerator or in your pantry? Use measure words to tell your group what you have.**

Example: *Food List: a quart of milk, 1/4 (one quarter) pound of cheese, four containers of yogurt*

STEP 2 **What can you say about the eating/food habits about the people in your group?**

Example: *Karla eats a lot of dairy products.*

EXERCISE 13

Correct the errors in the following sentences.

1. **Jane:** Can I talk to you for a minute?
   Kevin: Sure, I have little time.
2. John has much friends.
3. How many money do you have?
4. My teacher gives us many homeworks.
5. Her hairs are black.
6. Elsie is in great shape. She runs few miles a day.
7. We don't sell no newspapers here.
8. I have little friends. I want more friends.
9. There are much stores in this city.
10. I would like some informations please.
11. My best friend gives me many advices.
12. This school has little international students.
13. **Question:** How much time do you have?
    Answer: A lot of.
14. We have few time to finish this book.

Use Your English

ACTIVITY 1 speaking

Ask three students questions with *how much* and *how many* to complete the chart. Who has a healthy diet?

Examples: *How much coffee do you drink a day?* *I drink three cups a day.*
How much sugar do you put in your coffee? *Two teaspoons.*

FOOD HABIT SURVEY	STUDENT 1	STUDENT 2	STUDENT 3
coffee or tea/drink/a day			
sugar/put in coffee or tea			
meat/eat/a week			
soda/drink/a day			
fruit/eat/a day			
glasses of water/drink/a day			
eggs/eat/a week			
Other			

ACTIVITY 2 speaking

Work in a group of four. Ask questions about how much people in other countries eat using the categories below. Add two foods of your own.

Examples: Question: *How much meat do people eat in India?*
Answer: *People eat a lot of meat/a little meat/no meat in India.*

pasta	yogurt	chocolate	cheese	beans	tea	fish	water
fruit	bread	sweets	eggs	rice	meat	soda	coffee

ACTIVITY 3 speaking

Play a circle game with all the students in the class. Make a statement starting with "I want to buy . . ." One student says an item that begins with the letter *A* and uses a measure word. The second student repeats the statement and adds a second item that starts with the letter *B*. The third student does the same and adds on an item with the letter *C*, and so on.

Example: Student 1: *I want to buy a bag of apples.*
Student 2: *I want to buy a bag of apples and a loaf of bread.*
Student 3: *I want to buy a bag of apples, a loaf of bread, and a head of cabbage.*

ACTIVITY 4 writing/speaking

Work in a group of four. Choose a recipe you like and write the ingredients without writing the quantity. The other students ask you questions with *how much* and *how many* to fill in the exact quantity. Make a book of the class's favorite recipes.

Example: Recipe: *Italian Tomato Sauce*
Ingredients: *tomatoes*
garlic
Questions: *How many tomatoes do you use?*
How much garlic is there?

ACTIVITY 5 writing

Your friend wants to come and live where you are living now. Write a letter to your friend explaining why this is or is not a good idea. Use the vocabulary in the box on page 186 to help you.

Example: *I live in a really wonderful neighborhood. There isn't much crime. There are a lot of trees and parks. There are many good restaurants.*

crime	parks	trees	traffic
hospitals	flowers	noise	houses
grass	spacious apartments	bookstores	drugstores
good restaurants	movie theaters	job	clean streets
ethnic markets	good schools	open spaces	people from my country
friendly neighbors			

ACTIVITY 6 research on the web

STEP 1

Search the Internet for nutrition labels for three different foods. Use a search engine such as Google®, Yahoo®, or Ask®. Enter the keywords *database, nutrition,* and *label.* Print out the nutrition labels. Then write the nutrition facts on the chart below.

	EXAMPLE	LABEL 1	LABEL 2	LABEL 3
Food	Strawberry yogurt			
Number of Servings	one			
Calories per Serving	210			
Total Fat	2 g			
Saturated Fat	1 g			
Cholesterol	5 mg			
Sodium	75 mg			
Total Carbohydrates	41 g			
Fiber	1 g			
Sugars	29 g			
Protein	6 g			

STEP 2

Tell the class about the foods. Are they healthy or not?

ACTIVITY 7 listening

CD Track 10

Sara is calling Food Express, the new grocery home delivery service in her neighborhood, to order groceries for the weekend.

STEP 1 Listen to her order and check the things she wants.

_____ tortilla chips	_____ salsa	_____ sour cream	_____ chopped meat	_____ butter
_____ milk	_____ bananas	_____ eggs	_____ yogurt	_____ hot dogs
_____ ice cream	_____ onions	_____ apple pie	_____ tomatoes	
_____ avocados	_____ soda	_____ coffee	_____ cookies	

STEP 2 Read the statements below about Sara. Circle *True*, *False*, or *Maybe*.

1. Sara overeats.	T	F	M	4. Sara lives in a city.	T	F	M
2. Sara has a busy lifestyle.	T	F	M	5. Sara is having a party.	T	F	M
3. Sara likes sweets.	T	F	M	6. Sara's guests like Mexican food.	T	F	M

ACTIVITY 8 reflection

Take this survey on how much effort you are making in English. Write three statements about how you can improve your language learning.

1. How much time do you spend on your homework? a. a lot b. a little c. not very much
2. How many English-language news articles do you usually read a week? a. many b. a few c. none
3. How much English do you speak outside of class? a. a lot b. a little c. none
4. How many English-speaking friends do you have? a. many b. some c. none
5. How many American television shows do you watch? a. many b. a few c. none
6. How many English songs do you know? a. many b. a few c. none

UNIT 12

ADVERBS OF MANNER

UNIT GOALS

- Understand the meaning of adverbs of manner
- Know the position of adverbs of manner in a sentence
- Know how to spell adverbs of manner
- Focus on either an action or a person

OPENING TASK

Do You Want to Give James Watson Life Insurance?

STEP 1

You work for the Legit Life Insurance Company. James Watson wants to buy life insurance. Study the questionnaire he filled out. Decide: Does the Legit Life Insurance Company want to insure James Watson?

Legit Life Insurance Company Health and Accident Questionnaire

Name	James Watson
Sex	Male
Date of birth	3/3/46
Height	5 feet 9 inches
Weight	240 pounds
Occupation	Traveling salesman/7 days a week
Tobacco use	1–2 packs of cigarettes a day
Alcohol use	2 drinks a day/ treatment required in 1996
Date of last doctor's visit	10/8/02
Reason for visit; treatment	Chest pain; medication
Medical conditions	Heart problems; high blood pressure; corrective lenses
Driving record	
Moving violations in last 3 years	3 speeding tickets; 1 failure to stop at a red light
Accidents in last 3 years	4
Alcohol-related convictions in last 7 years	1 – 12/23/05

STEP 2

Why do you think the Legit Life Insurance Company wants or doesn't want to insure James Watson? Tell the class.

Example: *Legit Life Insurance Company doesn't want to insure James Watson because he smokes heavily.*

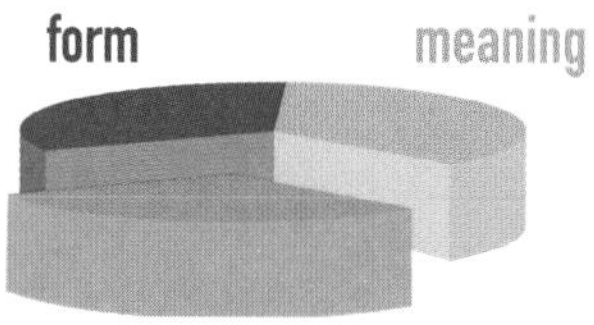

FOCUS 1 Adverbs of Manner

Manner is *how* or the *way* people do something.

EXAMPLES	EXPLANATIONS
(a) He is a **careful** driver.	*Careful* is an adjective. It describes the noun *driver*. The adjective goes before the noun.
(b) He drives **carefully**.	*Carefully* is an adverb of manner. It describes the verb *drive*. The adverb answers the question "how?" The adverb goes after the verb.
(c) He drives his new car **carefully**. NOT: He drives carefully his new car.	When there is an object after the verb, the adverb goes after the object (*his car*).

Spelling of Adverbs of Manner

ADJECTIVE	ADVERB	RULE
slow beautiful	slowly beautifully	Add *ly*.
heavy	heavily	Adjectives that end in *y*: change *y* to *i* and add *ly*.
fantastic	fantastically	Adjectives that end with *ic*: add *ally*.
terrible	terribly	Adjectives that end with *le*: drop the *e*, and add *y*.

EXERCISE 1

How are the speakers saying the sentences below? Match each sentence with the best adjective from the box below. Then write the adverb in the blank.

Example: quiet: "Shhh, don't say a word." she said <u>quietly.</u>

polite	sad	nervous	quick	shy
incorrect	impolite	happy	angry	kind

1. "I just got engaged!" she said ________________.
2. "My dog just died," he said ________________.
3. "I'm in a hurry," she said ________________.
4. "I no make mistakes," he said ________________.
5. "May I make a telephone call?" she asked ________________.
6. "Bring me a menu, fast!" he said ________________.

7. "This is the last time I'm telling you! Clean up your room!" she said ____________.

8. "WWWWWWWWWWWill yyyyou mmmmmmmmmarry mmmmmmmmmmme?" he asked ____________.

9. "Please, don't ask me to speak in front of the class," she said ____________.

10. "Can I help you?" he asked ____________.

EXERCISE 2

STEP 1 **Find three sentences that describe each occupation. Write the letters next to the occupation.**

1. I am a teacher.	c	a. I respond to medical emergencies very quickly.
	______	b. I defend my clients successfully.
	______	c. I prepare lessons carefully.
2. I am a lawyer.	______	d. I draw beautifully.
	______	e. I take care of international problems urgently.
	______	f. I give medical treatment to people carefully.
3. I am an artist.	______	g. I paint well.
	______	h. I speak three languages fluently.
	______	i. I speak clearly.
4. I am the	______	j. I drive very fast.
Secretary General	______	k. I talk to my students politely.
of the United	______	l. I use colors creatively.
Nations.		m. I study the law closely.
5. I am an emergency	______	n. I write on the blackboard neatly.
medical technician	______	o. I act diplomatically.
in an ambulance.	______	

STEP 2 **Go back to the sentences. Underline all the adverbs of manner.**

form

FOCUS 2 Forms of Adverbs of Manner

Some adverbs are different in form.

EXAMPLES		EXPLANATIONS
(a) She's a **fast** driver. (c) We have an **early** dinner. (e) We eat a **late** lunch. (g) We are **hard** workers.	(b) She drives **fast**. (d) We have dinner **early**. (f) We eat lunch **late**. (h) We work **hard**.	Some adverbs have the same form as adjectives.
(i) Joel's a **good** cook.	(j) He cooks **well**.	Some adverbs are irregular.
(k) He works **hard**. (l) He **hardly** works.		Do not confuse *hard* with *hardly*. In example (l), *hardly* is an adverb of frequency. It means "he doesn't work very much."
(m) She is lovely. (n) Marco is lonely. (o) That dress is ugly. (p) Maria is friendly. (q) The party is lively.		Some words that end in *-ly* are not adverbs. They are adjectives.

EXERCISE 3

Read the descriptions of people on the left. Use the adjectives in parentheses on the right, to complete the statements using adverbs. For (e), add one of your own.

1. Arlene is a wonderful hostess.

a. She treats her guests (gracious) ____graciously____.

b. She accepts gifts (grateful) ________________.

c. She speaks (polite) ________________.

d. She thanks her guests (sincere) ________________.

e. She cooks (   ) ________________.

2. George is a model student.

a. He studies (serious) ________________.

b. He participates (active) ________________.

c. He speaks (clear) ________________.

d. He works (cooperative) ________________.

e. He does his homework (   ) ________________.

3. Bill doesn't have good social skills.

a. He always comes (late) ______________________.
b. He interrupts others (rude) ______________________.
c. He treats others (disrespectful) ______________________.
d. He behaves (selfish) ______________________.
e. He speaks (   ) ______________________.

4. Nick is not a good leader.

a. He doesn't speak (confident) ______________________.
b. He doesn't think (critical) ______________________.
c. He doesn't speak (truthful) ______________________.
d. He doesn't act (responsible) ______________________.
e. He doesn't work (   ) ______________________.

EXERCISE 4

Work with a partner. Take turns asking and answering the questions below. The first one has been done for you.

1. Why is Carrie an excellent teacher?
   a. teach/energetic *She teaches energetically.*
   b. pronounce words/clear
   c. prepare/careful
2. Why is Mark a good secretary?
   a. type/fast
   b. get to work/early
   c. take phone messages/accurate
3. Why is Mike a good truck driver?
   a. drive/safe
   b. watch the road/constant
   c. drive/defensive
4. Why is Gloria Estefan a popular performer?
   a. sing/passionate
   b. dance/good
   c. perform/enthusiastic
5. Why is Miyuki a good language learner?
   a. study/hard
   b. guess/intelligent
   c. ask questions/regular

EXERCISE 5

Make definitions by matching the types of people with an appropriate adverb.

1. Insomniacs sleep	a. generously
2. Passionate people feel	b. negatively
3. Charitable people give	c. bravely
4. Optimists think	d. restlessly
5. Pessimists think	e. creatively
6. Soldiers fight	f. peacefully
7. Pacifists solve problems	g. strongly
8. Artists think	h. positively

FOCUS 3 Focusing on a Person or an Action

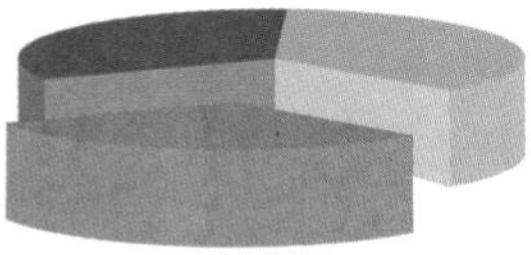

use

EXAMPLES	EXPLANATIONS
(a) Isabelle is a **good** writer.	When you want to focus on a person, place, or thing, use an **adjective**.
(b) Isabelle **writes** well.	When you want to focus on an action, use an **adverb**.
(c) She is a **very good** writer. (d) She writes **very well**.	You can use *very* in front of most adjectives or adverbs.

EXERCISE 6

Do these sentences focus on the person or the action? Check the correct column.

	PERSON	ACTION
1. Meryl Streep is a fantastic actress.		
2. My students learn easily.		
3. Steven reads slowly.		
4. Karl is a fast runner.		
5. My children are good cooks.		
6. James Watson drives carelessly.		
7. My accountant is an honest person.		
8. Anh speaks to his parents impolitely.		
9. Linda dresses beautifully.		
10. Your friend is a generous person.		

EXERCISE 7

Circle the correct adjective or adverb to complete the statements below. Think about whether the sentences focus on the person or the action.

1. Helene is a (a. great/greatly) friend. She's a very (b. thoughtful/thoughtfully) person. She listens to her friends' problems (c. attentive/attentively).
2. Tim is a skilled filmmaker. He has a (a. wonderful/wonderfully) imagination. He tells stories (b. creative/creatively). He makes films (c. successful/successfully).
3. Jared is a spoiled child. He doesn't speak to his parents (a. respectful/respectfully). He gets angry (b. easy/easily). He behaves (c. bad/badly) in school.
4. I'm worried about my friend Jay. He's a (a. lazy/lazily) person. He's a (b. terrible/terribly) employee. He doesn't do his work very (c. careful/carefully).

EXERCISE 8

Correct the mistakes in the following sentences.

1. Sarah comes to work in a suit every day. She dresses elegant.
2. Melanie speaks fluently French.
3. Sam studies three hours every night. He studies hardly.
4. Dinner started at 8:00. They arrived at 9:30. They came very lately.
5. Johan plays the piano very good.
6. She speaks slow.
7. She sings lovely.
8. The city traffic is heavily.

Use Your English

ACTIVITY 1 speaking

Work in a group. One person in the group chooses an adverb of manner, but does not tell the other students the adverb. The students in the group tell the person to do something "in that manner." The person mimes the action and the other students guess the adverb.

Example: 1. The first student chooses the adverb *slowly*.
2. Students in the group say: "Walk to the door in that manner."
3. The first student mimes.
4. Students in the group guess: slowly.

Example adverbs: *slowly, fast, nervously, happily, angrily, loudly, sadly, romantically, passionately, carefully, politely, impolitely, rudely, energetically, gracefully, shyly*

ACTIVITY 2 writing

Work in a group. List what makes a good student, a good parent, a good friend, and a good worker. Choose one topic and write a paragraph to describe yourself. Share this with a group.

Example: *I'm a very good student. I study hard. . .*

ACTIVITY 3 speaking

Look back to the Opening Task insurance form on pages 188–189. With a partner, role-play a conversation between an insurance agent and James Watson or a person like James Watson. The person tries to convince the agent to give him or her insurance. Then explain to the class why your partner can or cannot get insurance easily.

ACTIVITY 4 listening

CD Track 11

Listen to the three speakers talk about their jobs. Write the number of the speaker next to the correct job.

______ a customer service representative   ______ a cartoonist   ______ a judge

ACTIVITY 5 reflection

STEP 1 Compare teaching styles in your native country to teaching styles in the United States. What do teachers do differently? How do students behave differently? Write the differences in the outer edges of the circles. Write the similarities in the middle area created by the overlapping circles. Discuss your ideas with your classmates.

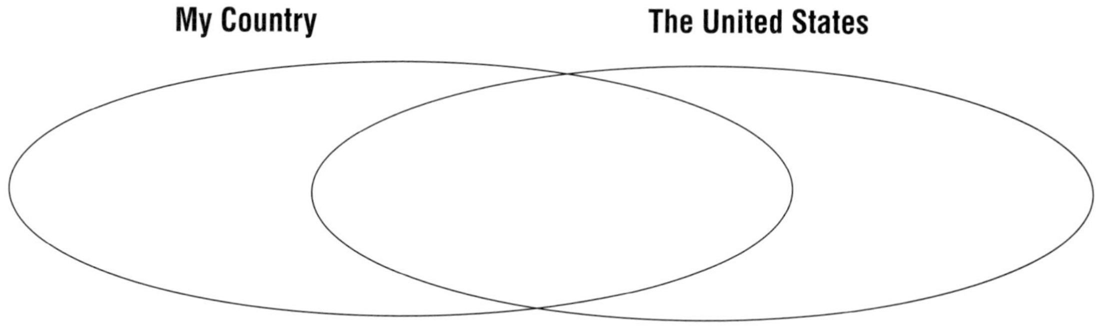

Example: *In the United States, students participate actively in class.*

STEP 2 Write a paragraph to describe the teaching style you like. What do you want a teacher to do? What helps you learn?

ACTIVITY 6 research on the web

STEP 1 A letter of recommendation is a letter that tells about a person's abilities and qualities. When you want to get a job or apply for college, a good letter of recommendation can help you. Search the Internet for examples of recommendation letters. Use a search engine such as Google®, or Yahoo®, or Ask®. Enter the keywords *recommendation, letter,* and *sample.*

STEP 2 Print out the recommendation letters you find. Study the letters. Are they good letters? Why or why not?

STEP 3 Write your own recommendation letter for someone you know.

Example: *Samuel Rodriguez is an excellent employee. He always completes his work quickly and diligently. . . .*

UNIT 13

DIRECT AND INDIRECT OBJECTS, DIRECT AND INDIRECT OBJECT PRONOUNS

UNIT GOALS

- Use direct objects and direct object pronouns correctly
- Use indirect objects correctly
- Form two sentence patterns with indirect objects
- Know where to place the indirect object in a sentence to focus on new information
- Know which verbs require *to* with indirect objects

OPENING TASK

Giving Gifts

STEP 1

The people on the next page are celebrating different life events. Look at the gifts on the next page and decide which gift you want to give to each person. Write the gift in the chart.

STEP 2

Tell a partner which gift you want to give each person and why.

Example: *I want to give the microwave to my sister. It's a practical gift, and she doesn't have one.*

Gifts

a.

Digital Camera

b.

Flowers

c.

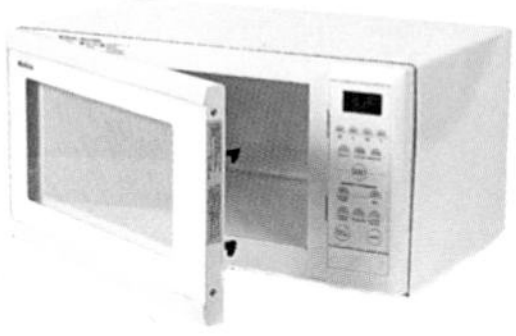

Microwave

d.

Stuffed Animal

e.

Compact Discs

f.

Earrings

PERSON	EVENT	GIFT
1. Your friend	Baby Shower: for a woman who is going to have a baby	
2. Your brother	Graduation: for a student finishing high school or college	
3. Your parents	Anniversary: for a married couple celebrating ______ years of marriage	
4. Your friend	Birthday: to celebrate the day a person was born	
5. Your sister	Bridal Shower: for a woman who is getting married	
6. Your niece	Sweet 16: for a young woman on her 16th birthday	

form meaning

FOCUS 1 Direct Objects

EXAMPLES			EXPLANATIONS
Subject	Verb	Direct Object	
(a) My friend	sings.		Some sentences have only a subject and a verb.
(b) He	loves	music.	Some sentences have a subject, a verb, and an object. The direct object can be a noun.
(c) He	buys	compact discs.	A direct object answers the question "What?" *Compact discs* is the direct object.
(d) He	loves	the Beatles.	A direct object also answers the question "Who(m)?" *The Beatles* is the direct object.

EXERCISE 1

Graduation from college is a very important event in the United States. Match the sentences with the correct direct object(s).

1. On this day, students wear	a. pictures with their cameras.
2. Graduates invite	b. flowers and gifts.
3. Important people make	c. special robes and hats.
4. Colleges give	d. the graduates.
5. Everyone congratulates	e. jobs.
6. Graduates often receive	f. family and friends.
7. Family and friends take	g. speeches.
8. New graduates find	h. diplomas.

FOCUS 2 Direct Object Pronouns

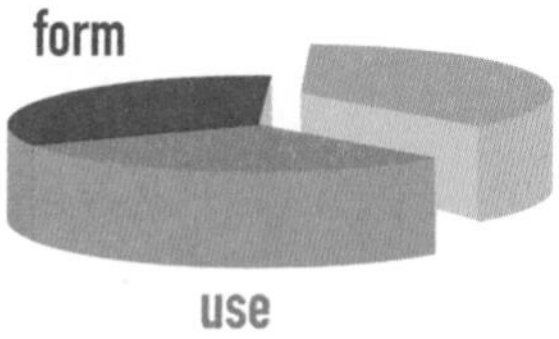

EXAMPLES			EXPLANATIONS
Subject	**Verb**	**Direct Object**	
(a) My mother	loves	my father.	The direct object can also be a **pronoun**.
(b) My mother	loves	**him.**	
(c) My mother loves **my father.** She thinks about **him** all the time.			Object pronouns refer to a noun that comes before. In (c), *him* refers to "my father." In (d), *her* refers to "my mother."
(d) My father loves **my mother**. He always thinks about **her**.			

SUBJECT	VERB	OBJECT	SUBJECT	VERB	OBJECT PRONOUN
I You	need	a friend	She	likes	me. you.
He She It	needs				him. her. it.
We You They	need				us. you. them.

EXERCISE 2

December 25th, Christmas Day, is a very big holiday for many Americans. People usually give each other gifts. Read this summary of a famous American story called "The Gift of the Magi" by O. Henry about giving gifts at Christmas. Then close your book and retell the story to a partner.

Della and Jim are a young married couple. She loves him, and he loves her very much. They are not rich, but they have two things of value. Jim has a gold watch from his grandfather. It's a family treasure. He loves it. Della has very beautiful long hair. Jim loves it.

At Christmas time, they both look for the perfect gifts. They find them, but they have no money to buy them. Della cuts her hair, and she sells it. She buys a chain for Jim's watch. She likes her gift, and she's excited about it. At the same time, Jim sells his watch to buy two beautiful combs for Della's hair. Jim knows that Della will love them.

Della's present is for Jim's watch, but he doesn't have it anymore. Jim's present is for Della's hair, but she doesn't have it anymore.

Most Americans know this popular story. It tells us that the greatest gift is love.

EXERCISE 3

Cross out the incorrect subject or object pronouns, and write the correct pronouns above them. Some sentences are correct.

In countries around the world, students and their families celebrate Teachers' Day. (1) They respect their teachers. (2) They appreciate they. (3) They thank they. Teachers' Day is a special event. (4) People celebrate she in different ways.

In India, teachers take a break on Teachers' Day. (5) They don't teach their classes. (6) The senior students teach it.

In Taiwan, this special day honors teachers and a man named Confucius. (7) She was a philosopher. (8) All Chinese people admire she. (9) She was a model teacher.

In Vietnam, students visit their teachers at home. (10) They thank they with gifts and food. (11) I am a teacher and a student. (12) This holiday pleases I.

Teachers touch all people. (13) We love they. (14) Them help us. (15) They prepare we for a changing world.

form meaning

FOCUS 3 Indirect Objects

EXAMPLES				EXPLANATION
Subject	Verb	Direct Object	Indirect Object	
(a) I	want to give	the microwave	to **the newlyweds.**	Some sentences have two objects: a direct object and an indirect object. *The microwave* is the direct object. It tells **what** I want to give. *The newlyweds* is the indirect object. It tells **to whom** I want to give the microwave.
(b) I	buy	flowers	for **my grandmother.**	*My grandmother* is the indirect object. It tells **for whom** I buy flowers.
(c) I	want to give	the microwave	**to the newlyweds.**	The indirect object can be a noun or a pronoun.
(d) I	want to give	the microwave	to **them.**	
(e) I make dinner **for** my grandmother.				***For* and *To*** *For* tells us one person does the action to help or please another person.
(f) I want to give the earrings **to** my niece.				*To* tells us about the direction of the action: The earrings go from you to your mother.

EXERCISE 4

Here are more people you would like to give gifts to or do something for. Write sentences telling what you want to give or do for each person.

Example: your roommate / He loves to cook.
I want to give a new cookbook to my roommate.
I want to make a gourmet dinner for him.

1. your grandfather / He loves to work in the garden.
2. your friend / She loves to travel.
3. your sister / She has a new job.
4. your brother / He is very athletic.
5. your classmate / It's her 21st birthday.
6. your husband / He plans to retire.

FOCUS 4 Position of the Indirect Object

All verbs that take indirect objects can follow Pattern A.

Pattern A

SUBJECT	VERB	DIRECT OBJECT	INDIRECT OBJECT
(a) I	give	presents	to my mother on her birthday.
(b) I	give	presents	to her.
(c) I	give	them	to her.
(d) We	make	a cake	for our twin daughters on their birthday.
(e) We	make	a cake	for them.
(f) We	make	it	for them.

Some of these verbs also follow Pattern B. In Pattern B, put the indirect object before the direct object. Do not use *to* or *for* with the indirect object.

Pattern B

SUBJECT	VERB	INDIRECT OBJECT	DIRECT OBJECT
(g) People	send	their friends	birthday cards.
(h) People	send	them	birthday cards.
(i) I	give	the guests	party favors.
(j) I	give	them	party favors.

NOTE: An indirect object pronoun can come before a direct object. Do not put an indirect object pronoun before a direct object pronoun.

Example: *I make my friend a cake. I make her a cake.*
NOT: *I make her it.*

Some verbs that follow both Pattern A and B

bake	do	hand	offer	read	teach
bring	find	lend	owe	sell	tell
buy	get	mail	pass	send	throw
cook	give	make	pay	show	write

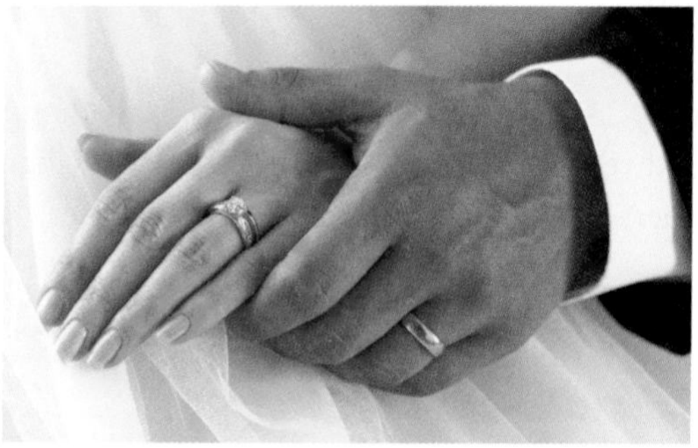

EXERCISE 5

Wedding Customs Around the World

STEP 1 **Read about the wedding customs in different countries around the world. Underline the direct object. Circle the indirect object.**

1.	Japan	Guests give the couple money in a special envelope.
2.	Yemen	The women in the family prepare a special meal for the guests.
3.	Hungary	The bride gives her husband seven scarves.
4.	Germany	After the ceremony, the bride and groom throw the children coins.
5.	Spain	The groom gives his bride 13 coins.
6.	U.S.	American brides and grooms give wedding rings to each other.
7.	Jamaica	After the wedding, the bride and groom send leftover slices of rum cake to guests who didn't come.
8.	Thailand	The family gives money to the Buddhist temple.

STEP 2 **Go back to the sentences in Step 1. Write *A* next to the sentences that follow Pattern A. Write *B* next to the ones that follow Pattern B. Then change the Pattern A sentences to Pattern B sentences, and change the Pattern B sentences to Pattern A sentences.**

1. ______________________________
2. ______________________________
3. ______________________________
4. ______________________________
5. ______________________________
6. ______________________________
7. ______________________________
8. ______________________________

EXERCISE 6

New Year's Resolutions. Every January 1st, North Americans decide to change their lives and do things differently. Read and rewrite the following resolutions. Change each underlined noun to a pronoun. Then add the information in parentheses. Read the statements aloud.

Example: Every year, I give my father a tie. (golf clubs)
This year, I want to *give him golf clubs.*

1. Used car salesman:
   I always sell my customers bad cars. (good cars)
   This year, I want to . . .
2. Child away at college:
   I always e-mail my parents once a month. (once a week)
   This year, I want to . . .
3. People with money problems:
   Every year, the bank sends my husband and me a big credit card bill. (a very small bill)
   This year, I want the bank to . . .
4. Boyfriend:
   I usually buy my girlfriend flowers for her birthday. (a diamond ring)
   This year, I want to . . .
5. Teenager:
   Sometimes I tell lies to my mother. (the truth)
   This year, I want to . . .
6. Mother:
   I never read books to my children at night. (every night)
   This year, I want to . . .
7. Student:
   I always give my homework to Mr. Green late. (on time)
   This semester, I want to . . .
8. Car owner:
   Every year, I wash my car once every 6 months. (2 months)
   This year, I want to . . .
9. Girlfriend:
   I usually bake my boyfriend a chocolate cake for his birthday. (a blueberry pie)
   This year, I want to . . .
10. Father:
    I usually send New Years cards to my relatives. (my friends)
    This year, I want to ...

Now say three things you want to do differently this year.

EXERCISE 7

Work with a partner. Write sentences about North American customs with the words below. The first one is done for you as an example.

BIRTH: When a baby is born:

1. mother / flowers / the / to / give / friends *Friends give flowers to the mother.*
2. cigars / gives / friends / father / his / the
3. send / and / parents / friends / family / to / birth / announcements / their / the
4. baby / family / friends / gifts / the / buy / and
5. knit / for / grandmothers / sweaters / new / the / baby
6. grandfathers / for / toys / make / baby / the
7. child / the / the / parents / everything / give

ENGAGEMENT/MARRIAGE: When a couple gets engaged or married:

8. diamond / man / a / woman / the / gives / ring / the / to / sometimes
9. friends / couple / an / party / the / for / have / engagement
10. gifts / woman / give / friends / at the bridal shower / the
11. at the wedding / to / couple / gifts / give / the guests / the

DEATH: When someone dies:

12. send / family / some / flowers / people / the
13. people / sympathy cards / the / send / family / to
14. some / to / give / people / money / charities
15. some / food / for / family / bring / people / the

FOCUS 5 Position of New Information

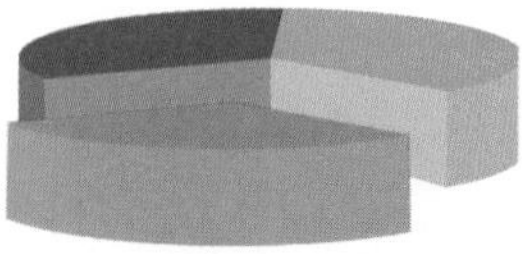

New information comes at the end of a sentence. You can write these sentences in two different ways. Both are grammatically correct, but the emphasis is different.

EXAMPLES	EXPLANATIONS
(a) Whom do you give earrings to? I usually give earrings to **my mother.**	The emphasis is on **who(m)**. *My mother* is the new information.
(b) What do you usually give your mother? I usually give my mother **earrings.**	The emphasis is on **what.** *Earrings* is the new information.

EXERCISE 8

Answer the following questions. The new information is in parentheses ( ).

Examples: Who(m) do you usually give presents to at Christmas? (my family)
I usually give presents to my family.
What do you usually give your father? (a good book)
I usually give him a good book.

1. Who(m) do you want to give presents to at work? (three of my co-workers)
2. What do you usually give your parents for their anniversary? (tickets to a play)
3. Who(m) do you tell jokes to? (my friend)
4. What do you send your sister every year? (some photographs)
5. Who(m) do you need to mail the party invitations to? (the children in my daughter's class)
6. What do you usually buy for your son on his birthday? (video games)
7. What do you usually bring to your friend's house for dinner? (a bouquet of flowers)
8. What do you usually send your guests after a party? (thank-you notes)

EXERCISE 9

Choose the best sentence.

Examples: You are waiting for a friend in front of a restaurant.
You do not have your watch. You want to know the time.
You see someone coming. You ask him:
(a.) Could you please tell me the time?
b. Could you please tell the time to me?

1. You are alone at a restaurant. You finish your meal. You see the waiter. You ask him:
   a. Could you please give the check to me?
   b. Could you please give me the check?
2. You are celebrating someone's birthday with a group of friends. You finish your meal. You want to be sure you pay the check. You tell the waiter:
   a. Please give the check to me.
   b. Please give me the check.
3. What do your children usually do for you on Mother's Day?
   a. They usually serve breakfast in bed to me.
   b. They usually serve me breakfast in bed.
4. You are at a friend's house for dinner. The food needs salt. You say:
   a. Please pass me the salt.
   b. Please pass the salt to me.
5. You realize you don't have any money for the bus. You ask a friend:
   a. Could you lend a dollar to me?
   b. Could you lend me a dollar?

6. You are in class. It is very noisy. You say to a classmate:
   a. Do me a favor. Please close the door.
   b. Do a favor for me. Please close the door.
7. Why does your class look so sad on Mondays?
   a. Because our teacher gives us a lot of homework on weekends.
   b. Because our teacher gives a lot of homework to us on weekends.
8. You want to apply to the City University. You have the application form in your hand. The Director is helping you. The Director says:
   a. Please send the application form to the City University.
   b. Please send the City University the application form.
9. You come home from the supermarket. Your car is full of groceries. You need help. You say to your roommate:
   a. Can you please give a hand to me?
   b. Can you please give me a hand?
10. There are three children at a table. They are finishing a box of cookies. A fourth child sees them and runs toward them. The child says:
    a. Wait! Save me one!
    b. Wait! Save one for me!

form

FOCUS 6 Verbs That Require *To* or *For* with Indirect Objects

EXAMPLES		EXPLANATION
S + V + D.O.+I.O. (a) My mother reads stories to us. S + V + I.O.+D.O. (b) My mother reads us stories.		Many verbs follow both Pattern A and B. (See Focus 4 on pages 204–205.)
D.O. + I.O. (c) The teacher explains the grammar to us. (d) NOT: The teacher explains us the grammar. D.O. + I.O. (e) The teacher pronounces the words for us. (f) NOT: The teacher pronounces us the words.		Some verbs only follow Pattern A.
Verbs with *to:* *describe* *explain* *report* *introduce*	Verbs with *for:* *answer* *fix* *repeat* *carry* *open* *solve* *cash* *prepare* *spell* *clean* *pronounce* *translate* *do* *repair*	Verbs that follow Pattern A ONLY. Always use *to*/*for* for indirect objects.

EXERCISE 10

Work with a partner. Ask polite questions with "Could you please… ?" with *to* or *for.*

Example: *Could you please open the window for me?*
Could you please explain the problem to me?

1. explain the difference between direct objects and indirect objects

2. pronounce this word

3. fix my computer

4. carry my books

5. introduce your roommate

6. spell your last name

EXERCISE 11

Read the following sentence or question pairs aloud. Mark an X next to any sentence that is **not** possible. In some pairs, both patterns are possible.

Example 1: **Pattern A:** My husband sends flowers to me every Valentine's Day.
Pattern B: My husband sends me flowers every Valentine's Day.
(Both patterns are possible.)

Example 2: **Pattern A:** The teacher always repeats the question to the class.
Pattern B: The teacher always repeats the class the question. X
(Only Pattern A is possible.)

PATTERN A	PATTERN B
1. Tell the truth to me.	Tell me the truth.
2. Please explain the problem to me.	Please explain me the problem.
3. Spell that word for me, please.	Spell me that word, please.
4. I need to report the accident to the insurance company.	I need to report the insurance company the accident.
5. My father usually reads a story to my little brother every night.	My father usually reads my little brother a story every night.
6. He always opens the door for me.	He always opens me the door.
7. Let me introduce my friend to you.	Let me introduce you my friend.
8. Cynthia gives money to the Red Cross.	Cynthia gives the Red Cross money.
9. The students write letters to their parents every week.	The students write their parents letters every week.
10. Please repeat the instructions to the class.	Please repeat the class the instructions.
11. Can you describe your hometown to me?	Can you describe me your hometown?
12. Can you carry that bag for me?	Can you carry me that bag?
13. Could you make a photocopy for me?	Could you make me a photocopy?
14. Could you fix my computer for me?	Could you fix me my computer?
15. Please cash this check for me.	Please cash me this check.

Use Your English

ACTIVITY 1 speaking

Think of the different things people have. Then give clues so that your classmates can guess the objects.

Example: **Clues:** The Japanese and Germans make a lot of them. We drive them. What are they?
Answer: *Cars!*

ACTIVITY 2 speaking/writing

Work in groups of three. What customs do you have in your country for events such as birth, engagement, marriage, death? Tell your group what people do in your country. Write the information in the chart.

Example: *In India, when a couple gets married, the bride usually wears red.*

EVENT	COUNTRY 1: ________	COUNTRY 2: ________	COUNTRY 3: ________
When a baby is born...			
When a couple gets married...			
When someone dies...			
When a person turns 13 (or 15 or 16)...			
When a person graduates from college...			
Other:			

ACTIVITY 3 speaking

This is an activity for the whole class. On small slips of paper, write the numbers 1 to 16, and put them in an envelope. One student is the "caller" and the other students pick numbers. Only the caller looks at the grid below. The first student picks a number from the envelope. The caller calls out the command in that square for the student to follow. Then a second student picks out a number, and the caller calls out the command. The caller names different students as needed. Continue until all the commands are given.

Example: You pick the number 7.
Caller: *Lend some money to Maria.*

1. Whisper a secret to the person next to you.	2. Give a penny to the person on your left.	3. Write a funny message to someone in the class.	4. Hand your wallet to the person on your right.
5. Make a paper airplane for the person across from you.	6. Tell a funny joke to someone.	7. Lend some money to a person in the class.	8. Describe your best friend to someone.
9. Explain indirect objects to a person near you.	10. Tell your favorite color to the person on your right.	11. Introduce the person on your left to the person on your right.	12. Offer a piece of gum to someone.
13. Teach your classmates how to say "I love you" in your language.	14. Open the door for someone in the class.	15. Throw your pen to the person across from you.	16. Pass a secret message to one person in the class.

ACTIVITY 4 listening/speaking

CD Track 12

STEP 1 Listen to the conversation between Linda and Amy. Then read the statements below. Check *True* or *False.*

	TRUE	FALSE
1. Linda is giving her mother perfume on Mother's Day.		
2. Linda's mother tells Linda what gift she wants.		
3. Amy's mother always tells her daughter what gift she wants.		
4. Linda's father only takes Linda's mother to a restaurant on Mother's Day.		
5. Linda's father does not buy his wife a gift.		

STEP 2 Compare your answers with a partner's. If a statement is false, make a true statement.

STEP 3 Tell your classmates what you do and give to a person on a special day like Mother's Day or a birthday.

ACTIVITY 5 research on the web

People in the United States often send greeting cards to friends and family for birthdays, holidays, and life events. Search the Web for information on this American custom. Use a search engine such as Google®, Yahoo®, or Ask®. Enter the keywords *greeting*, *card*, *facts*, and *U.S.* Write down 3–5 interesting facts about greeting cards. Share your facts with the class.

Example: *Americans send 180 million greeting cards to loved ones on Valentine's Day.*

ACTIVITY 6 reflection

STEP 1 Think about what you do in a conversation when you have a problem understanding the speaker or expressing your meaning. Check the things you do.

a. When I don't understand the speaker:

_______ 1. I ask the speaker a question.

_______ 2. I ask the speaker to explain his/her meaning to me.

_______ 3. I say to the speaker, "Please repeat that."

_______ 4. I repeat the speaker's meaning in my own words to check my understanding.

_______ 5. I guess the speaker's meaning.

_______ 6. I don't do anything.

b. When I have a problem speaking / expressing my meaning:

_______ 1. I ask the listener to pronounce words for me.

_______ 2. I ask the listener to translate a word or a sentence for me.

_______ 3. I repeat my sentence for the listener.

_______ 4. I tell the listener my meaning in a different way.

_______ 5. I draw a picture for the listener.

_______ 6. I don't do anything.

STEP 2 Evaluate what you do in conversations. How can you improve your conversation skills?

UNIT 14

CAN, KNOW HOW TO, BE ABLE TO, CONNECTORS: *AND/BUT/SO/OR*

UNIT GOALS

- Use *can* to express ability
- Ask questions with *can*
- Ask for help with English using *can*
- Understand the difference between *can/know how to/be able to* for expressing learned or natural ability
- Use sentence connectors: *and, but, so,* and *or* correctly

OPENING TASK

In his book *Frames of Mind*, about multiple intelligences, Howard Gardner defines different types of intelligences.

STEP 1

Read the statements related to six of Gardner's types of intelligence. Check the things that you can do. Then ask your partner questions about your partner's ability.

	ME ...	MY PARTNER ...
1. Visual Intelligence ("Picture" Smart)		
a. do a puzzle		
b. interpret a graph		
c. read a map		
2. Verbal Intelligence ("Word" Smart)		
a. tell a story		
b. speak three languages		
c. write		
3. Physical Intelligence ("Body" Smart)		
a. dance		
b. play sports		
c. act		

	ME ...	MY PARTNER ...
4. Musical Intelligence ("Music" Smart)		
a. sing		
b. play a musical instrument		
c. write music		
5. Logical Intelligence ("Logic" Smart)		
a. work with numbers and shapes		
b. think scientifically		
c. solve problems with logic		
6. Interpersonal Intelligence ("People" Smart)		
a. work well in a group		
b. understand others		
c. communicate with all kinds of people		

STEP 2

Ask your partner questions about his/her abilities. What type of intelligence do you think your partner has? Tell the class why.

form

FOCUS 1 *Can*

Can is a special kind of verb called a modal verb. Modal verbs come before the base form of the verb. Modals do not take *-s* in the third person singular (with subjects he-she-it). *Can* expresses ability.

AFFIRMATIVE	NEGATIVE	NEGATIVE CONTRACTION
I You He She **can** speak English. We You They	I You He She **cannot** speak Chinese. We You They	I You He She **can't** speak French. We You They
(a) She can DANCE. (b) He can SING.	In the affirmative, we pronounce *can* as /ken/ and stress the base form of the verb.	
(c) He CAN'T DANCE. (d) She CAN'T SING.	In the negative, we stress both *can't* and the base form of the verb.	

EXERCISE 1

Go back to the Opening Task on pages 216–217. With a partner, take turns saying what you can or can't do.

Examples: *I can read a map.*
I can't play a musical instrument.

EXERCISE 2

"Musical Savants" are special people. They have some social, learning, and physical disabilities, but they also have one extraordinary ability. For example, Eric is a blind musical savant.

Complete the sentences with an affirmative or a negative form of *can* and a verb in the box.

create	remember	play	write	communicate	read

1.  He ______________________.

2.  He ______________________.

3.  He ______________________ the piano.

4.  He ______________________ any new music he hears, and he can play it.

5.  He ______________________ new music.

6.  He ______________________ through music.

form

FOCUS 2 Questions with *Can*

YES/NO **QUESTIONS**	**INFORMATION QUESTIONS**
(a) **Can** you use a computer? Yes, I can. / No, I can't.	(c) What **can** you do on the computer? I can do research on the Internet.
(b) **Can** he cook? Yes, he can. / No, he can't.	(d) Who **can** cook in your family? My mother can. My father can't boil water!

EXERCISE 3

STEP 1 **Write *yes/no* questions with *can*. Then, under *Your Response*, check *Yes* or *No* to give your opinion about each question. Leave the columns under *Total* blank for now.**

	YOUR RESPONSE		TOTAL	
	YES	NO	YES	NO
1. a woman/work as a firefighter Can a woman work as a firefighter?				
2. women/fight bravely in wars _______________________________?				
3. a man/be a good nurse _______________________________?				
4. men/raise children _______________________________?				
5. women/be good police officers _______________________________?				
6. a woman/be a construction worker _______________________________?				
7. a man/keep house neatly _______________________________?				
8. a woman/be a good leader of a country _______________________________?				
9. men/communicate well with women _______________________________?				

STEP 2 **Go back to Step 1. Read the questions aloud. Do a survey in your class. Count how many students say "yes" and how many say "no." Write the *total* number of *Yes* and *No* answers in the *Total* column. Do you agree or disagree with your classmates? Give reasons for your answers.**

Example: *Women can be good police officers. They can be tough. They can be brave. They can help people in trouble.*

EXERCISE 4

Work in a group of four to six people. Find out who in your group can do the following things. Take turns asking the questions. Keep the conversation going by asking follow-up questions. Report the results to your class.

Example: Who/type?
Student 1: Who can type?
Student 2: I can type.
Student 1: How fast can you type?
Student 2: I can type 90 words per minute.

1. Who/cook? ________________

____

2. Who/speak more than one language? ________________

____

3. Who/play a musical instrument? ________________

____

4. Who/solve math problems? ________________

____

5. Who/teach? ________________

____

6. Who/draw? ________________

____

7. Who/run a marathon? ________________

____

8. Who/play card games? ________________

____

FOCUS 3 Asking for Help with English

use

EXAMPLES	EXPLANATIONS
(a) **Can I say,** "She can to swim" **in English?**	When you are not sure your English is correct, use the expression: *Can I say . . . in English?*
(b) **A:** How can I say, ". . ." in English?  B: That's called "sweeping."	When you don't know how to say something in English, ask the question: *How can I say, ". . ." in English?*

EXERCISE 5

Look at the pictures. First, mime each action. Then ask your classmates questions to find out how to say each word. Do three of your own.

Example: *How can I say* (mime the action) *in English?*

1. 
2. 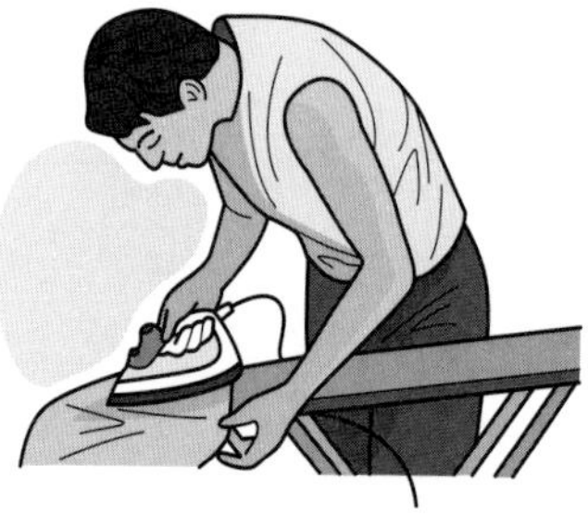
3. 
4. 
5. 
6. 

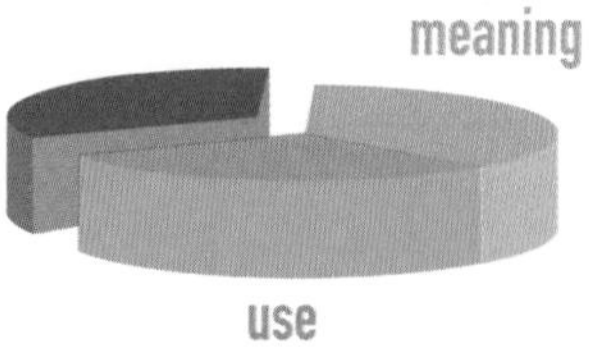

FOCUS 4 Expressing Ability: *Can, Know How to*, and *Be Able to*

EXAMPLES	EXPLANATIONS
(a) She **can** cook. (b) She **knows how to** cook. (c) She **is able to** cook.	To express learned ability, use *can, know how to,* or *be able to.*
(d) A blind person **can't** see. (e) A blind person **isn't able to** see. (f) NOT: A blind person **doesn't know how** to see.	To express natural ability, use *can* or *be able to* only. *Be able to* is more formal than *can.* Use *be able to* in all tenses; not *can.*

EXERCISE 6

Make affirmative or negative statements with the words below. To express learned ability, make one statement with *can / can't* and one statement with *know(s) how to / don't/doesn't know how to.* To express natural ability, make only one statement with *can/can't.*

Examples: a. A chef/cook
A chef can cook.
A chef knows how to cook.
b. Humans/learn a new language
Humans can learn a new language.

1. A blind person/see
2. A dog/live for twenty-five years
3. Infants/walk
4. A deaf person/hear
5. Fish/breathe on land
6. A man/have a baby
7. Doctors/cure all diseases
8. Men/take care of babies
9. Roses/grow without water
10. Painters/work with color and light

EXERCISE 7

Fill in the blanks in the sentences. For learned ability, use the affirmative or negative form of *be able to*. For natural ability, use the affirmative or negative form of *can*.

Evelyn Glennie is a Scottish percussion musician. She (1) ________________ play over 1,800 percussion instruments. Surprisingly, Evelyn Glennie is also profoundly deaf. Being "profoundly deaf" means she (2) ________________ hear only a little. She (3) ________________ hear the sounds of people speaking, but she (4) ________________ understand the words. Evelyn (5) ________________ read lips to understand people's words, but how can she be a musician? Evelyn (6) ________________ hear music with her ears. But she believes that hearing is a form of touching. When our ears don't work, we (7) ________________ feel the sound vibrations. In this way, a deaf person (8) ________________ touch sounds. Evelyn (9) ________________ also see sounds. When she sees something move or vibrate, she (10) ________________ create that sound in her mind. Evelyn Glennie (11) ________________ hear. But she (12) ________________ perform at international concerts. She (13) ________________ teach. She (14) ________________ communicate with people through the language of music. Evelyn Glennie is an amazing musician.

EXERCISE 8

Test your knowledge. Make *yes/no* questions with *be able to*. Then discuss your answers.

Example: people/live without food and water for one month
Are people able to live without food and water for one month?
No, they aren't. People are able to live without food for one month. But they aren't able to live without water for one month.

1. a computer/think

 ____

2. robots/raise children

 ____

3. an airplane/fly from New York to Paris in four hours

 ____

4. cats/see in the dark

 ____

5. a river/flow uphill

 ____

6. we/communicate with people from other planets

 ____

7. a person/learn a language in one week

 ____

8. doctors/cure AIDS

 ____

9. a 2-year old child/read

 ____

10. the United Nations/stop wars

 ____

11. humans/travel to outer space

 ____

12. you/think of any more questions

 ____

FOCUS 5 Sentence Connectors: *And/But/So/Or*

And, but, so, and **or** are sentence connectors. We use them to connect two complete sentences.

EXAMPLES	EXPLANATIONS
(a) I can roller-skate, **and** I can ski.	**And** adds information.
(b) I can dance, **but** I can't sing. He can swim, **but** his brother can't.	**But** shows contrast.
(c) I can't cook, **so** I often go out to eat.	**So** gives a result.
(d) You can go, **or** you can stay.	**Or** gives a choice.
(e) I can speak English, but I can't speak Chinese. (f) I can speak Spanish, and my sister can speak Japanese.	When you connect two complete sentences, use a comma (,) before the connector.
(g) I can say it in English, or I can say it in French. (h) I can say it in English or French.	When the subject is the same for the two verbs, it is not necessary to repeat the subject or *can*.
(i) **Nick** can watch a movie, or **he** can play soccer.	When the subject is the same for the two verbs, you can use a pronoun in the second clause.
(j) My sister can play the piano, but I **can't.** (k) I'm able to eat spicy food, but my wife **isn't.** (l) Jim knows how to fix computer problems, but Ted **doesn't.**	When the subjects are different but the verb is the same, it is not necessary to repeat the base form of the verb (e.g., *play the piano, eat spicy food, fix computer problems*).

EXERCISE 9

You want to spend a Saturday with a classmate. Choose a partner. Ask each other questions to decide what kind of day you want to have. Then add three questions of your own.

Example: **You:** *Do you want to meet early for breakfast or wait until later to meet?*
Your partner: *Let's meet early for breakfast.*

1. meet early for breakfast/wait until later to meet
2. skip lunch/have a picnic lunch
3. go to a museum/spend some time outdoors (in a park or at the beach)
4. surf the Internet/play soccer
5. cook dinner together/eat out
6. rent a DVD/go to a movie
7. ______________________________
8. ______________________________
9. ______________________________

EXERCISE 10

How technologically smart are you? Write sentences using *can* or *know how to* with *and* or *but.*

1. take a photo/edit a digital photo
2. write a check/ do banking online
3. listen to a CD/burn a CD
4. use a computer/write a computer program
5. surf the Web/evaluate good Web sources for a research project
6. use an MP3 player/download music
7. play the piano/play an electronic keyboard
8. send an e-mail/send an attachment to an e-mail
9. chat online/send a text message

EXERCISE 11

Fill in the blanks with *and, but, so,* or *or.*

Daniel Tammet is a mathematical savant. He lives in England. He can multiply big numbers in his head. He loves numbers (a) ________________ loves to count, (b) ________________ the problem is, he can't stop. He tries to count the pebbles at the beach, (c) ________________ there are too many pebbles to count, (d) ________________ Daniel gets tired. As a result he doesn't like the beach. At the supermarket, Daniel counts every fruit (e) ________________ every vegetable, (f) ________________ he doesn't like the supermarket. Daniel is a mathematical genius, (g) ________________ he can't drive a car (h) ________________ understand people's feelings.

Daniel can never change his daily schedule. He needs to brush his teeth (i) ________________ drink his tea at the same time every day, (j) ________________ it is difficult for Daniel to keep a regular job.

Like Eric in Exercise 2, Daniel has extraordinary abilities, (k) ________________ he also has extraordinary disabilities.

Use Your English

ACTIVITY 1 speaking

Read the job advertisement in the newspaper for a baby sitter. Interview your partner for the job. Ask questions with *can*, *know how to*, and *be able to*.

Examples: *Do you know how to cook?*
Can you work full-time?

> **142 Employment**
>
> **WANTED: Baby sitter ★**
> Responsible person. Full-tme work five days a week 8:00-5:00, some evenings and weekends. Must speak English and be able to drive. Laundry, light housekeeping, and cooking required. Experience with children necessary. References requested.

ACTIVITY 2 writing

What can you do that your parents or other people you know cannot do? Write six sentences.

Examples: *My mother can't ride a bicycle, but I can.*
My sister knows how to sew, but I don't.

ACTIVITY 3 writing/speaking

Do you think it's better to be a man or a woman? Write as many reasons as you can for your opinion, and then discuss them.

Example: *It's better to be a woman. A woman can have children.*

ACTIVITY 4 speaking

Make a list of ten jobs. Say what you can or are able to do. The class decides what job is good for you. Use *and* and *but*.

Example: You say: *I can help sick people and get along with them. I am able to follow directions.*
Your group: *Then you can be a nurse!*

ACTIVITY 5 speaking

STEP 1

Ask a classmate if he or she can do one of the activities in the box below.

Example: *Can you touch your toes without bending your knees?*

STEP 2

If the person says *yes*, write his/her name in the box. Then go to another student and ask another question.
If the person says *no*, ask the other questions until he or she says *yes*. Then write his or her name in the box.

STEP 3

Each student who answered *yes* must perform the action!

touch your toes without bending your knees __________	dance salsa __________	whistle __________
sing a song in English __________	say "Hello" in four languages __________	tell a joke in English __________
draw a horse __________	pronounce this word: "psychology" __________	juggle __________

ACTIVITY 6 listening/speaking

CD Track 13

STEP 1

Listen to Ken's interview for a job. Then read the statements. Check *Yes* or *No*.

	YES	NO
1. Ken can speak Spanish.		
2. Ken can understand Latin American people.		
3. Ken is able to listen to others patiently.		
4. Ken is able to understand people's needs.		
5. He can solve problems.		
6. He can cooperate with others.		
7. He can use a computer.		

STEP 2

According to this conversation, what kind of intelligence does Ken have?

a. Musical b. Interpersonal c. Physical

ACTIVITY 7 reflection

STEP 1

What can you do in English? Check *Yes* or *No*. Add two additional abilities.

	YES	NO
1. I am able to introduce someone.		
2. I know how to ask about prices.		
3. I can describe people and places.		
4. I can make a polite request.		
5. I'm able to give directions.		
6. I can give advice.		
7. I know how to ask for information about English.		
8. ______________________________		
9. ______________________________		

STEP 2

Now, exchange books with a partner. Tell what your partner can or can't do in English.

Example: *My partner is able to introduce someone.*

UNIT

15

PRESENT PROGRESSIVE TENSE

UNIT GOALS

- **Make affirmative and negative statements in the present progressive tense**
- **Know how to spell verbs ending in *-ing***
- **Choose between the simple present and the present progressive**
- **Know which verbs are not usually used in the progressive**
- **Ask *yes/no* questions in the present progressive**

OPENING TASK

A Bad Day at the Harrisons'

Robin and Regis have three children. Their babysitter cannot come today, so Regis is staying at home and taking care of the children and the house.

Why is Regis having a bad day?

Talk about what is happening in the picture. Use the verbs in the box.

VERBS
bark
play cowboy on his father's back
burn
go crazy
watch TV
do homework
cry
ring
fight over a toy
walk into the apartment

REGIS
JIMMY
ROBIN
ROVER
BABY
SUZY
MATH

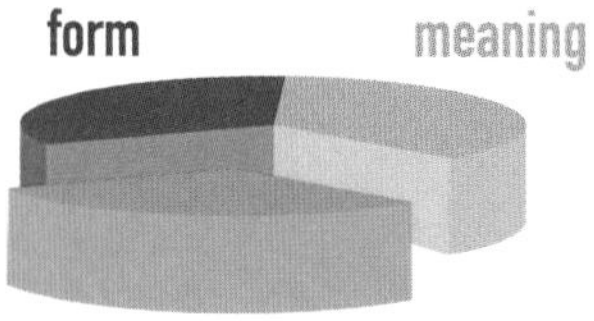

FOCUS 1 Present Progressive: Affirmative Statements

EXAMPLES	EXPLANATIONS
(a) The food **is burning.** (b) The baby **is crying.** (c) The dog and the baby **are fighting.**	Use the present progressive to talk about an action that is happening right now; an action in progress.
(d) **The baby is crying and fighting** with the dog.	We usually do not repeat the subject and the verb *be* when the subject is doing two or more things.

SUBJECT	*BE*	BASE FORM OF THE VERB + *-ING*
I	am	
He She It	is	working.
We You They	are	

Affirmative Contractions

SUBJECT + *BE* CONTRACTION	BASE FORM OF THE VERB + *-ING*
I'm	
He's She's It's	working.
We're You're They're	

EXERCISE 1

Underline all the present progressive verbs in the text.

Example: *Regis <u>isn't having</u> a good day.*

Today is not a normal day at the Harrisons'. Usually, Robin's babysitter comes at 3:00 P.M., and Robin leaves for class. Robin teaches from 4:00 P.M. until 8:00 P.M., but today, Robin is attending an all-day meeting at the college. Her babysitter is sick today, so Regis is spending the day at home. He's taking care of the children and the house. He's trying very hard, but everything is going wrong. Regis isn't having a good day. Actually, poor Regis is going crazy. He's thinking about Robin. He's learning something today. It's not easy to stay home with the children. He's beginning to understand this.

form

FOCUS 2 Spelling of Verbs Ending in *-ing*

VERB END	RULE	EXAMPLES	
1. consonant + *e*	Drop the *-e*, add *-ing*.	write	writing
2. consonant + vowel + consonant (one syllable verbs)	Double the consonant, add *-ing*.	sit	sitting
Exception: verbs that end in *-w*, *-x*, and *-y*.	Do not double *w*, *x*, and *y*.	show fix play	showing fixing playing
3. consonant + vowel + consonant. The verb has more than one syllable, and the stress is on the last syllable.	Double the consonant, add *-ing*.	beGIN forGET	beginning forgetting
If the stress is not on the last syllable	Do not double the consonant.	LISten HAPpen	listening happening
4. *-ie*	Change *-ie* to *y*, add *-ing*.	lie die	lying dying
5. All other verbs	Add *-ing* to the base form of verb.	talk study do agree	talking studying doing agreeing

EXERCISE 2

Fill in the blanks with the present progressive.

Today's a normal day at the Harrisons'. It is 4:00. Robin (1) ________________ (prepare) dinner in the kitchen. She (2) ________________ (slice) onions and (3) ________________ (wipe) the tears from her eyes. The house is quiet, so she (4) ________________ (listen) to some music. She (5) ________________ (think) about her class tonight. She (6) ________________ (wait) for her babysitter to arrive. The baby (7) ________________ (sleep). The dog (8) ________________ (lie) on the floor and (9) ________________ (chew) on a bone. Jimmy (10) ________________ (play) with his toys. Suzy (11) ________________ (clean) her room. Nothing unusual (12) ________________ (happen). Everything is under control.

EXERCISE 3

Trends in the Changing Family: Young Adults

Complete all the statements in columns A and B. Then find the statement in column B that matches and explains each statement in column A. Read the two statements together.

A	B
1. More and more, young people (move) ________________ back home after college.	a. They (build) ________________ their careers first, before getting married.
2. Young men and women (delay) ________________ marriage.	b. The cost of raising a child (increase) ________________.
3. Many young couples (live) ________________ together, but they (not/get) ________________ married.	c. Working mothers (feel) ________________ too much stress.
4. Many families (get) ________________ smaller.	d. Couples (worry) ________________ about the high divorce rate.
5. Some women (quit) ________________ their jobs to stay home with their children.	e. Young people (save) ________________ money by living at home with their parents.

EXERCISE 4

Who's talking? Fill in the blanks with the present progressive of the verb. Then match each statement to a picture.

Example: *"You're* driving *(drive) me crazy. Turn off the TV!"*

1. "That crazy dog ________________ (bite) me!"

a. 

2. "What ________________ (happen) here! I ________________ (walk) into a zoo!"

b. 

3. "Quiet! You ________________ (make) a lot of noise. I can't hear the TV."

c. 

4. "Stop that, Jimmy. You ________________ (hurt) me."

d. 

5. "Oh no! The food ________________ (burn)!"

e. 

6. "I ________________ (die) to take off my shoes. My feet ________________ (kill) me."

f. 

form

FOCUS 3 Present Progressive: Negative Statements

SUBJECT + BE + NOT			NEGATIVE CONTRACTION			BE CONTRACTION + NOT	
I	am		*			I'm	
He			He			He's	
She	is		She	isn't		She's	
It's		not working.	It		working.	It's	not working.
We			We			We're	
You	are		You	aren't		You're	
They			They			They're	

*There is no standard English contraction with *I am not.*

EXERCISE 5

Make negative statements using contractions.

Example: Robin/take care of the children today.
Robin isn't taking care of the children today.

1. Robin/wear comfortable shoes today
2. Robin's babysitter/watch the children today
3. The baby and the dog/get along
4. Regis/pay attention to the dinner on the stove
5. The children/listen to Regis
6. Suzy/do her homework
7. Suzy/help Regis
8. Regis/laugh
9. Regis/relax
10. Regis/enjoy his children today

EXERCISE 6

Trends in the Changing Family: Older Adults

The term "baby boomer" refers to a person born in the United States between 1946 and 1964. After World War II, there was a "baby boom," or population explosion. Read each statement. Make affirmative or negative statements in the present progressive.

1. Baby boomers (begin) ________________ to turn 60.
2. They (try) ________________ to stay young forever.
3. Some baby boomers (prepare) ________________ to retire and relax.
4. They (plan) ________________ to travel the world.
5. Others (not/seek) ________________ to retire.
6. They (not/quit) ________________ their jobs.
7. Some (think) ________________ about changing careers.
8. They (go) ________________ back to school to learn new skills.
9. They (hope) ________________ to do interesting, meaningful work.
10. Some men (become) ________________ fathers again at 60.
11. Other baby boomers (become) ________________ grandparents.
12. Baby boomers (expect) ________________ to live to 100!

FOCUS 4 Choosing Simple Present or Present Progressive

The simple present and the present progressive have different uses.

USE THE SIMPLE PRESENT FOR:	USE THE PRESENT PROGRESSIVE FOR:
• habits and repeated actions (a) Suzy usually does her homework in the evening.	• actions in progress now (c) Suzy's watching TV right now.
• things that are true in general (b) Women usually take care of children.	• actions that are temporary, not habitual (d) Regis is taking care of the children today. • situations that are changing (e) These days, men are spending more time with their children.
Time Expressions *always* *rarely* *often* *never* *usually* *every day/week/year* *sometimes* *once a week* *seldom* *on the weekends* *all the time* *three times a year*	Time Expressions *right now* *now* *today* *at the moment* *this week* *this evening* *this year* *this month* *these days* *nowadays*

EXERCISE 7

Read each statement. If the statement is in the simple present, make a second statement in the present progressive. If the statement is in the present progressive, make a second statement in the simple present. Discuss the differences in meaning.

SIMPLE PRESENT	PRESENT PROGRESSIVE
1a. Suzy usually does her homework in the evening.	1b. Tonight she isn't doing her homework. She's watching cartoons.
2a. ______________________	2b. Tonight, Robin isn't cooking dinner.
3a. Robin usually takes care of the children.	3b. ______________________
4a. ______________________	4b. Today, Regis is spending the day at home.
5a. The babysitter usually takes care of the children when Robin goes to work.	5b. ______________________

6a. ______________ ______________	6b. Right now, the baby and the dog are fighting.
7a. The babysitter doesn't usually go crazy.	7b. ______________ ______________
8a. Robin usually arrives home at 6:00 P.M.	8b. ______________ ______________

EXERCISE 8

Complete each statement with a verb in either the simple present or the present progressive. Be ready to explain your choice of verb.

In the traditional American family, men usually (1) ______________ (work) and women (2) ______________ (stay) home and (3) ______________ (take) care of the children. Women (4) ______________ (depend) on men financially.

Today, families (5) ______________ (change). The roles of men and women (6) ______________ (change), too. Nowadays, about 50 percent of American women (7) ______________ (work) outside the home. Some women (8) ______________ (get) high-paying jobs. Women (9) ______________ (become) more financially independent. These days, some women (10) ______________ (have) and (11) ______________ (raise) children without men.

On the other hand, some married women with children and jobs (12) ______________ (feel) stressed. These women (13) ______________ (quit) their good jobs. They (14) ______________ (stay) home with their children. Married men (15) ______________ (share) the housework. They (16) ______________ (help) their wives. They (17) ______________ (spend) more time with their children.

Men and women (18) ______________ (struggle) to balance work and family.

FOCUS 5 Verbs Not Usually Used in the Progressive

There are some verbs we usually do not use in the present progressive. These verbs are *not* action verbs. They are called nonprogressive (or stative) verbs.

EXAMPLES	NONPROGRESSIVE (STATIVE) VERBS
(a) Robin **loves** her job. (b) NOT: Robin is loving her job. (c) The children **need** help. (d) NOT: The children are needing help.	**Feelings and Emotions** *(like, love, hate, prefer, want, need)*
(e) Regis **understands** his wife.	**Mental States** *(think, believe, understand, seem, forget, remember, know, mean)*
(f) Regis **hears** the telephone ringing.	**Senses** *(hear, see, smell, taste, feel, sound)*
(g) Robin and Regis **own** a house.	**Possession** *(belong, own, have)*

You can use the present progressive with some of these verbs, but they have a different meaning.

SIMPLE PRESENT	PRESENT PROGRESSIVE
(h) I **think** you're a good student. (*Think* means "believe.")	(i) I **am thinking** about you now. (Here *thinking* shows a mental action.)
(j) I **have** two cars. (*Have* means "possess.")	(k) I'm **having** a good time. (*Have* describes the experience.)
(l) This soup **tastes** delicious. (*Taste* means "has a delicious flavor.")	(m) **I'm tasting** the soup. (*Taste* here means the action of putting soup in one's mouth.)

EXERCISE 9

Fill in the blanks with the present progressive or simple present form of the verb. Read the dialogues aloud. Use contractions.

Example: **Regis:** *I'm going* (go) crazy in this house.
Robin: *I think* (think) you need a vacation!

1. **Regis:** Suzy, I need your help here.
   Suzy: But, Dad, you (a) ________________ (need) my help every five minutes! I (b) ________________ (watch) TV right now!
2. It is 3:00 P.M. The telephone rings.
   Regis: Hello.
   Laura: Hello, Regis. What are you doing home in the middle of the day?
   Regis: Oh, hi, Laura. I know I (a) ________________ (be) never home during the day, but today I (b) ________________ (try) to be a househusband!
   Laura: Oh really? Where's Robin?
   Regis: Robin (c) ________________ (attend) a meeting at the college, so I (d) ________________ (take) care of the kids.
3. Jimmy interrupts Regis's telephone conversation:
   Regis: Hold on a minute, Laura . . . Jimmy (a) ________________ (pull) on my leg! Jimmy, I (b) ________________ (talk) to Mommy's friend Laura right now. You (c) ________________ (know) Laura. She (d) ________________ (come) to see Mommy every week. Now, just wait a minute, please . . .
   Laura: Is everything O.K., Regis?
   Regis: Oh, yes. We (e) ________________ (do) just fine. Bye!
4. It is 5:30 P.M. The telephone rings.
   Regis: Hello.
   Robin: Hi, honey! The meeting (a) ________________ (be) over. I (b) ________________ (be) on my way home. What (c) ________________ (happen)? I hope the children (d) ________________ (behave).
   Regis: They (e) ________________ (behave) like wild animals, Robin. I (f) ________________ (yell) at them all the time, but they don't listen to me. I (g) ________________ (not/have) a very good day today.
   Robin: You (h) ________________ (sound) terrible! Can I bring you anything?
   Regis: Yes, a bottle of aspirin!

EXERCISE 10

Work with a partner. Choose any picture (do not go in order). Describe the picture by making one statement with *seem, look,* or *feel* and an adjective from the box. Make another statement with the present progressive to say what the person is doing. Your partner must guess the number of the picture you are talking about. Take turns.

Example: You say: *The woman looks nervous. She's biting her nails.*
Your partner says: *Picture Number 5.*

sad	sick	scared	tired
angry	happy	cold	hot
bored	surprised	nervous	confused

1.

4.

7.

10.

2.

5.

8.

11.

3.

6.

9.

12.

form

FOCUS 6 Present Progressive: *Yes/No* Questions and Short Answers

***YES/NO* QUESTIONS**			**SHORT ANSWERS**					
Am	I	working?	Yes,	you	are.	No,	you	aren't.
Are	you		Yes,	I	am.	No,	I'm	not.
Is	he she it		Yes,	he she it	is.	No,	he she it	isn't.
Are	we you they		Yes,	we you they	are.	No,	we you they	aren't.

EXERCISE 11

Refer to the picture in the Opening Task on page 233. With a partner, take turns asking and answering questions about the Harrisons. Give short answers. Use the verbs from the box below.

Example: Suzy / her father
You: *Is Suzy helping her father?*
Your partner: *No, she isn't.*

watch	ring	play	bite	come
enjoy	burn	help	fight	smile

1. children / their father
2. the baby and the dog
3. Suzy / TV
4. their dinner
5. the phone
6. Jimmy / cowboy
7. the dog / Regis
8. Robin / home
9. Robin
10. Regis / his children

EXERCISE 12

Work with a partner. Ask your partner *yes/no* questions about changing trends in your partner's country. Add two questions of your own.

Example: young people / delay marriage *Are young adults delaying marriage in your country?*

1. couples / live together before marriage
2. women / stay home with their children
3. fathers / spend time with their children
4. men / share housework
5. women / become financially independent
6. women / raise children without men
7. more couples / get divorced
8. couples / pay babysitters to take care of their children
9. men and women / try to balance work and family
10. grandparents / live with their grown children and grandchildren
11. ______________________________
12. ______________________________

form

FOCUS 7 Present Progressive: *Wh*-Questions

WH-WORD	*BE*	SUBJECT	VERB + -*ING*	ANSWERS
What	am	I	doing?	(You're) getting ready for the beach.
When Where Why How	are	you	going?	(I'm going) at 2:00. (We're going) to Malibu Beach. (We're going) because we don't have school today. (We're going) by car.
Who *Who* asks about the subject.	is		going with us?	Clara (is going with us).
Who(m) *Whom* asks about the object.	is	she	meeting?	(She's meeting) her friends.

For a review of *who* and *whom*, refer to Unit 9, Focus 5.

EXERCISE 13

Write the question that asks for the underlined information.

1. Q: Who is watching television?

   A: Suzy is watching television.

2. Q: Who(m) is Regis taking care of tonight?

   A: Regis is taking care of the children.

3. Q: ____________________

   A: Suzy is watching television because she doesn't want to do her homework.

4. Q: ____________________

   A: Robin is meeting her colleagues at the college.

5. Q: ____________________

   A: Robin's thinking that she's lucky to be at work!

6. Q: ____________________

   A: They're eating peanut butter and jelly sandwiches for dinner because Regis's dinner is burnt.

7. Q: ____________________

   A: Regis is watching the children today.

8. Q: ____________________

   A: Regis is taking two aspirin because he has a terrible headache.

9. Q: ____________________

   A: Robin's meeting is taking place at the college.

10. Q: ____________________

    A: Robin is coming home right now.

11. Q: ____________________

    A: Regis is feeling very tired right now.

12. Q: ____________________

    A: The children are making a lot of noise.

EXERCISE 14

Correct the errors in the following sentences.

Example: Is the pizza tasting good?
Does the pizza taste good?

1. The baby and the dog are fight.
2. He's having a new TV.
3. Why you are working today?
4. Are you needing my help?
5. What Robin is thinking?
6. Is she believing him?
7. Right now, he plays cowboy on his father's back.
8. Regis's dinner is not smelling delicious.
9. Where they are going?
10. People no are saving money nowadays.
11. You working hard these days.
12. How you doing today?

Use Your English

ACTIVITY 1 writing/speaking

STEP 1 Your teacher will divide the class into two groups. Group A looks only at the statements in Column A and covers Column B. One student at a time will mime an action. Students in Group B must cover Column A and guess the action. Group B students can ask questions of Group A. Then each Group B student mimes an action from Column B and Group A guesses the action and so on.

COLUMN A	COLUMN B
1. You are opening the lid of a jar. The lid is on very tight.	1. You are reading a very sad story.
2. You are watching a very funny TV show.	2. You are watching your country's soccer team playing in the final game of the World Cup.
3. You are trying to sleep, and a mosquito is bothering you.	3. You are sitting at the bar in a noisy club. At the other side of the bar, there is someone you like. You are trying to get that person's attention.
4. You are crossing a busy street. You are holding a young child by the hand and carrying a bag of groceries in the other hand.	4. You are a dinner guest at a friend's house. Your friend is not a good cook. You don't like the food!
5. You are trying to thread a needle, but you're having trouble finding the eye of the needle.	5. You are cutting up onions to cook dinner.

STEP 2 Make up three situations like those above. Write each situation on a separate piece of paper, and put all the situations in a hat. Every student will then pick a situation and mime it for the others to guess.

ACTIVITY 2 writing

In this unit and Exercise 12, we see that family life is changing in many places. Is family life changing in your home country or in a country that you know? Write sentences expressing habits and things that are generally true or things that are changing for:
Mothers Children Grandparents Men Fathers Teenagers Couples Women
Discuss your statements in a group or with the whole class.

ACTIVITY 3 listening/speaking

CD Track 14

STEP 1

You are going to listen to a news report about changing trends in the American family. Before you listen, read the statements below. What do you <u>think</u> is true? Under *Pre-listening*, check *True* or *False* for each statement.

STATEMENTS	PRE-LISTENING		POST-LISTENING	
	TRUE	FALSE	TRUE	FALSE
1. The number of traditional nuclear families is increasing in America.				
2. Hispanic and Asian immigrants are not building traditional nuclear families in the United States.				
3. Americans are only marrying people from their own racial and cultural groups.				
4. The number of children per family is increasing.				
5. More and more unmarried partners are living together.				
6. No children are living with single parents.				
7. More people are choosing to live alone.				

STEP 2

Now listen to the news report. Under *Post-Listening*, check *True* or *False* according to what you <u>hear</u>. Then compare your answers in Steps 1 and 2. What is surprising about the American family? Discuss this in your group.

ACTIVITY 4 speaking

Work with a partner. Discuss how your lives in the United States today are different from your lives in the countries you come from.

Example: *In my country, I live with my parents. Here, I'm living with three roommates.*

ACTIVITY 5 writing/speaking

STEP 1 Look at the photo on the right. Give this person a name, a nationality, an occupation, an age, and so on. Write a story about this person. What is the woman doing? Where is she? How does she look? What is she thinking about? Why is she there?

STEP 2 Tell the class your story.

ACTIVITY 6 reflection

Work with a partner. Ask each other *yes/no* questions about your experiences learning English in this class. Check *yes* or *no.*

Example: *Are you enjoying this class?*

YES/NO QUESTION	YOU		YOUR PARTNER	
	YES	NO	YES	NO
1. enjoy this class				
2. your English improve				
3. this book help you				
4. make progress in listening and speaking				
5. feel more confident in English				
6. your classmates help you in class				
7. raise your hand more in class				
8. have any specific problems in English				
9. your writing ability improve				
10. your vocabulary increase				
11. use English more				
12. think more about grammar				

UNIT 16

ADJECTIVE PHRASES

Another, The Other, Other(s), The Other(s), and Intensifiers

UNIT GOALS

- Understand and know how to use adjective phrases
- Ask questions with *which*
- Understand and use *another, the other, other(s),* and *the other(s)*
- Use intensifiers with adjectives

OPENING TASK

Match Maker

Find the couples. Match one person on the left with a perfect partner on the right by describing both of them. Do not point to the picture.

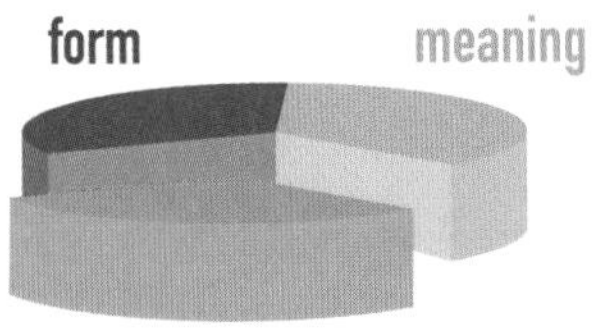

FOCUS 1 Adjective Phrases

EXAMPLES			EXPLANATIONS
Noun	Adjective Phrase	Verb	
(a) The man (b) The diamond ring	**in the suit** **on her finger**	is a businessman. is beautiful.	Adjective phrases are groups of words that describe nouns.
The man has a basketball. The man is an athlete. (c) The man	 **with the ball**	 is an athlete.	Adjective phrases combine two sentences.
(d) The **man** with the glasses **is** a businessman. (e) The two **people** on the motorcycle **are** free.			The verb agrees with the subject, not with the noun in the adjective phrase.

EXERCISE 1

Underline the subject and the verb in each sentence. Put parentheses around the adjective phrases.

Example: *The man (in the suit) works in an office.*

1. The man with the bandana drives a motorcycle.
2. The woman with the shopping bags is his girlfriend.
3. The young man with the laptop is a computer programmer.
4. The woman with the dog is in love with the man with the laptop.
5. The gentleman with the briefcase is a businessman.
6. The woman in the dress works for a flower shop.
7. The man with the basketball is physically fit.
8. The woman with the nose ring loves music.
9. The people in the picture on page 253 live in the same apartment building.

EXERCISE 2

These ten people below sit in specific chairs on page 256. Match each person to a chair. Then write a sentence with an adjective phrase to describe where each is sitting. The first one has been done for you.

1.

2.

3.

4.

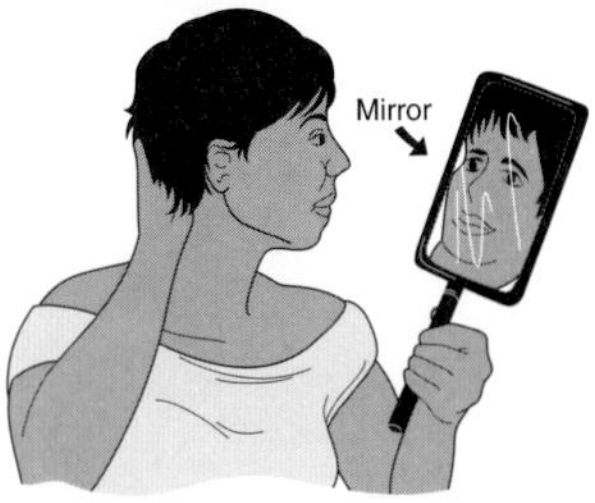

5.

6.

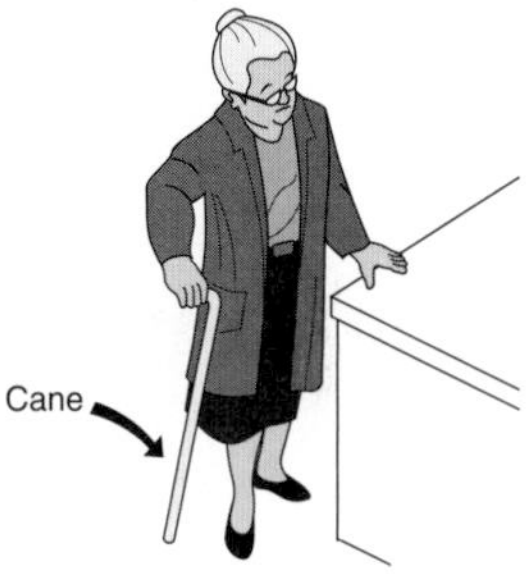

7.

8.

9.

10.

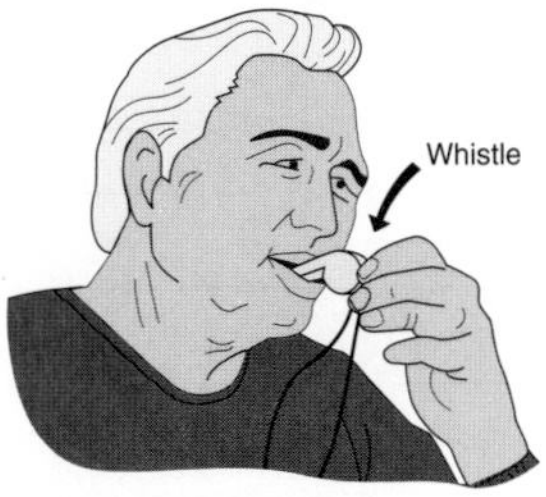

a.
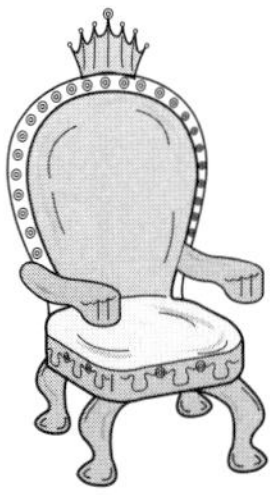

b.

c.
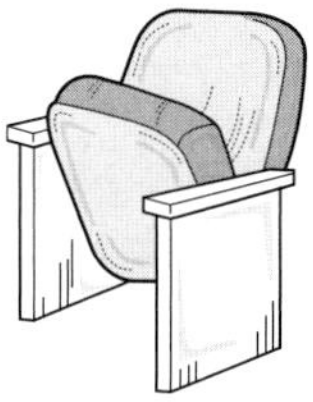

d.

e.

f.
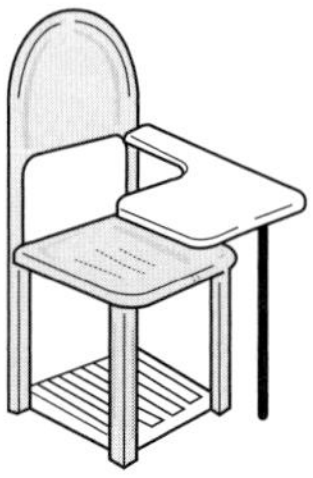

g.

h.
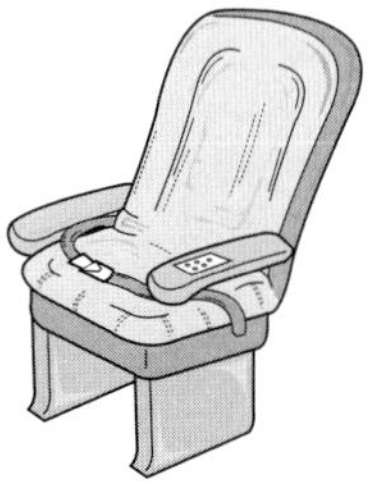

i.

j.
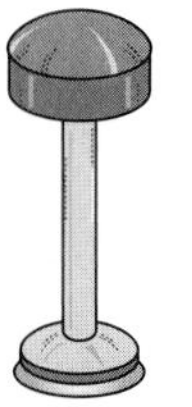

	Person	Chair	
1.	1	B	The man with the megaphone sits in chair B.
2.	2		
3.	3		
4.	4		
5.	5		
6.	6		
7.	7		
8.	8		
9.	9		
10.	10		

EXERCISE 3

Combine each of the sentence pairs on the next page into one sentence using an adjective phrase. Then find the person in the picture, and write the number of your sentence on the person. The first one has been done for you.

Kindergarten Chaos

1. The girl has a bow in her hair. She is kicking her partner.

   The girl with the bow in her hair is kicking her partner.

2. The boy has a striped shirt and black pants. He is throwing a paper airplane across the room.

   ____

3. The girls are near the window. They are waving to their friends outside.

   ____

4. The boy is in a baseball uniform. He is standing on the teacher's desk.

   ____

5. The boys are in the back of the room. They are fighting.

   ____

6. The boy is in the corner. He is reading.

   ____

7. The boy is in the closet. He is crying.

   ____

8. The girl has an MP3 player. She is singing.

   ____

9. The man has a rope around him. He is the new teacher.

   ____

10. The man is in a suit and tie. He is the school principal.

   ____

FOCUS 2 Questions with *Which*

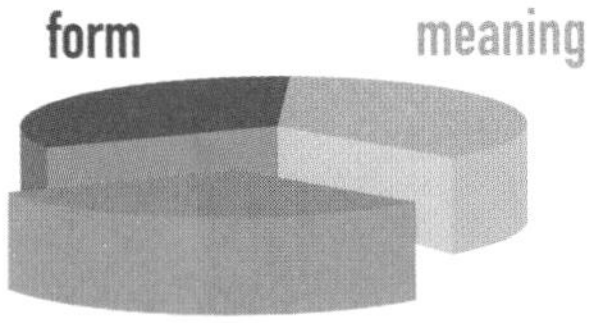

EXAMPLES	EXPLANATIONS
(a) **Which** man is wearing shorts? the athlete (b) **Which** men are conservative? the businessman and the computer programmer	Use ***which*** when there is a choice between two or more people or things.
(c) **Which** car do they like? They like the small **one**. (d) **Which** shoes do they like? the comfortable **ones**	Substitute the words ***one*** or ***ones*** for nouns so you do not repeat the noun.
(e) **Which** restaurant do they want to try? the one with the organic food	You can also use adjective phrases after *one* and *ones*.

EXERCISE 4

Julie's house was robbed. She is very upset, and she is talking to her husband Charles on the phone, describing the damage. Work with a partner. Find the differences between the pictures. One person says Julie's statements. One person is the husband, and asks questions to get more specific information.

Example: **Julie:** *The window is broken.*
Charles: *Which window?*
Julie: *The one over the kitchen sink.*

Before

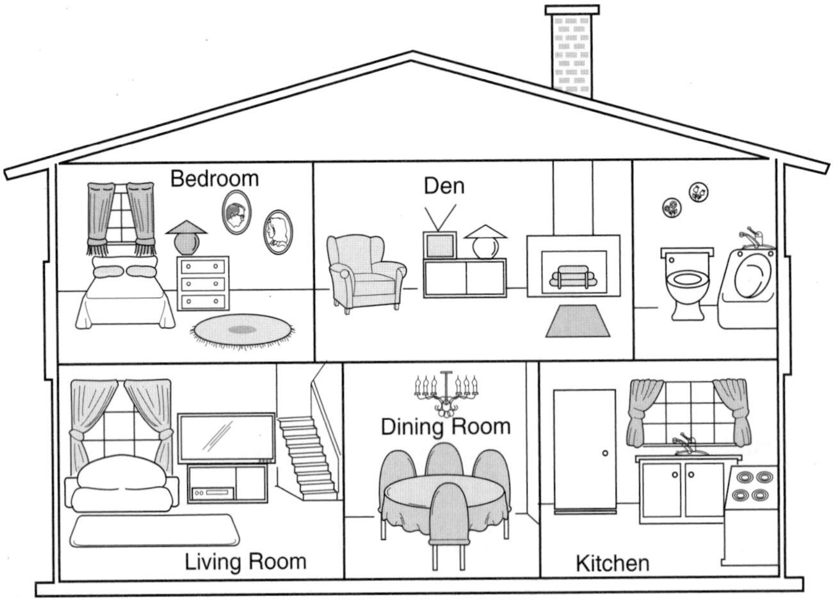

After

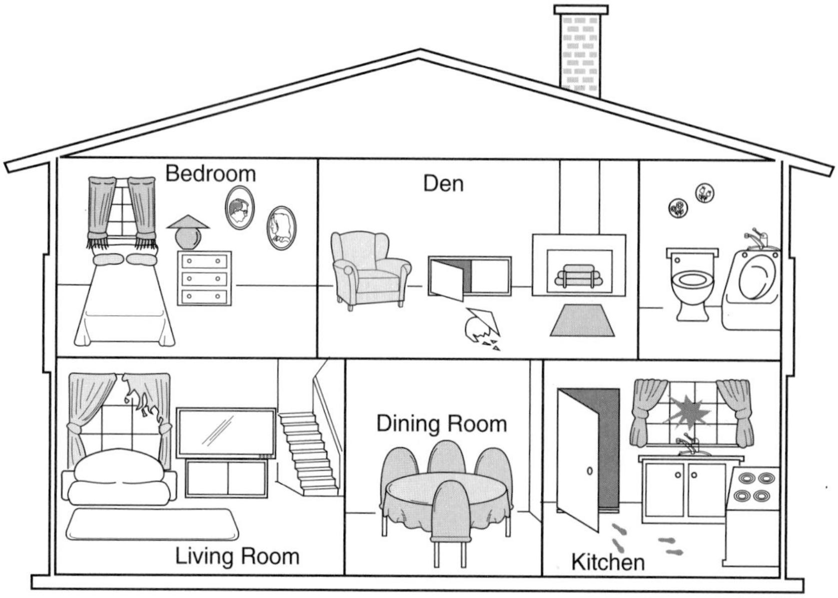

1. The floor is dirty.
2. The curtains are torn.
3. The TV is missing.
4. The door is open.
5. The lamp is broken.
6. The DVD player is missing.
7. The cabinet is empty.
8. The rug is missing.
9. The chandelier is gone.

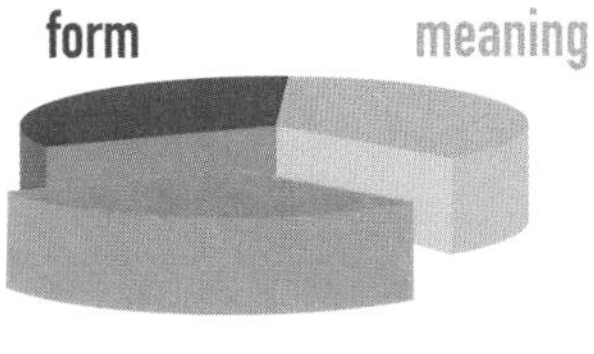

FOCUS 3 *Another, The Other, Other(s), The Other(s)*

EXPLANATION	EXAMPLE	MEANING
You can use ***another***:		
before a singular noun	(a) That cookie was so delicious. Can I have **another cookie**?	One more cookie; one more from a group
alone (as a pronoun).	(b) Can I have **another**?	
You can use ***other***:		
before a plural noun	(c) **Child:** There are no more cookies in the box, Mom! **Mom:** Don't worry. There are two **other boxes** in the pantry.	More than one more
alone (as a pronoun).	(d) There are two **others** in the pantry.	
You can use ***the other***:		
before a singular noun	(e) I found one box. Where is **the other box**?	The specific one you spoke about; the last one in the group
alone (as a pronoun)	(f) Where's **the other**?	
before a plural noun	(g) **Sister:** How many more cookies can I have? **Brother:** You can have one more. **The other cookies** are for me!	The specific ones you spoke about; the last ones in a group
alone (as a pronoun)	(h) **The others** are for me!	

EXERCISE 5

Thor is visiting Earth from another planet. Ed Toppil interviews Thor on television. Fill in the blanks with *another, the other, other(s),* or *the other(s).*

Ed: We on Earth are really excited to know there is (1) ________________ planet out there, Thor. Many of us know there are (2) ________________, but we can't find them. Do you know of any (3) ________________ planets?

Thor: Yes, we do. We know two (4) ________________: Limbix and Cardiax. I have photos of the people from both of (5) ________________ planets. The Limbix are the ones on the left. The Cardiax are (6) ________________ ones. We also now know the planet Earth. We are sure there are (7) ________________ out there, but (8) ________________ are very far away.

Ed: I am surprised that you speak English so well, Thor. Do the Thoraxes have (9) ________ language, too?

Thor: Yes, of course. We speak Thoracic, but English is a universal language, you know, so we all learn it in school. People on (10) ________ two planets speak English, too!

Ed: So what brings you to Earth?

Thor: Well, Ed, we are looking for (11) ________ intelligent beings in the universe.

Ed: On Earth?!! I don't know if you can find many intelligent beings on Earth, Thor! But we can discuss this at (12) ________ time. Right now, let's stop for a station break.

EXERCISE 6

Thor tours America. Fill in *another, other(s),* or the *other(s).*

1. Thor is in a department store with Ed Toppill.

Ed: You only have one tie, Thor. You need to buy (a) ________ one.

Thor: Why?

Ed: Because Americans are consumers. They like to buy things.

Thor: But I don't like any (b) ________ ties here.

Ed: O.K. Look at (c) ________ over there. Maybe you can find (d) ________ one.

2. Thor is in a candy store with a child:

Thor: Which candy is good here?

Child: This one is good, but first taste (a) ________ one in the brown and green paper. It's out of this world!

Thor: Hmmmm, excellent. Is it O.K. to take (b) ________ one?

3. **Soaprah:** So, Thor, tell us about your family. Are you married?

Thor: Yes. I am, and I have two children. One is a specialist in interplanetary communication and (a) ________________ owns a spaceship factory.

Soaprah: And what does your wife do?

Thor: My wife is a spaceship pilot.

Soaprah: What about (b) ________________ people on Thorax? What do they do?

Thor: (c) ________________ do different jobs. We have doctors, teachers, artists, and so on. We don't have any tax collectors.

Soaprah: Are there any (d) ________________ professions you don't have?

Thor: We don't have any lawyers, I'm happy to say.

Soaprah: That sounds great to me, too!

Thor: Do you have any (e) ________________ questions?

Soaprah: I have a million (f) ________________ questions! But our time is up. It was nice meeting you, Thor. Thanks so much for coming

FOCUS 4 Intensifiers

Intensifiers are words that make adjectives stronger. The chart below includes some examples of intensifiers.

SUBJECT	*BE*	INTENSIFIER	ADJECTIVE	NOTES
(a) Earth	is	very	beautiful.	
(b) The people on Earth	are	really	interesting.	The word *really* is often used in informal English.
(c) The people on Thorax	are	quite	happy.	
(d) The people on Earth	are	rather/pretty fairly	diverse.	*Pretty* has the same meaning as *rather*, but is very informal.
(e) Thorax	isn't	very really	beautiful.	*Very* and *really* are the only intensifiers we use in negative sentences.

SUBJECT	*BE*	ARTICLE	INTENSIFIER	ADJECTIVE	NOUN
(f) Earth	is	a	very really	special	place.
(g) Thorax	is	a	rather/pretty fairly	small	planet.
(h) Thorax	isn't	a	very really	attractive	place.

SUBJECT	*BE*	INTENSIFIER	ARTICLE	ADJECTIVE	NOUN
(i) Thorax	is	quite	a	small	planet.

EXERCISE 7

Test Thor's knowledge. How many of the objects can Thor (and you) guess?

1. This is fairly long and thin.
   People eat it.
   It is very popular in Italy. What is it? ______________________
2. This is a liquid.
   People usually drink it hot.
   They like its rather strong, rich smell.
   It's brown. What is it? ______________________
3. This is an electrical appliance.
   It is quite common in people's homes.
   Sometimes it is very hot.
   You put bread into it. What is it? ______________________
4. This is very cold.
   It's also pretty hard.
   People put it in drinks on hot days.
   It's quite slippery. What is it? ______________________
5. This is quite a big metal box.
   It's electrical and pretty practical.
   It's very useful in tall buildings.
   People go inside the box.
   The box goes up and down. What is it? ______________________
6. This is a very popular piece of plastic.
   With it, we can buy rather expensive things without cash.
   It isn't very big. What is it? ______________________
7. There are different kinds of candy.
   All of them are good.
   But this one is really special.
   It comes in brown or white.
   It's pretty fattening.
   It's quite delicious. What is it? ______________________
8. This thing is quite colorful.
   It isn't very common.
   It sometimes follows rainstorms.
   It is quite a beautiful sight. What is it? ______________________

EXERCISE 8

Ed Toppil continues his interview with Thor. Write an intensifier in each blank. There is more than one possible answer.

Ed: So tell me, Thor, what do you think of our planet?

Thor: Well, Earth is a beautiful planet, but it's (1) ____quite____ a strange place. Many of your leaders are not doing a (2) ________ good job. Some people on Earth are (3) ________ rich. Others are (4) ________ poor. There can be a (5) ________ big difference between people. On Thorax, we are all equal. Money isn't (6) ________ important. Learning is (7) ________ important. That's why we're visiting Earth. Your knowledge can be (8) ________ useful to us. Also, your art and music are (9) ________ beautiful.

Ed: That's (10) ________ interesting. I'm sure we can learn many (11) ________ useful and exciting things from you, too, Thor.

EXERCISE 9

How necessary or important is each item to you? Give your opinion using intensifiers. Explain your answers.

Example: a cell phone
A cell phone is very important to me. I can call my friends anytime I want.

1. family
2. a life partner
3. designer clothes
4. a university degree
5. children
6. my native language
7. my culture
8. music
9. friends
10. a fancy car

EXERCISE 10

Read the statements and comments. Fill in an intensifier in each blank. Sometimes, there can be more than one possible answer.

Statement	Comment
1. I want to see the movie *Friday the 13th.*	Don't! That's a ________ scary movie!
2. Our teacher is planning an end-of-term party.	That's ________ a nice thing for her to do.
3. How do you like your new digital camera?	It looks easy to use, but it's actually ________ difficult.
4. I like this restaurant very much.	Me, too! This is ________ a delicious dinner.
5. My brother wants to get a motorcycle.	That's not a ________ good idea.
6. He's working in Vietnam.	Really! That's ________ a fascinating place!
7. They have eight children.	Wow! That's a ________ large family.
8. Eric and Tina are doing well in my class.	In mine, too. They're________ bright students.
9. I'm bored again today.	I'm afraid this is not a ________ exciting vacation.
10. Do you know Newport, Rhode Island?	Oh, yes. The mansions in Newport are ________ big—just like castles.

EXERCISE 11

Correct the errors in the following sentences.

1. The five of us plan to meet at 8:00 tomorrow. I'll tell Mary. You tell the other.
2. This cake is delicious! Can I have other slice?
3. The girl with the brown eyes are my sister.
4. Some of the students are here. Where are the others students?
5. The test wasn't quite difficult.
6. The supermarket is on the another side of the street.
7. There were three books on my desk. One is here. Where are others?
8. I need to go to other school.
9. Please give me the other chance.
10. The exercises in this unit is interesting.

Use Your English

ACTIVITY 1 writing/speaking

STEP 1 Write a paragraph (at least six sentences) about your home country or city. Use the topic sentence given below.
TOPIC SENTENCE:
My home country/city, _________, is a very wonderful place to visit.

Examples: *The beaches in the south are very beautiful.*
The market in the center of the city is always crowded.

STEP 2 Now tell the class about your country or city.

ACTIVITY 2 writing/speaking

STEP 1 In a group, write sentences about ten students in the class. Use adjective phrases. Use intensifiers when possible. Do not use names.

STEP 2 Read your sentences to the class. The class guesses the person you are talking about.

Examples: *The student from Bogotá is very friendly.*
The student next to Miyuki is quite a good dancer.
The student with the big smile is from Ecuador.

ACTIVITY 3 speaking/writing

STEP 1 Check (✔) the adjectives that describe you, and write *very/quite/rather/pretty/fairly/not very* under **You** in the chart below.

STEP 2 Ask your partner questions to find out which adjectives describe him or her. Then ask questions with how and write *very/quite/rather/pretty/fairly/not very* under **Your Partner** in the same chart.

Example: **You ask:** *Are you shy?*
Your partner answers: *Yes, I am.*
You ask: *How shy are you?*
Your partner answers: *I'm very shy.*

	YOU		YOUR PARTNER	
Adjective		**very really quite rather pretty fairly not very**		**very really quite rather pretty fairly not very**
shy			✔	very
curious				
quiet				
romantic				
outgoing				
old-fashioned				
organized				
jealous				
talkative				
athletic				
adventurous				
sensitive				
caring				
mature				

ACTIVITY 4 writing

Use the information in Activity 3 to write five sentences about you or about your partner using *very/quite/rather/pretty/fairly/not very.*

Example: My partner is a very romantic person. He is pretty old-fashioned, and he is very jealous.

ACTIVITY 5 speaking

Imagine you are starting life on a new planet. Look at the following list of people. Then choose only ten people to move to the new planet. Say how necessary each one is and why. Say why the others are not necessary and why.

Example: A doctor is very necessary because we want to stay healthy.

an actor	an artist	a police officer	a political leader
a scientist	a religious leader	a young man	a young woman
a historian	a writer	a musician	a lawyer
a farmer	a teacher	a journalist	a pilot
a doctor	a mechanic	a computer specialist	a dancer
a military person	a stockbroker	an elderly person	an engineer

ACTIVITY 6 writing/speaking

Guess the object! Write descriptions of objects using intensifiers like those in Exercise 7. Ask your classmates to guess the object.

ACTIVITY 7 listening/speaking

CD Track 15

STEP 1

Listen to Steffi describing the photograph of her family reunion. Label the picture with the names of the people and their relationship to Steffi.

Steffi's Family Reunion

STEP 2

Bring in your own photo of a family gathering or a group of friends. Describe the people in the picture to your classmates.

ACTIVITY 8 research on the web

STEP 1 Your partner needs a vacation. Look for a beautiful place for a dream vacation on the Internet. Use a search engine such as Google® or Ask® or Yahoo® and look for photos of three places you think your partner will like. Use keywords such as *vacation*, *beach*, and *island*. Print out the photos.

STEP 2 Show your partner the photos. Ask your partner to choose which vacation place he or she likes the best and (without pointing) to give reasons for his or her choice.

Example: *I like the place with the big beach and pretty trees. The water looks quite warm and blue. The water in the other picture looks quite dark and cold. That beach isn't very attractive.*

ACTIVITY 9 reflection

What is helpful to you as you learn English? Check the things that help you learn English. Discuss why or why not with a partner. Add two of your own.

	YES	NO
1. A school with many computers		
2. A class with other students from my country		
3. Books with audiotapes		
4. A language lab with recording equipment		
5. A reading text with pictures		
6. A teacher with challenging materials		
7. A grammar book with clear explanations and examples		
8. A dictionary with phonetic symbols		
9. Movies with captions		
10. Conversation groups with students from different countries		

UNIT

17

PAST TENSE OF *BE*

UNIT GOALS

- **Make affirmative and negative statements with the verb *be* in the past tense**
- **Ask and answer *yes/no* and *wh*-questions with *be* in the past tense**

OPENING TASK

Test Your Memory

Look at the photos of famous people from the past. Make affirmative and negative statements about each person's nationality and occupation. Use the information in the boxes.

NATIONALITY
French
Indian
British
American

OCCUPATION
president
princess
religious leader
civil rights leader
scientist
rock singer

NAME	NATIONALITY	OCCUPATION
 1. Martin Luther King, Jr.		
 2. The Beatles		
 3. Diana		
 4. Mahatma Gandhi		
 5. Pierre and Marie Curie		
 6. George Washington, Thomas Jefferson, Abraham Lincoln, Theodore Roosevelt		

form

FOCUS 1 Past Tense of *Be*: Affirmative Statements

SUBJECT	VERB	
I	was	famous.
He She It	was	famous.
We You They	were	famous.
There	was	a famous actress in that film.
There	were	many political leaders at the meeting.

EXERCISE 1

Use the past tense of *be* to make correct statements about the famous people in the Opening Task.

1. The Beatles __________________ a famous British rock group in the 1960s.
2. Mahatma Gandhi __________________ a nationalist and Hindu religious leader in India.
3. Marie and Pierre Curie __________________ French scientists.
4. George Washington, Thomas Jefferson, Abraham Lincoln, and Theodore Roosevelt __________________ presidents of the United States.
5. Martin Luther King, Jr. __________________ American civil rights leader.
6. Diana __________________ a British princess, the wife of Prince Charles.

form

FOCUS 2 Past Tense of *Be:* Negative Statements

NEGATIVE STATEMENTS			NEGATIVE CONTRACTIONS		
SUBJECT	*BE + NOT*		SUBJECT	*BE + NOT*	
I	was not	famous.	I	wasn't	famous.
He She It	was not		He She It	wasn't	
We You They	were not		We You They	weren't	
There	was	no time to eat.	There	wasn't	any time to eat.
There	were	no good restaurants.	There	weren't	any good restaurants.

EXERCISE 2

STEP 1 **What do you know about Albert Einstein? Read the statements below. Circle (T) for *true* or (F) for *false* for each statement.**

1. Albert Einstein was Austrian. T F
2. As a boy, he wasn't a very good student. T F
3. He was friendly. T F
4. He was interested in his classroom subjects. T F
5. He was a good reader. T F
6. He was a great thinker. T F

STEP 2 **Read the text below about Albert Einstein. Compare the text to your answers in Step 1. Correct any incorrect sentences in Step 1.**

Albert Einstein was born in Germany on March 14, 1879. As a young student, Einstein wasn't very good in school. He wasn't focused in class. His memory was bad. He wasn't a good reader, and spelling was difficult for him. His teachers said he was mentally slow. Other students said young Albert Einstein was unsociable. But everyone was wrong about Einstein. In truth, Albert Einstein was bored in school. The subjects in class weren't interesting to him. Albert Einstein was a scientific genius. By 1920, he was famous around the world. He was the Nobel Prize winner for Physics in 1921.

EXERCISE 3

Read Michael and Carol's views about their trip to Disneyworld, a famous American place. Fill in the blanks with the affirmative or negative of *be* in the simple past. Then role-play the dialogue aloud.

Alice: Oh, hi, Michael. Hi, Carol. How (1) ______was______ your trip last week?

Carol: Hi, Alice. Oh, it (2) ________________ fun.

Michael: Fun! That vacation (3) __________ (not) fun, it (4) __________ terrible!

Carol: But Michael, how can you say that? I think the children and I (5) ________________ very satisfied with our vacation.

Michael: Carol, the weather (6) ________________ boiling hot.

Carol: It (7) __________ (not) boiling hot, it (8) __________ very comfortable.

Michael: The food (9) ________________ (not) very good . . .

Carol: The food (10) ________________ fine, Michael.

Michael: The people (11) ________________ rude.

Carol: They (12) __________ (not) rude/They (13) __________ polite and friendly.

Michael: The kids (14) ________________ very difficult.

Carol: The kids (15) __________ (not) difficult. They (16) __________ great.

EXERCISE 4

A positive person sees the world in a positive way and believes that good things will happen. A negative person usually sees only the bad things in life. Make sentences using *was/were* for the situations below. These adjectives may help you. Use other adjectives you know.

terrible	ugly	romantic	delicious	beautiful	small	extraordinary	polite
rude	friendly	sunny	fantastic	loud	rainy	ordinary	spacious

SITUATION	A POSITIVE PERSON SAYS:	A NEGATIVE PERSON SAYS:
1. Yesterday evening, you were at a famous restaurant with friends.	a. The place ________________. c. The food ________________. e. The waiters ________________.	b. The place ________________. d. The food ________________. f. The waiters ________________.
2. Last Saturday, you went to a trendy club.	a. The music ________________. c. The dance floor ____________.	b. The music ________________. d. The dance floor ____________.
3. Last summer, you were on vacation in Vietnam with your friends.	a. The weather ______________. c. The scenery ______________. e. The people ______________.	b. The weather ______________. d. The scenery ______________. f. The people ______________.

FOCUS 3 *Yes/No* Questions and Short Answers with *Be* in the Simple Past

YES/NO QUESTIONS			SHORT ANSWERS				
VERB	SUBJECT		AFFIRMATIVE			NEGATIVE	
Was	I	right?	Yes,	you	were.	No,	you were not. you weren't.
Were	you	right?	Yes,	I	was.	No,	I was not. I wasn't.
Was	he she it	right?	Yes,	he she it	was.	No,	he/she/it was not. he/she/it wasn't.
Were	we you they	right?	Yes,	you we they	were.	No,	you/we/they were not. you/we/they weren't.
Was there any good food at Disneyworld?			Yes,	there was.		No,	there was not. there wasn't.
Were there long lines at Disneyworld?			Yes,	there were.		No,	there were not. there weren't.

EXERCISE 5

Detective Furlock Humes is questioning a police officer about a crime. Fill in the blanks with *there* + *be* in the simple past.

Examples: ___Was there___ a crime last night?

___Yes, there were___ several police officers at the house.

Police Officer: The body was here, Detective Humes.

Furlock: (1) ________________ a weapon?

Police Officer: Yes, (2) ________________ a gun next to the body.

Furlock: (3) ________________ any fingerprints on the gun?

Police Officer: No, sir, (4) ________________.

Furlock: (5) ________________ any motive for this crime?

Police Officer: We don't know, sir.

Furlock: How about witnesses? (6) ________________ any witnesses to the crime?

Police Officer: Yes, sir. (7) ________________ one witness—a neighbor. She said (8) ________________ loud noises in the apartment at midnight.

Furlock: Where is she? Bring her to me . . .

EXERCISE 6

Take turns asking and answering the *yes/no* question about the events below. Give the correct information about the event if it is incorrect.

Example: Margaret Thatcher/the first female Prime Minister of Great Britain.
Was Margaret Thatcher the first female Prime Minister of Great Britain?
Yes, she was.

1. Tom Hanks/the first man to walk on the moon
2. AIDS/a widespread disease in 1949
3. Yugoslavia/a country in 1980
4. Europeans/the first people on the American continent
5. Nelson Mandela/in prison for many years in South Africa
6. The Wright Brothers/the first men to cross the Atlantic Ocean by plane
7. a big earthquake/in Pakistan, in 2005
8. any women/in the Olympic Games in 1920

form meaning

FOCUS 4 *Wh*-Questions with *Be*

WH-QUESTION	*BE*	SUBJECT	ANSWERS
When		JFK's assassination?	November 22, 1963
Where		the assassination?	It was in Dallas, Texas.
Who	was	the assassin?	Lee Harvey Oswald, we think.
What		his motive	There were different theories.
How		the day?	Very sad
Why	were	people sad?	Because Kennedy was a popular president
Whose gun	was	it?	Lee Harvey Oswald's

EXERCISE 7

Fill in the *wh*-question word the correct form of *be* to complete each question.

Andrea: (1) ______________ you on the day of Kennedy's assassination?
Helene: I was in school. There was an announcement over the loud speaker.
Andrea: (2) ______________ you with at the time?
Helene: I was with my friend Patty.
Andrea: (3) ______________ school that day?
Helene: It was terrible. We were all very upset and silent.
Andrea: (4) ______________ you all silent?
Helene: Because it was hard to belive he was dead.
Andrea: And at home? (5) ______________ things at home?
Helene: At home, things were bad. My parents were in shock too.

EXERCISE 8

Look at the photo, and write a *wh*-question for each answer.

1. ____?
   These people were mountain climbers.
2. ____?
   They were in the Himalayas.
3. ____?
   They were there for the adventure and the challenge.
4. ____?
   They were there in 1996.
5. ____?
   The name of the mountain was Mount Everest.
6. ____?
   It was their dream to climb Mt. Everest.
7. ____?
   The trip was a disaster; eight people died on this trip.

EXERCISE 9

Famous Women Information Gap

You look at Chart A below. Your partner looks at Chart B on page A-20. Ask and answer each question about the woman/women. Fill in the information you learn on the chart.

Example: Question 1a: *Who was Anne Frank?*
Answer 1a: *She was a young victim of the Nazis during World War II. . . .*

Chart A

1. Anne Frank 	a. who b. why/a victim c. what . . . famous for	She was a young victim of the Nazis during World War II.
2. Susan B. Anthony & Elizabeth Cady Stanton 		d. two important "suffragists" in the United States e. their fight for voting and equal rights for women f. in the late 1800's and early 1900's
3. Amelia Earhart 	g. who h. what/famous for i. when/her flight	
4. Indira Gandhi 		j. what/famous for k. whose daughter l. what/her father/famous for

EXERCISE 10

Correct the errors in the following sentences.

1. Do was Mahatma Gandhi a religious leader in India?
2. The Beatles wasn't fashion designers.
3. Was hot the weather at Disneyworld last week?
4. Where the earthquake was in 2005?
5. Why the people were on Mount Everest?
6. Was good the service at the restaurant?
7. No was any good restaurants in Disneyworld.
8. How it was the trip to Disneyworld?

EXERCISE 11

What are your earliest childhood memories? Think about some of your favorite things from your childhood. Work in a group of four. Take turns asking questions about your favorite things below.

Example: *When you were a child, what was your favorite food?*
When you were a child, who was your favorite relative?

1. food
2. relative
3. holiday
4. hobby
5. toy/game
6. TV program
7. teacher
8. friend
9. birthday
10. day of the week
11. subject in school

Use Your English

ACTIVITY 1 speaking

Work with a partner. Ask your partner the questions below and your own questions to find out about a place that is special to him or her.

Questions: *What place was special to you? When were you there?*
Why were you there? What was special about this place?
How was the weather? Were the people friendly? How was the food?

ACTIVITY 2 speaking/writing

With the information from Activity 1, write a paragraph about your partner's special place. Then, tell the class something interesting about your partner's special place.

Example: *Last summer, my partner was in Greece. She was there with her friend. Greece was very beautiful and interesting.*

ACTIVITY 3 speaking

Work in a group.

STEP 1 Write each of the dates/times below on a separate piece of paper. Mix all the papers together.

On December 31, 1999	In the 90's	In the summer of 2001
On September 11, 2001	In the 80's	In the fall of 2002
On December 26, 2004	In the 70's	On my birthday in 2005

STEP 2

Pick a piece of paper, and say something about your life at that time and your life now. Take turns with the classmates in your group.

Example: *In the 90's, I was a doctor in the Philippines, but now I am an ESL student in the United States.*

ACTIVITY 4 research on the web

STEP 1

Go to the Internet to find out information about the famous people listed below. Use a search engine such as Google®, Yahoo®, or Ask® and enter each name in the search box. Other useful sites to find this information is www.answers.com or Wikipedia.com. Find out what the person was famous for and where the person was from. Write the information in the chart.

FAMOUS PERSON	FAMOUS FOR	COUNTRY
Che Guevara		
Sigmund Freud		
Jonas Salk		
Louis Armstrong		
Helen Keller		
Charlie Chaplin		
Frank Sinatra		
Marilyn Monroe		
Lucille Ball		
Ho Chi Minh		
Mother Teresa		
Pablo Picasso		
Winston Churchill		
Abbott and Costello		

STEP 2 Write the names of the famous people from the chart above on large index cards. Place the cards face down on the desk. Each student chooses a card and tapes the card to another student's back. Each student asks *yes/no* questions to try to guess who he/she was. Use these clues to help you:

Nationality	*Was I American? Latin American? European? Asian?*
Gender	*Was I a man? A woman?*
Occupation	*Was I an actor/actress? A doctor? A political activist?*

ACTIVITY 5 listening/speaking

CD Track 16

Listen to the story of the Titanic. Write an answer to each question below.

1. Who were the passengers on the Titanic?
2. How many people were there on the ship?
3. How was the weather the night of the accident?
4. What was the cause of the accident?
5. How cold was the water?
6. Why were there many deaths?

ACTIVITY 6 reflection

Compare yourself as a language learner from the time when you started learning English to now. Are you a better language learner now? Write your reflection and then discuss this with a partner.

Example: *I think I'm a better language learner now. Before I was afraid to speak English. Now I'm confident. . . . .*

UNIT

18

PAST TENSE

UNIT GOALS

- Make affirmative and negative statements with regular and irregular simple past tense verbs
- Know how to spell and pronounce regular past tense verbs
- Understand the meaning and position of past time expressions
- Ask and answer *yes/no* and *wh*-questions in the past tense

OPENING TASK

Solve the Mystery: Who Took Ms. Kudo's Flash Drive?

STEP 1

Read the mystery.

For almost everyone at the college, Ms. Kudo was the best ESL teacher. She won many awards for her excellent teaching and materials. She taught her students about language, culture, and history. She discussed film and television in class. She helped the students do Internet research in the computer lab. They wrote every day in her class. They went on trips together. The students enjoyed her classes and really learned. Everyone liked her—except for one student, Leo, and one of the teachers, Mr. Dim.

Leo was not a serious ESL student. He made no effort to learn, so Ms. Kudo refused to have him in her class. The Director put Leo in Mr. Dim's class, but Leo wasn't happy there. Leo blamed Ms. Kudo for his unhappiness. The teacher, Mr. Dim, disliked Ms. Kudo.

He felt jealous of all Ms. Kudo's teaching awards. Mr. Dim felt he was a good teacher, but nobody noticed him.

Ms. Kudo saved all her ideas and teaching materials on her flash drive. She kept her flash drive in her school bag. Everyone knew that. On the first day of the new semester, Ms. Kudo's flash drive disappeared. She looked everywhere, but she didn't find it. Instead, she found a type-written letter.

The letter said:

> Ms. Kudo:
>
> Today, I very sad. I no can stay in English Language Center because no am important in here. Always Ms. Kudo, Ms. Kudo. And me? What I am? What I can do? How I continue to teach here? I also teach good. No is easy for me here. I take your flash drive because I have angry. Please understand my . . .

Ms. Kudo reported the theft to the Director. She gave the Director the letter.

STEP 2

Read the sentences and check *True* or *False*.

	TRUE	FALSE
1. Someone wanted to hurt Ms. Kudo.		
2. Ms. Kudo's students didn't like her.		
3. Leo was happy in Mr. Dim's class.		
4. Ms. Kudo wanted Leo in her class.		
5. Mr. Dim felt jealous of Ms. Kudo.		
6. Leo blamed himself for being unhappy.		
7. The note was well written.		

STEP 3

Who took Ms. Kudo's flash drive? How do you know? Discuss your answers with the class.

form

FOCUS 1 Forming and Spelling Regular Past Tense Verbs

SUBJECT	BASE FORM + *-ED*
I He She It We You They	**started** three years ago.

Regular verbs can change spelling in the simple past tense.

IF THE VERB ENDS IN:	SPELLING RULE
(a) a consonant **want** **need**	Add *ed* **wanted** **needed**
(b) a vowel + *y* **enjoy** **play**	Add *ed* **enjoyed** **played**
(c) a consonant + *e* **like** **smile**	Add *d* **liked** **smiled**

IF THE VERB ENDS IN:	SPELLING RULE
(d) a consonant + *y* **study** **worry**	Change *y* to *i*, add *ed* **studied** **worried**
(e) consonant + vowel + consonant (one syllable verbs) **stop** **drop**	Double the consonant, add *ed* **stopped** **dropped**
(f) *x* or *w* (one syllable verbs) **show** **fix**	Do not double the consonant, add *ed* **showed** **fixed**
(g) two-syllable verbs with the stress on the last syllable **ocCUR** **preFER**	Double the consonant, add *ed* **occurred** **preferred**
(h) two-syllable verbs with the stress on the first syllable **LISten** **VISit**	Do not double the consonant, add *ed* **listened** **visited**

EXERCISE 1

Go back to the Opening Task on pages 286–287, and underline all the **regular** past tense verbs in the mystery story and letter.

Example: *She* ___discussed___ *film and television in class.*

EXERCISE 2

Fill in the blanks with the past tense of the verbs.

1. Ms. Kudo ________________ (enjoy) teaching.
2. Ms. Kudo ________________ (use) film and television in class.
3. She ________________ (help) her students do research on the Internet.
4. The students ________________ (study) new ideas and vocabulary.
5. They ________________ (learn) about culture and history.
6. They ________________ (discuss) many topics in class.
7. The students ________________ (work) on group projects.
8. Many students ________________ (register) for her class every semester.
9. Ms. Kudo ________________ (receive) many awards for her excellent teaching.
10. Almost everyone ________________ (like) Ms. Kudo.
11. One day, a crime ________________ (occur) at the English Language Center.
12. Ms. Kudo's flash drive ________________ (disappear).

form

FOCUS 2 Pronunciation of the *ed* Ending

VERB END	EXAMPLES	
Group I After voiceless sounds,* the final *ed* is pronounced /t/.	/t/ *asked* *kissed* *stopped*	 *washed* *sniffed* *matched*
Group II After voiced sounds,** the final *ed* is pronounced /d/.	/d/ *robbed* *killed* *played* *gazed* *shared*	 *waved* *rained* *begged* *harmed*
Group III After /t/ and /d/, the final *ed* is pronounced /Id/.	/Id/ *pointed* *wanted* *waited*	 *needed* *ended* *added*

*When you make a **voiceless** sound, your vocal chords don't vibrate. (Put your hand on your throat. Say the sound. If you don't feel a vibration, the sound is voiceless.)

** When you make a **voiced** sound, your vocal chords vibrate. (Put your hand on your throat. Say the sound. If you feel a vibration, the sound is voiced.)

EXERCISE 3

STEP 1 **Put each verb in the simple past, and read each sentence aloud. Check the column that shows the pronunciation of each verb.**

Bookworm Benny was an excellent student.	/T/	/D/	/ID/
1. Teachers always ___liked___ (like) Bookworm Benny.			
2. He ___________ (work) hard in school.			
3. He always ___________ (finish) his work first.			
4. The teacher always ___________ (call) on him.			
5. He always ___________ (answer) questions correctly.			
6. He ___________ (remember) all his lessons.			
7. He never ___________ (talk) out of turn.			
8. The other students ___________ (hate) Benny.			
9. One day, they ___________ (decide) to get him into trouble.			
10. They ___________ (roll) a piece of paper into a ball.			
11. They ___________ (wait) for the teacher to turn his back.			
12. They threw the paper ball at the teacher. It ___________ (land) on the teacher's head.			
13. The teacher was really angry. He ___________ (yell) at the class.			
14. "Who did that?" he ___________ (ask).			
15. All the students ___________ (point) to Benny.			
16. But the teacher ___________ (trust) Benny.			
17. The teacher ___________ (punish) the other students.			

STEP 2 **The pictures about Bookworm Benny on the next page are not in the correct order. Number the pictures in the correct order. Then retell Bookworm Benny's story using only the pictures.**

a. Number ________

b. Number ________

c. Number ________

d. Number ________

e. Number ________

EXERCISE 4

This exercise contains the solution to the Opening Task mystery. Fill in the blanks with the past tense of the verbs shown in the box below.

look	remember	call	type	learn
realize	confess	want	discuss	lock
notice	remove	complain		

When the Director of the English Language Center (1) ____learned____ about Ms. Kudo's flash drive, she was surprised. She (2) ________________ to understand this crime.

To solve the mystery, the Director (3) ________________ herself in her office to think. She (4) ________________ that Mr. Dim was jealous of Ms. Kudo. She also (5) ________________ a conversation with Leo about moving to Mr. Dim's class. Leo (6) ________________ about Mr. Dim's class. Then, the Director (7) ________________ at the note again. She (8) ________________ all the grammar mistakes! The Director (9) ________________ Leo to her office.

She (10) ________________ the problem with him. Finally, Leo (11) ________________ to the crime. Leo said, "I (12) ________________ the note. I (13) ________________ the flash drive from her bag."

(See Exercise 5 on page 297 for a possible ending)

form

FOCUS 3 Irregular Past-Tense Verbs: Affirmative Statements

Many verbs in the past tense are irregular. They do not have the *ed* form.

SUBJECT	VERB	
I He She It We You They	went	to Miami last year.

You can learn irregular past tense forms in groups.

BASE FORM	SIMPLE PAST
/I/ sound	**/æ/ sound**
begin	began
drink	drank
ring	rang
sing	sang
sink	sank
swim	swam

BASE FORM	SIMPLE PAST
	ought/aught
buy	bought
bring	brought
catch	caught
fight	fought
teach	taught
think	thought

BASE FORM	SIMPLE PAST
	Base form and past-tense forms are the same.
cost	cost
cut	cut
hit	hit
hurt	hurt
put	put
quit	quit
shut	shut
let	let
-ow	-ew
blow	blew
grow	grew
know	knew
throw	threw
/iy/ sound	/ɛ/ sound
feed	fed
feel	felt
keep	kept
lead	led
leave	left
meet	met
read	read
sleep	slept
-d	-t
lend	lent
send	sent
spend	spent
bend	bent
build	built

BASE FORM	SIMPLE PAST
	Change of vowel
become	became
come	came
dig	dug
draw	drew
fall	fell
forget	forgot
forgive	forgave
get	got
give	gave
hold	held
hang	hung
run	ran
sit	sat
win	won
	/o/ sound
break	broke
choose	chose
sell	sold
tell	told
speak	spoke
steal	stole
drive	drove
ride	rode
wake	woke
write	wrote

BASE FORM	SIMPLE PAST
	Other These verbs have unique changes in the past form.
be	was
bite	bit
do	did
eat	ate
find	found
fly	flew
go	went
have	had
hear	heard
hide	hid
lose	lost
make	made
pay	paid
say	said
see	saw
shake	shook
shoot	shot
stand	stood
take	took
tear	tore
understand	understood
wear	wore

(See Appendix 8 on page A-8 for an alphabetical list of common irregular past tense verbs.)

EXERCISE 5

Here is one possible ending to the mystery story. Fill in the correct simple past tense verb forms.

In the end, the Director (1) ________________ (give) Leo a second chance. True, Leo (2) ________________ (hurt) everyone, but the Director (3) ________________ (feel) Leo was able to change. Ms. Kudo (4) ________________ (forgive) Leo. She (5) ________________ (take) Leo into her class. She (6) ________________ (spend) many afternoons in school with Leo. Leo (7) ________________ (become) more serious. His English (8) ________________ (get) better.

The Director also (9) ________________ (speak) to Mr. Dim about his teaching. She (10) ________________ (tell) Mr. Dim to visit Ms. Kudo's class. Mr.Dim (11) ________________ (sit) in Ms. Kudo's class many times. As a result, Mr. Dim (12) ________________ (begin) to teach differently.

EXERCISE 6

Liisa and Katja are from Finland. They had a **dream vacation** in New York last fall. Fill in the blanks with the simple past tense of the verbs in parentheses.

1. Liisa and Katja ____flew____ (fly) to New York on Sunday, November 4.
2. They ________________ (find) many interesting things to do in the city.
3. They ________________ (eat) great food every day.
4. They ________________ (go) to the Statue of Liberty.
5. They ________________ (take) a ferry to the Immigration Museum at Ellis Island.
6. They ________________ (stand) in the middle of Times Square.
7. They ________________ (spend) an evening at a jazz club.
8. Liisa ________________ (buy) gifts for her friends in Finland.
9. They ________________ (see) an exhibit at the Museum of Modern Art.
10. They ________________ (meet) a nice woman at the museum.
11. They ________________ (speak) English with her all afternoon.
12. They ________________ (think) New York was a beautiful, friendly city.

EXERCISE 7

Monique and Daniel are from France. Their vacation in New York was a **nightmare**. Fill in the blanks with the simple past tense of the verbs in parentheses.

1. On Sunday, November 4, Monique and Daniel's flight to New York was late, so they ______sat______ (sit) in the airport in Paris for four hours.
2. The airline company ________________ (lose) all their luggage, so on Monday they ________________ (go) shopping for new clothes.
3. On Tuesday, they ________________ (get) stuck in the subway when their train ________________ (break) down.
4. On Wednesday, they ________________ (pay) ninety dollars to rent a car, and ________________ (drive) to the Aquarium.
5. They ________________ (leave) the car on the street and ________________ (get) a $115.00 parking ticket!
6. Monique ________________ (lose) her digital camera in the Aquarium.
7. On Thursday, they ________________ (buy) a new camera downtown.
8. On Friday, they ________________ (go) ice skating at Rockefeller Center. Monique had the new camera around her neck.
9. Monique ________________ (fall) on the ice ________________ (hurt) her knee.
10. She ________________ (break) her new camera.
11. Monique was wet and frozen, so she ________________ (catch) a cold.
12. On Saturday, there ________________ (be) a snowstorm; the city ________________ (be) silent and still. There ________________ (be) no transportation.
13. All the theaters ________________ (shut) their doors, so Monique and Daniel missed their night at a Broadway show.
14. On Sunday, they ________________ (take) a taxi to the airport and finally ________________ (leave) for home.

FOCUS 4 Time Expressions in the Past

Time expressions tell us when the action occurred in the past.

TIME EXPRESSION	EXAMPLES	EXPLANATIONS
in 1998 on Sunday at 6:00 the day before yesterday	(a) **On Sunday,** they flew to New York.	Time expressions can come at the beginning or at the end of a sentence.
an hour **ago** two days **ago** six months **ago** a year **ago**	(b) Liisa and Kate went to Spain **two years ago.**	
yesterday morning **yesterday** afternoon **yesterday** evening	(c) **Yesterday morning,** a flash drive disappeared from the Center.	Use a comma after the time expression if it is at the beginning of the sentence.
last night **last** week **last** month **last** year **last** summer	(d) We took two summer school classes last summer.	Do not use a comma before a time expression at the end of a sentence.

EXERCISE 8

On Tuesday, November 13th, Monique and Daniel talked to their friend Colette about their trip. Complete the sentences with time expressions.

Colette: Hi, guys! When did you get back?

Monique: We got home (1) ________________ 8:00 yesterday morning.

Colette: So, how was your trip?

Daniel: Well, let's say that (2) ________________ week was a week to remember! Our plane arrived in New York four hours late (3) ________________ Sunday. Today's Tuesday, right? Well, exactly a week (4) ________________, we got stuck in the New York City subway for two hours! Then, (5) ________________ Wednesday, we got a parking ticket for $115.00. What else? Oh, (6) ________________ Thursday, we bought a new digital camera and Monique accidentally broke it. The day we left there was a big snowstorm.

Monique: As you can see, (7) ________________ week was difficult! We were happy to come home (8) ________________ Sunday. Our trip to New York four years (9) ________________ was much better!

EXERCISE 9

Make true statements about yourself. Use each of the time expressions below.

Example: Six months ago, ______I took a trip to Mexico______.

1. Two months ago, ________________________.
2. In 2001, ________________________.
3. Last year, ________________________.
4. Last summer, ________________________.
5. Two days ago, ________________________.
6. On Sunday, ________________________.
7. The day before yesterday, ________________________.
8. Yesterday morning, ________________________.
9. At six o'clock this morning, ________________________.
10. An hour ago, ________________________.

form

FOCUS 5 Past Tense: Negative Statements

SUBJECT	*DID + NOT/DIDN'T*	BASE FORM OF VERB
I He She It We You They	did not didn't	work.

EXERCISE 10

Make affirmative or negative statements aloud about the people in this unit.

Example: the teacher/like Benny
The teacher liked Benny
the teacher/get angry at Benny.
The teacher didn't get angry at Benny

1. The other students/like Bookworm Benny
2. The teacher/trust Benny
3. The students/try to get Benny into trouble
4. The students' plan for Benny/succeed
5. Liisa and Katja/lose their luggage
6. Liisa's digital camera/break
7. Liisa and Katja/get stuck on the subway
8. Liisa and Katja/enjoy their vacation in New York
9. Leo/notice the grammar mistakes in his note
10. Mr. Dim/ feel jealous of Ms. Kudo
11. Leo/steal Ms. Kudo's flash drive
12. The Director/punish Leo
13. Monique and Daniel/spend an evening at a jazz club
14. Monique and Daniel/visit the Statue of Liberty
15. Monique and Daniel/enjoy their vacation in New York

form

FOCUS 6 Past Tense: *Yes/No* Questions and Short Answers

Yes/No Questions

DID	SUBJECT	BASE FORM OF THE VERB	
Did	I he she we you they	visit	New York last year?

Short Answers

AFFIRMATIVE			NEGATIVE		
Yes,	I he she we you they	did.	No,	I he she we you they	did not. didn't.

EXERCISE 11

Ask a partner *yes/no* questions about Ms. Kudo's story.

Example: understand the mystery
You: *Did you understand the mystery?*
Your partner: *Yes, I did.*

1. like the mystery story
2. enjoy being a detective
3. think Mr. Dim was the thief
4. guess that Leo was the thief
5. find the grammar mistakes in Leo's note
6. correct the mistakes in the note
7. agree with the Director's decision
8. want the Director to punish Leo?

EXERCISE 12

Look at the cartoons about Jinxed Jerry, a man with very bad luck. He went on a two-week Caribbean cruise last winter and there was a hurricane at sea.

STEP 1 **Ask a partner *yes/no* questions with the words below. The pictures can help you answer the questions.**

Example: Jerry/go on a cruise last winter
You: *Did Jerry go on a cruise last winter?*
Your partner: *Yes, he did.*

1. Jerry's ship/get to the Caribbean
2. Jerry/know how to swim
3. Jerry/die
4. he/find an island
5. he/meet anyone on the island
6. the island/have stores
7. he/have enough food
8. he/write postcards home
9. he/make tools
10. he/build a good boat

STEP 2 **Remember, Jerry has very bad luck. Ask each other *yes/no* questions and guess the end of the story.**

11. Jerry's luck/change
12. a helicopter/find Jerry
13. Jerry/find his way back home
14. the story/have a happy ending
15. Jerry/ever take another cruise again

See the Appendix for the conclusion to Exercise 12 (page A-22).

form

FOCUS 7 Past Tense: *Wh*-Questions

WH-WORD	*DID*	SUBJECT	BASE FORM OF VERB	ANSWERS
What		I	do last summer?	You went to Paris.
When		you	make plans?	(I made plans) last month.
Where		he	go last summer?	(He went) to Scotland.
Why		the ship	sink?	(It sank) because there was a storm.
How	did	she	get to Paris?	(She got there) by plane.
How long		they	stay in New York?	(They stayed there for) two weeks.
How long ago		you	visit Alaska?	(I visited Alaska) ten years ago.
Who(m)		Liisa and Katja	meet in New York?	(They met) a friendly woman.

WH-WORD AS SUBJECT	PAST TENSE VERB	ANSWERS
What	happened to Jerry's ship?	It sank.
Who	had a terrible vacation?	Monique and Daniel (did).

EXERCISE 13

Write *wh*-questions about Jerry. Then ask your partner the questions. Your partner gives an answer or says "I don't know."

Example: Jerry/eat on the island?
Q: *What did Jerry eat on the island?*
A: *(He ate) fruit from the trees and fish from the sea.*

1. Jerry/want to go on vacation
   Q: Where ______________________________?
   A: ______________________________

2. Jerry/go on vacation
   Q: When ______________________________?
   A: ______________________________

3. Jerry/leave home

Q: How long ago ____?

A: ____

4. Jerry's ship/sink

Q: Why ____?

A: ____

5. Jerry/do after the ship sank

Q: What ____?

A: ____

6. Jerry/meet on the island

Q: Who(m) ____?

A: ____

7. Jerry/build the boat

Q: How ____?

A: ____

8. Jerry/put on the boat

Q: What ____?

A: ____

9. Jerry/feel when he finished the boat

Q: How ____?

A: ____

10. the story end (in your opinion)

Q: How ____?

A: ____

EXERCISE 14

STEP 1 **Make questions that ask for the underlined information. Use *who*, *whom*, *why*, *how* or *what*.**

Example: Q: *Who won awards for teaching?* A: *Ms. Kudo won awards.*

1. Q: ____?
   A: The Director solved the mystery by reading the note carefully.
2. Q: ____?
   A: Leo lied. Mr. Dim didn't lie.
3. Q: ____?
   A: Leo stole Ms. Kudo's flash drive.
4. Q: ____?
   A: Leo hurt everyone: Ms. Kudo, Mr. Dim, the Director, and himself.
5. Q: ____?
   A: The Director made the decision about Leo.
6. Q: ____?
   A: The Director gave Leo a second chance because she believed Leo was able to change.
7. Q: ____?
   A: The moral of the story was "crime doesn't pay."

STEP 2 **What did you think of the Director's decision? Check (a) or (b), and give reasons for your answers in writing. Discuss with the class.**

______ a. I liked the Director's decision. ______ b. I disagreed with the Director's decision.

EXERCISE 15

Correct the errors in the following sentences.

1. This morning, I waked up early.
2. I saw him yesterday night.
3. Leo didn't felt happy.
4. They don't met the Mayor of New York last week.
5. What Leo wanted?
6. Leo didn't noticed his mistakes.
7. Who did signed the note?

8. What did the Director?
9. What did happened to Leo?
10. Where Liisa and Katja went on vacation?
11. Who did go with Liisa to New York?
12. How Jerry built a boat?
13. They no had dinner in a Greek restaurant.
14. Whom did trust the teacher in the Bookworm Benny story?
15. Doina escaped from Romania before a long time.

EXERCISE 16

Information Gap. This is a true story about a very special woman named Doina. Work with a partner. You look at Text A below. Your partner looks at Text B on page A-21. Take turns asking questions to get the information in the blanks.

Example: Your partner: *(Look at Text B)* *1. Where did Doina grow up?*
You: *(Look at Text A)* *1. She grew up in Romania.*

TEXT A:

1. Doina grew up in Romania.
2. She married ________________ (who/m).
3. She had a daughter.
4. Doina was unhappy because she was against the government in Romania.
5. She thought of ________________ (what) every day.
6. She taught her daughter how to swim.
7. On October 9, 1988, she and her daughter swam across the Danube River. They swam to ________________ (where).
8. The police caught them.
9. Doina and her daughter went ________________ (where).
10. They tried to escape several months later.
11. Finally, they left Romania ________________ (how).
12. They flew to New York in 1989.
13. Doina went to school ________________ (why).
14. She wrote the story of her escape from Romania in her ESL class.

Use Your English

ACTIVITY 1 speaking

STEP 1 Work in groups. One person in the group thinks of a famous person from the past.

STEP 2 The others in the group can ask up to twenty *yes/no* questions to guess who the person is. After twenty questions, the group loses if they haven't guessed.

Example: *Did this person sing?*
Did this person live in North America?
Was this person a woman?

ACTIVITY 2 speaking

STEP 1 **Who is telling the truth?** Work in groups of three. Each student tells a **true personal story.** The group chooses one of the stories. Then the other two students learn as much as they can about that story.

STEP 2 The first group sits in front of the room. Each of the three students tells the same beginning of the story to the class. The rest of the class asks the three students questions to find out who is telling the truth.

Example: **Student 1, 2 and 3 each says:** *When I was ten years old, I went on a long trip.*
The class asks each person a question: *Student 1, where did you go? Student 2, who(m) did you go with? Student 3, why did you go there?*

STEP 3 The class takes a vote on who(m) they think is telling the truth. Finally, the student with the true story stands up.

ACTIVITY 3 writing/speaking

Write your own ending for the story about Jinxed Jerry. Compare your ending with your classmates'. Who has the best ending? When you are finished, look at the cartoons that tell the end of Jerry's story on page A-22. Discuss how your ending compares with the ending in the cartoon.

ACTIVITY 4 speaking

Interview a partner about a past vacation. Ask as many *wh*-questions as you can. Report back to the class about your partner's trip.

Example: *Where did you go?*
When did you go?
How did you get there?
What did you do there?
How long did you stay?
With whom did you go?
Why did you go there?

ACTIVITY 5 listening/speaking

CD Track 17

STEP 1 Listen to another possible ending of the Opening Task mystery story.

STEP 2 How is this ending different from the ending in Exercise 5 (page 297)? In which ending did the Director make the best decision? Why?

ACTIVITY 6 speaking

Jeopardy Game. Your teacher will choose one student to be the host. Only the host can look at the complete game board (page A-21). The rest of the class will be divided into two teams. Team 1 chooses a category and an amount of money from the blank game board below. The host reads the answer. Team 1 has one minute to ask a correct question. If Team 1 can't, Team 2 gets a chance to ask a question. There may be more than one correct question for each answer. Your teacher decides on the "correctness" of the question and answer. The team with the most money wins.

Example: Team 1 chooses: *"People" for ten dollars.*
Host reads: *Ms. Kudo*
Team 1 asks: *Who forgave Leo?*

Game Board

$$$	CATEGORY 1 PEOPLE	CATEGORY 2 *WH*-QUESTIONS	CATEGORY 3 *YES/NO* QUESTIONS
$10			
$20			
$30			
$40			
$50			

ACTIVITY 7 writing/speaking

The stories in this unit are about unlucky things that happen to people and how people escape from difficult situations. Think about a time when something unlucky happened to you or when you escaped from a difficult situation. Write your story, and then tell the class what happened. Your classmates can ask you questions.

ACTIVITY 8 research on the web

Sir Ernest Shackleton was a famous explorer. In 1914, Shackleton left London with his crew to explore Antarctica on his ship *Endurance.* He and his ship disappeared a few months later. They finally returned to London two years later. What happened?

STEP 1 Write a list of *wh*-questions about Shackleton and *Endurance.*

STEP 2 Search the Internet for answers to your *wh*-questions. Use an online information source such as Ask.com or Wikipedia.com. Enter keyword groups like these: *Shackleton; Shackleton* and *biography; Shackleton* and *time line.* Share your answers with the class.

ACTIVITY 9 reflection

Think of the ESL/EFL classrooms in your own experience. What kind of classroom language learning activities did you do/not do in your country? What kind of activities did the students in Ms. Kudo's class do? What classroom activities did you do/not do in this country? Which activities did you find most useful? Discuss this as a class.

UNIT 19

REFLEXIVE PRONOUNS, RECIPROCAL PRONOUN: *EACH OTHER*

UNIT GOALS

- Use reflexive pronouns correctly
- Know which verbs are commonly used with reflexive pronouns
- Know how to use *each other*

OPENING TASK

Advice Columns

STEP 1

Read the letters to "Dear Darcy" in Part A. Match each one to a "Letter of Advice" in Part B. Fill in the name of the person who wrote each letter in the blanks in Part B.

PART A: Letters to Dear Darcy

Dear Darcy,

My wife and I never go out anymore. We have a new baby, and my wife doesn't want to get a babysitter. I need a social life. I'm starting to talk to myself! Can you help me?
—Bored in Boston

Dear Darcy,

I'm married and have two children. I'm trying to be a superwoman. I work outside the home. I also do all of the housework, the shopping, and the cleaning. I help my children with their schoolwork. I never have time for myself. I am tired and unhappy. Please help!
—Supermom in Seattle

Dear Darcy,

My mom and dad got divorced last month. They fought with each other a lot, and finally, my dad moved out. Maybe I wasn't a good daughter to them. Maybe the breakup was my fault. I can't forgive myself.
—Guilty in Gainesville

PART B: Letters of Advice

a. Dear ______________,
Don't blame yourself. You did not cause these problems. Your parents need to learn to talk to each other.

b. Dear ______________,
You need to explain how you feel to her. Tell her you want to go out once a week. Life is short. Find a babysitter. Go out and enjoy yourselves!

c. Dear______________,
You need to make time for yourself. Go out with your friends. Do yourself a favor and join a gym. Take care of yourself, too. Buy yourself something special.

STEP 2

Read the letter from *Lonely in Los Angeles.* Then read Darcy's response and circle the correct pronouns.

Dear Darcy,

I'm a rather shy and lonely international student in high school. I'm doing well in school, but I don't have many friends. The students in my classes always talk to each other, but they never include me. I don't go out. I don't enjoy myself. I don't even like myself very much anymore.

—Lonely in Los Angeles

Dear Lonely in Los Angeles,

Remember, the teenage years are difficult. At 16, many teenagers don't like (1) (they/them/themselves). You're doing well in school. Be proud of (2) (you/yourself). Try to like (3) (you/yourself) first. Then others will like (4) (you/yourself). Teenagers need (5) (each other/themselves). Force (6) (you/yourself) to open up to others. Relax and try to enjoy (7) (you/yourself).

—Darcy

form

FOCUS 1 Reflexive Pronouns

Use a reflexive pronoun when the subject and object are the same.

Example: Sara bought **herself** a new car.
NOT: Sara bought Sara a new car.

EXAMPLES	REFLEXIVE PRONOUNS
(a) I bought **myself** a new car.	*myself*
(b) Look at **yourself** in the mirror.	*yourself*
(c) He doesn't take care of **himself.**	*himself*
(d) She blames **herself** for the accident.	*herself*
(e) A cat licks **itself** to keep clean.	*itself*
(f) We enjoyed **ourselves** at the theater.	*ourselves*
(g) Help **yourselves** to some food.	*yourselves*
(h) Babies can't feed **themselves.**	*themselves*

EXERCISE 1

Go back to Step 1 in the Opening Task on page 312. Underline all the reflexive pronouns and circle the subjects.

Example: (I) never have time for myself.

EXERCISE 2

Fill in each blank with a reflexive pronoun.

Example: I lost my wallet yesterday, and I just wanted to kick ____myself____.

1. **Mary:** Do you sometimes talk to (a) ______________?
   Bill: Well, yes. I talk to (b) ______________ pretty often. I always give (c) ______________ advice!
2. **Monica:** Thanks for such a lovely evening. We really enjoyed (a) ______________.
   Gloria: Well, thanks for coming. And the children were just wonderful. They really behaved (b) ______________ all evening. I hope you can come back soon.
3. **Jane:** I can't believe my bird flew out the window! It's my fault. I forgot to close the birdcage.
   Margaret: Don't blame ______________. He's probably happier now. He's free!

4. **Cynthia:** What's the matter with Bobby's leg?

   Enrique: He hurt ____________________ at the soccer game last night.

5. **Jason:** My girlfriend Judy really knows how to take care of ____________________. She eats well, exercises regularly, and gets plenty of sleep.

6. **Sylvia:** Hello Carol, hello Eugene. Come on in. Make (a) ____________________ at home. Help (b) ____________________ to some drinks.

7. **Mother:** Be careful! That pot on the stove is very hot. Don't burn ____________________.

8. **Cristina:** I know this chocolate is fattening, but it looks so delicious. I can't help ____________________!

   Billy: Oh, go ahead. One piece is okay!

FOCUS 2 Verbs Commonly Used with Reflexive Pronouns/*By* + Reflexive Pronoun

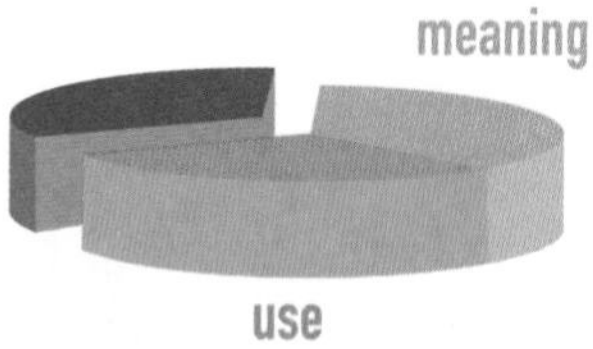

EXAMPLES	EXPLANATIONS
(a) I fell and **hurt myself.** (b) He **taught himself** to play the guitar. (c) Be careful! Don't **cut yourself** with that knife. (d) Did you **enjoy yourself** at the party?	These verbs are commonly used with reflexive pronouns: *hurt* — *cut* *tell* — *burn* *blame* — *enjoy* *teach* — *introduce* *behave* — *take care of*
(e) He got up, washed, and shaved.	The verbs *wash, dress,* and *shave* do not usually take reflexive pronouns. In sentence (e), it is clear he washed and shaved *himself* and not another person.
(f) He's only 2, but he wants to get dressed **by himself.** (g) I sometimes go to the movies **by myself**.	Use *by* + a reflexive pronoun to show that someone is doing something alone (without help or company).

EXERCISE 3

Write a sentence describing the action in each picture. Use the verbs in the box.

Examples: *The woman is introducing herself to the man.*
The woman introduced herself to the man.

1. 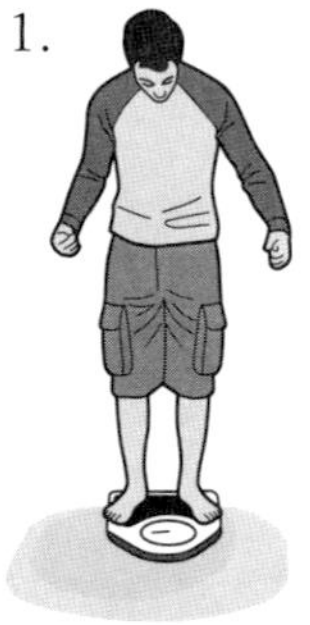

2. 

3. 

4. 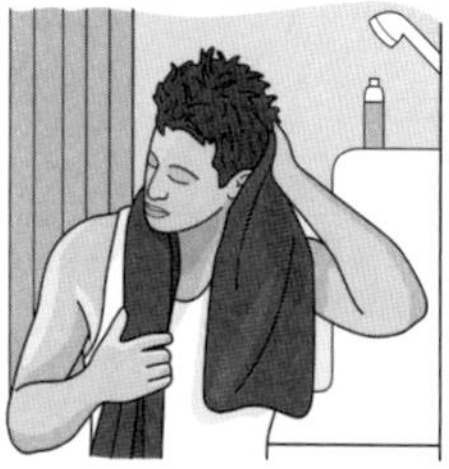

5. 

6. 

7. 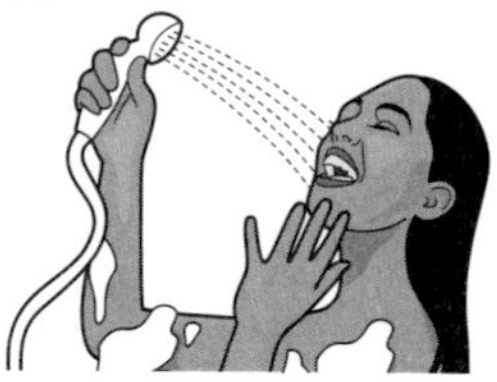

8. 

cut	dry	enjoy	look at/admire
clean/lick	hurt	sing to	weigh

1. ______________________________
2. ______________________________
3. ______________________________
4. ______________________________
5. ______________________________
6. ______________________________
7. ______________________________
8. ______________________________

meaning

FOCUS 3 Reciprocal Pronoun: *Each Other*

The reciprocal pronoun *each other* is different in meaning from a reflexive pronoun.

a. John and Ann blamed **themselves** for the accident.

b. John and Ann blamed **each other** for the accident.

EXERCISE 4

Match the sentence to the picture it describes. Write the letter of the picture next to the sentence.

1. The weather was very hot. The runners poured water on each other after the race.

   The runners poured water on themselves after the race.

2. They love themselves.

   They love each other.

3. The women are fanning themselves because it's so hot.

   The women are fanning each other because it's so hot.

a.

b.

c.

d.

e.

f.

EXERCISE 5

Work with a partner. Act out the following sentences to show the difference between *each other* and reflexive pronouns. Each pair will take turns performing the action in front of the class. The class decides if the action is (a) or (b).

1. a. You and your classmate are looking at yourselves in the mirror.
   b. You and your classmate are looking at each other.
2. a. You and your classmate are talking to yourselves.
   b. You and your classmate are talking to each other.
3. a. You're playing ball with a friend, and you break a neighbor's window. Blame yourself for the accident.
   b. You're playing ball with a friend, and you break a neighbor's window. Blame each other for the accident.
4. a. Introduce yourself to your partner.
   b. You and your partner introduce each other to another person.
5. a. You and your partner are admiring each other.
   b. You and your partner are admiring yourselves.

EXERCISE 6

Choose a reflexive pronoun or *each other* to complete the statements.

1. An egotistical person only thinks about ____himself/herself____.
2. Divorced people can be friends if they forgive ________.
3. Good friends protect ________.
4. Close friends tell ________ their secrets.
5. A self-confident person believes in ________.
6. In a good relationship, the two people trust ________.
7. A realistic woman doesn't lie to ________.
8. Independent people take care of ________.
9. Caring people help ________.
10. Angry people say things to hurt ________.
11. Young children can't always control ________.
12. An insecure boy doesn't have confidence in ________.

EXERCISE 7

Circle the correct pronoun in the "Dear Darcy" letters below.

Example: He / Him / Himself doesn't care about I / me / myself.

Dear Darcy,

(1) I / My / Mine boyfriend loves himself. (2) He / His / Him is very pleased with (3) he / him / himself. He always looks at (4) he / him / himself in store windows when he passes by. (5) Himself / He / Him only thinks about (6) his / himself / him. He never brings (7) my / me / myself flowers. The last time he told (8) my / me / myself that he loved me was two years ago. He's also very selfish with (9) he / his / him things. For example, he never lends me (10) him / himself / his car. He says that the car is (11) himself / him / his, and he doesn't want me to use it. Do (12) yourself / your / you have any advice for me?

—Unhappy

Dear Unhappy,

(13) You / Your / Yourself boyfriend certainly is very selfish. (14) You / Your / Yourself can't really change (15) he / himself / him. Get rid of (16) he / himself / him! Do (17) you / yourself / yours a favor. Find (18) you / yourself / yours a new guy!

—Darcy

EXERCISE 8

Correct the errors in the following sentences.

1. I hurt me.
2. They decided to work out the problem theirselves.
3. I shave myself every morning.
4. I have a friend in Poland. We write to ourselves every month.
5. We enjoyed at the circus.
6. After the argument, Alex didn't talk to Sam. Sam didn't talk to Harry. They didn't talk to themselves for a whole year.
7. He did it hisself.
8. Each other said hello.

Use Your English

ACTIVITY 1 writing/speaking

Who is the most independent person in your class?

STEP 1 Work in groups of three. Make up a survey with ten questions to ask your classmates.

Examples: *Do you like to do things by yourself? Do you ever travel by yourself? Do you ever go to the movies by yourself?*

STEP 2 Each student goes to everyone in class and asks the survey questions. Take notes on the responses.

STEP 3 Go back to your group and share the responses. Decide who is the most independent person in class. Compare your results with the results of the other people.

ACTIVITY 2 listening/speaking

CD Track 18

STEP 1 Listen to the Dear Darcy Radio Talk Show callers talk about their problems. Match each problem to the caller.

Caller 1 ______	a. Frantic about Finances
Caller 2 ______	b. Ms. No Confidence
Caller 3 ______	c. Lonely Without Love

STEP 2 Imagine you are the radio talk show host. What advice can you give to each of these people? Tell your classmates.

ACTIVITY 3 writing

STEP 1 Write a letter to Dear Darcy about a problem you have. Choose a problem you are comfortable sharing with your partner.

STEP 2 Work with a partner. Exchange your letters and write a response to the problem.

ACTIVITY 4 speaking

STEP 1 Talk about a good relationship you have with another person—friend or family. Describe what you do for each other, how you support each other, how you help each other, and how you feel about each other.

STEP 2 Talk about two nations or two groups within a nation and describe a political, economic, or social problem such as what they did to each other, how they hurt each other, and if they worked out a solution to their problems.

ACTIVITY 5 research on the web

Search the Internet for *advice* on *student English language learning*. Enter those keywords into a search engine such as Google®, Yahoo®, or Ask®. Choose one page of advice, print it out, and bring it to class. Make a list of good advice on English language learning. Do you and your classmates agree or disagree with the advice?

ACTIVITY 6 reflection

How do you see yourself as a language learner? Write a paragraph using the topic sentence: *"I see myself as a successful/unsuccessful language learner."* Use your sentence responses to the questions to support your topic sentence.

YOUR EMOTIONS	YOUR LEARNING STRATEGIES
1. Do you feel confident in yourself as a language learner?	7. Do you set goals for yourself?
2. Do you ever compare yourself to other students in the class?	8. Do you repeat new words to yourself?
3. Do you tell yourself you can do it?	9. Do you ask yourself questions about a reading or listening text?
4. Are you proud of yourself? Disappointed in yourself?	10. Do you correct yourself?
5. Do you push yourself to learn more?	11. Do you try to solve language problems by yourself?
6. Do you get angry at yourself about errors?	12. Do you listen to yourself on tape?

UNIT

20 FUTURE TIME

Will and *Be Going To, May* and *Might*

UNIT GOALS

- Talk about future time using *will, be going to, may*, and *might*
- Understand the meaning and position of future time expressions
- Choose between *will* and *be going to* when
  - talking about future intentions or plans
  - making predictions

OPENING TASK

Are You an Optimist or a Pessimist?

Do you see this glass as half full or half empty?

If you see it as half full, you are a positive person, or an optimist.

If you see it as half empty, you are a negative person, or a pessimist.

STEP 1

Work with a partner. Write statements about the future using the information below. Your statements can be affirmative or negative.

Within the next twenty-five years, . . .

1. Wars / end
____
2. People everywhere / have enough food to eat
____
3. Governments / take care of their people's needs
____
4. People in all countries / have a good life
____
5. Men and women around the world / be equal
____
6. People / take care of the earth
____
7. All the world's children / learn to read and write
____
8. People / live on the moon
____
9. Scientists / find a cure for AIDS
____
10. The world / speak one universal language
____

STEP 2

Look at your answers. Are you an optimist or a pessimist? (Note: more than five negative responses indicate that you are a pessimist!) Share your answers with the class.

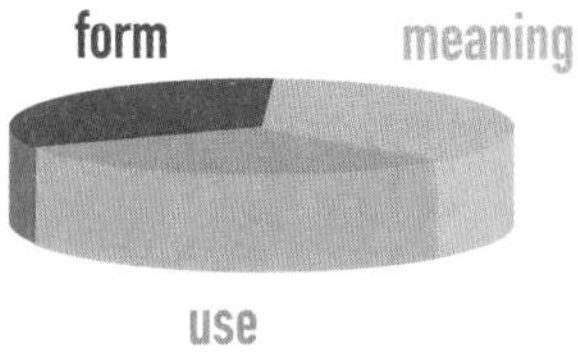

FOCUS 1 Talking About Future Time

Use *will* and *be going to* to make predictions about the future or to say what you think will happen in the future.

EXAMPLES	EXPLANATIONS
(a) One day, he **will** be rich.	Use *will* for a prediction (what we think will happen).
(b) Look at those big black clouds. It **is going to** rain. (c) NOT: It will rain.	Use *be going to* for a prediction based on the present situation (what we can see is going to happen).
(d) Teacher to student: Your parents **will** be very upset about this.	*Will* is more formal.
(e) Father to daughter: Your mother's **going to** be very angry about this.	*Be going to* is less formal.

EXERCISE 1

Match the sentences on the next page to these pictures.

a. 

b. 

c. 

d. 

e. 

f. 

g. 

1. _____ Look at that waiter! He's going to fall!
2. _____ This marriage isn't going to last.
3. _____ You will find gold on the streets of America!
4. _____ She's going to get a headache.
5. _____ I will always love you.
6. _____ You will grow up and be famous.
7. _____ Be careful, Julian. You're going to fall!

FOCUS 2 *Will*

AFFIRMATIVE STATEMENTS		NEGATIVE STATEMENTS	
I He She It We You They	**will arrive** next week. **'ll arrive** next week.	I He She It We You They	**will not arrive** next week. **won't arrive** next week.
There	**will be** peace in the world. **'ll be** peace in the world.	There	**will not be** any wars. **won't be** any wars.
Men	**will be able to** stay home with their children. **'ll be able to** stay home with their children.	Men	**will not be able to** have children. **won't be able to** have children.

YES/NO QUESTIONS			SHORT ANSWERS					
			Affirmative			Negative		
Will	I you he she it we you they	arrive next week?	Yes,	you I he she it you we they	will.	No,	you I he she it you we they	won't.

***WH*-QUESTIONS**	**ANSWERS**
(a) **Who will** get an Olympic medal?	The snowboarder.
(b) **What will** the homeless woman do with the money?	She'll **change her life**.
(c) **When will** scientists discover a cure for AIDS?	(They **will discover** a cure)* within six years.
(d) **Where will** the couple retire?	(They **will retire**) to Hawaii.
(e) **How will** the couple travel to Hawaii?	(They'll **travel**) by plane.
(f) **How** long **will** they be on the plane?	(They'll **be** on the plane) for five hours.
(g) **Why** will this doctor be successful?	because she cares about her patients.
(h) **Who(m) will** the doctor save?	(She'll **save**) many patients.

* Note: The parentheses (...) show the part of the answer that is often not said in spoken English.

EXERCISE 2

How will our lives be different in fifty years? Make predictions with *will* or *won't*. Discuss your predictions with a partner.

1. Cities ________________ be very crowded.
2. Many people ________________ eat only fruits and vegetables.
3. All countries ________________ share the world's money equally.
4. Most people ________________ move back to the countryside.
5. Cell phones ________________ be the size of our thumb.
6. Most people ________________ go to college.
7. All people of different races ________________ live together peacefully.
8. Robots ________________ take over some human jobs.
9. Crime ________________ go down.
10. People ________________ drive electric cars.
11. Students ________________ take classes from home by satellite.
12. Science ________________ continue to be very important.
13. Most people ________________ work sixty hours a week.
14. A woman ________________ be president of the United States.

EXERCISE 3

Think about the year 2025. Write *yes/no* questions with *will.* Interview two classmates and report their answers to the class.

	Classmate 1	Classmate 2
1. be in the United States *Will you be in the United States?* ____________________	________	________
2. speak English fluently ____________________	________	________
3. be back in your home country ____________________	________	________
4. have a good job ____________________	________	________
5. have children ____________________	________	________
6. live in the city or country ____________________	________	________
7. be happy ____________________	________	________
8. want something different ____________________	________	________
9. write to your friends from our ESL class ____________________	________	________
Add two questions of your own.		
10. ____________________	________	________
11. ____________________	________	________

EXERCISE 4

How will life be different in a hundred years? Work in a group of four. Take turns asking and answering *yes/no* questions with *will.* Discuss your predictions with the group.

Example: 1. *Will the climate change?*

a. The Environment

1. the climate / change
2. hurricanes and earthquakes / get stronger
3. pollution / get worse

b. The Family

1. The traditional family with a husband, wife, and two children / disappear
2. Men and women / continue to marry
3. Girls / have the same opportunities as boys

c. Science and Health

1. We / discover life on other planets
2. People / vacation on the moon
3. People / live to be 150 years old

EXERCISE 5

Work in groups of three. Make one question about the future with *there* + *be* in Column A. Make *yes/no* questions with *be able to* in Column B. Discuss your answers to these questions.

Example: 1. a. *Will there be wars?*
b. Will the UN be able to stop wars? Will soldiers be able to say "no" to war?

COLUMN A: THERE + BE	COLUMN B: BE ABLE TO
1. wars __________	1. a. The United Nations / stop wars __________ b. Soldiers / say "no" to war __________
2. new sources of energy __________	2. a. We / heat our homes __________ b. We / drive our cars __________
3. good governments __________	3. a. People / vote __________ b. People / speak freely __________
4. economic equality __________	4. a. The poor / feed their children __________ b. The poor / get health care __________
5. new medicines __________	5. a. Doctors / cure cancer __________ b. Doctors / treat new diseases like bird flu __________

EXERCISE 6

Wally the Worry Wart Meets Fanny the Fortune Teller

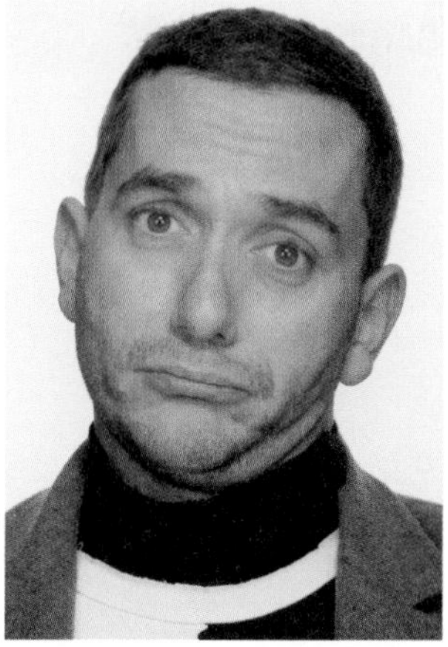

Wally the Worry Wart

Fanny the Fortune Teller

Work with a partner. You are Wally the Worry Wart. Your partner is Fanny the Fortune Teller. Ask your partner *yes/no* and *wh-questions* with *will.* Your partner will create a possible story for Mr. Worry Wart. Compare your stories with those of your classmates. Decide if your fortune teller partner is an optimist or a pessimist!

Example: You: *Will I go to college?*
Your partner: *Yes, you will. / No, you won't.*

Mr. Worry Wart's Questions

1. I / go to college
2. How / I / pay for college
3. I / graduate from college
4. What / I do after college
5. Who / give me a job
6. I / earn a good salary
7. Whom / I marry
8. Where / we live
9. We / be able to / have children
10. Our children / be healthy
11. My wife and I / be able to / retire
12. Who / take care of us
13. How many grandchildren / we have
14. How long / we live
15. I / be a worry wart forever

FOCUS 3 *Be Going To*

AFFIRMATIVE STATEMENTS			NEGATIVE STATEMENTS		
I	am 'm	**going to** leave.	I	am not 'm not	**going to** leave.
He She It	is 's		He She It	is not isn't	
We You They	are 're		We You They	are not aren't	

YES/NO QUESTIONS			SHORT ANSWERS					
Am	I	**going to** leave?	Yes,	you	**are.**	No,	you	**aren't.**
Are	you			I	**am.**		I	**'m not.**
Is	he she it			he she it	**is.**		he she it	**isn't.**
Are	we you they			we you they	**are.**		we you they	**aren't.**

WH-QUESTIONS			ANSWERS	
When Where What How How long Who(m)	**are you going to**	leave? go? do there? get there? stay? visit?	**I'm going to**	leave in two weeks. go to Colorado. go skiing. go by car. stay for one week. visit my cousin.
Who's	**going to**	drive?	My friend	(**is going to** drive).

NOTE: *Going to* is often pronounced "gonna" when we speak. We do not usually write "gonna."

EXERCISE 7

Look at the pictures. Then fill in the blanks with the affirmative or negative form of *be going to*.

1. 

"Watch out! That bag ______________ fall!"

2. 

"Hurry up! We ______________ miss the bus."

3. 

"This ______________ hurt you one bit."

4. 

"I am so tired! I ______________ take a nap."

5. 

"Hello, dear. I ______________ be home on time tonight."

6. 

George: What are you __________ have, Fred?

Fred: I __________ have a pizza, as usual.

7. 

"Watch her, Jack! She __________ fall into the pool!"

8. 

"They __________ have a baby today."

9. 

"Hello, boss. I'm sorry, I __________ be able to come in today. I have a terrible backache, and I can't get out of bed."

10. 

Ben: I have a test tomorrow. I __________ study.

Roommate: I have a test tomorrow too, but I __________ study. I __________ watch the game on TV!

EXERCISE 8

This is a conversation between Wally and Robert. Read the answers. Write a yes/no question or wh-question with *be going to*. The first one has been done for you.

Wally: My doctor says I have too much stress. I need to leave my job and get away somewhere.

Robert: (1) ______Where are you going to go______?

Wally: To California.

Robert: (2) ________________________________?

Wally: I don't know (what I'm going to do there).

Robert: (3) ________________________________?

Wally: (I'm going to stay) with some old friends.

Robert: (4) ________________________________?

Wally: For about a month.

Robert: (5) ________________________________?

Wally: By plane.

Robert: (6) ________________________________?

Wally: I don't know (if I'm going to come back to my job).

EXERCISE 9

STEP 1 Match the phrases to the correct person/people. Then, make a statement about each person's future, using *be going to.*

____ 1. A bald man	a. inherit one million dollars from an uncle
____ 2. An athlete	b. win an Olympic gold medal
____ 3. A teenager	c. have ten grandchildren
____ 4. A movie director	d. open his own restaurant
____ 5. A lifeguard	e. write best-selling books
____ 6. A chef	f. produce a new movie and win an Oscar
____ 7. A homeless man	g. find a cure for the common cold
____ 8. A scientist	h. save someone's life
____ 9. An elderly couple	i. grow hair on his head
____ 10. An author	j. graduate and become a famous rock star

STEP 2 Make one optimistic and one pessimistic prediction using *be going to* for each person.

Example: *The bald man is going to marry a beautiful woman.* (optimistic prediction)
The bald man is going to color his hair green. (pessimistic prediction)

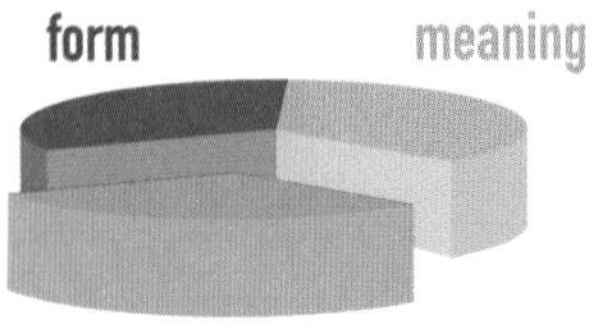

FOCUS 4 Time Expressions in the Future

EXAMPLES	EXPLANATIONS
(a) I'm going to visit you **tomorrow evening**. (b) **A month from now,** Fanny will be on a tropical island.	Future time expressions can come at the beginning or at the end of the sentence. Put a comma (,) after the time expression when it is at the beginning of the sentence.

Future Time Expressions

(later) this	morning	next	week	tomorrow	morning	soon
	afternoon		month		afternoon	later
	evening		year		evening	the day after tomorrow
			Sunday		night	a week from today
			weekend			tonight

EXAMPLES	EXPLANATIONS
I'll see you	We also use prepositional phrases of time to talk about future time.
(c) **in** fifteen minutes. two weeks. March. 2015.	Use *in* with part of a day or a longer period.
(d) **on** Tuesday. May 21st.	Use *on* with a specific day.
(e) **at** 4:00. midnight.	Use *at* with clock time.
(f) We are going to go to the Bahamas **for** three weeks.	*For* shows how long the action will last.
(g) I'll be there **until** 3:00. (At 3:00, I will leave. I will not be there after 3:00.) (h) I won't be there **until** Monday. (Before Monday, I won't be there. After Monday, I'll be there.)	*Until* shows the specific time in the future when the action will change.

EXERCISE 10

Look at Fanny's calendar. Imagine it is now 2:00 P.M. on Wednesday, April 10. Read the sentences about Fanny's plans, and fill in the blanks with a time expression or a preposition of time. There may be more than one correct answer.

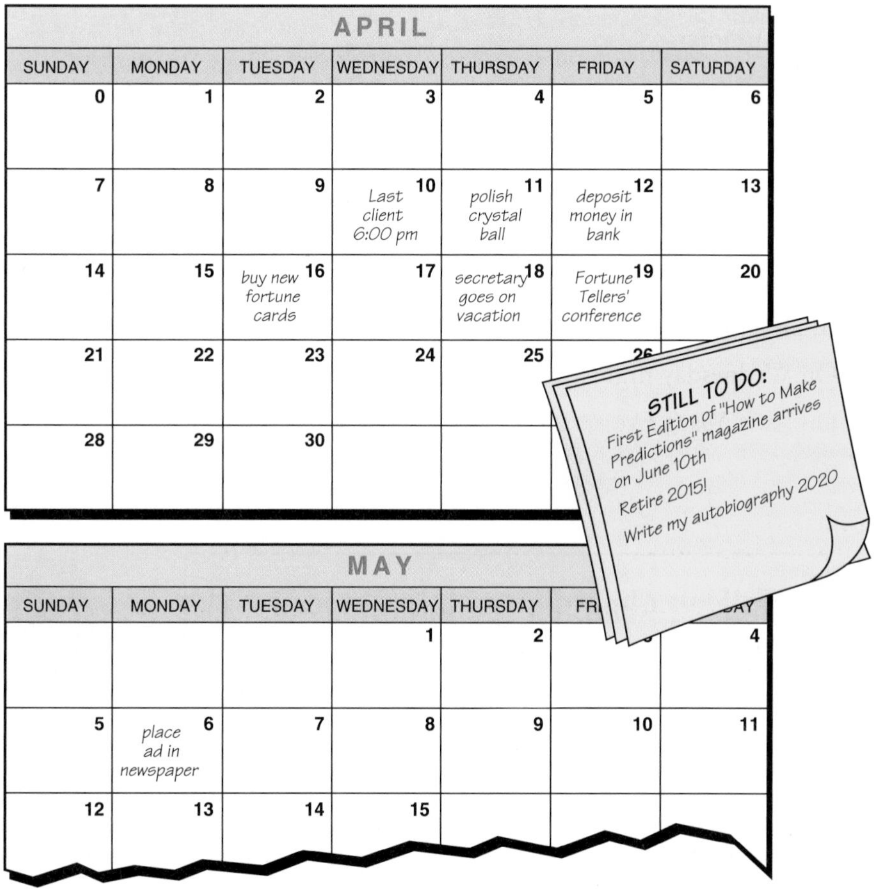

1. Fanny is going to see her last client <u>at 6:00 this evening/in four hours</u>.
2. She's going to attend the Fortune Tellers' Conference ______________________.
3. She's going to polish her crystal ball ______________________.
4. She's going to deposit all her money in the bank ______________________.
5. Her secretary is going to go on vacation ______________________.
6. She is going to buy new fortune cards ______________________.
7. She's going to put an advertisement about herself in the newspaper ______________________.
8. She will read her first *How To Make Predictions* magazine ______________________.
9. She will retire to a tropical island ______________________.
10. She will write a book called *How to Be a Successful Fortune Teller in 10 Easy Lessons* ______________________.

EXERCISE 11

Make statements about yourself. Use *be going to.*

Example: In a few days, I'm going to move out of my apartment.

1. In a few days, ______________________________.
2. Next summer, ______________________________.
3. The day after tomorrow, ______________________________.
4. This evening, ______________________________.
5. Tomorrow night, ______________________________.
6. This weekend, ______________________________.
7. At 9:00 P.M., ______________________________.
8. In December, ______________________________.
9. On Wednesday night, ______________________________.
10. On New Year's Eve, ______________________________.

FOCUS 5 Talking About Future Intentions or Plans

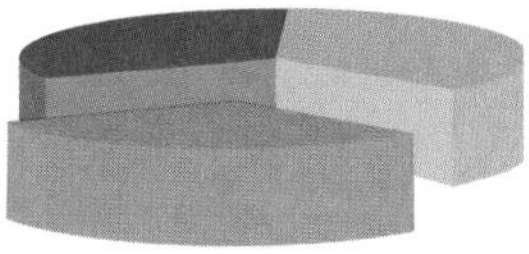

EXAMPLES	EXPLANATIONS
(a) **A:** The phone is ringing. **B:** O.K. I'**ll** get it.	Use *will* when you decide to do something **at** the time of speaking.
(b) **Mother:** Where are you going? **Daughter:** I'**m going to** take a drive with Richard tonight. Remember, Mom? You said it was okay . . . **Mother:** I did?	Use *be going to* when you made a plan to do something **before** the time of speaking.

EXERCISE 12

Work with a partner. You read the first five statements in Column A aloud. Your partner chooses an answer from Column B. After the first five, your partner reads from Column A and you choose the answer from Column B.

Example: Do you have any plans for tonight? a. Yes, we will go to the theater.
(b.) Yes, we're going to the theater.

Column A	Column B
1. Christine called. She's coming over for dinner.	a. Great! I'll cook. b. Great! I'm going to cook.
2. What are you doing with that camera?	a. I'll take your picture. b. I'm going to take your picture.
3. Do you need a ride home today?	a. No, thanks. Andrew will take me home. b. No, thanks. Andrew's going to take me home.
4. We don't have a thing to eat in the house.	a. I'll call up and order a pizza. b. I'm going to call up and order a pizza.
5. Help! The car died again.	a. Calm down. I'll be right there. b. Calm down. I'm going to be right there.
6. Why are you meeting Jenny in the library tonight?	a. She'll help me with my homework. b. She's going to help me with my homework.
7. Look, those thieves are robbing the bank!	a. I'll call the police. b. I'm going to call the police.
8. Mom, can you brush my hair?	a. I'll do it in a minute, sweetie. b. I'm going to do it in a minute, sweetie.
9. Are you off the phone yet?	a. I'll be off in a minute! b. I'm going to be off in a minute!
10. Why did Maria cancel her date for Saturday night?	a. Her parents will take her away for the weekend. b. Her parents are going to take her away for the weekend.

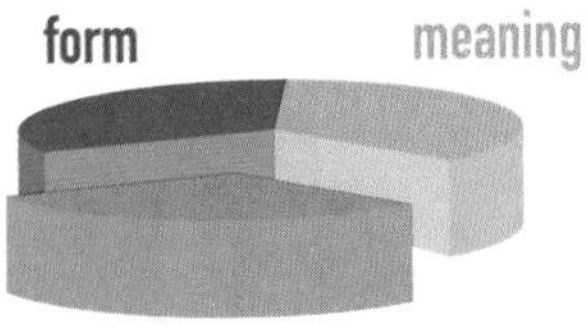

FOCUS 6 *May* and *Might*

Use *may* or *might* to say something is possible in the future

EXAMPLES	EXPLANATIONS
(a) I **will go** to Mexico next year.	(a) shows certainty The speaker is 100 percent sure.
(b) I **may/might go** to Mexico next year.	(b) shows possibility The speaker is 50 percent sure.

AFFIRMATIVE STATEMENTS			NEGATIVE STATEMENTS		
I He She We You They	**may** **might**	study abroad next year. be able to stay abroad.	I He She We You They	**may not** **might not**	take a vacation. be able to stay for two years.
It		rain later.	It		rain later.
There		be cheap flights to Mexico.	There		be any discounts on flights.

NOTE: There are no contractions for *may* or *might*.

EXERCISE 13

What's it like to be Wally the Worry Wart? Fill in the blanks with *may* or *might* in the affirmative or negative.

1. Wally on the Weather

Wally: Look at those clouds! It'll definitely rain today.

Wife: No, Wally. It (a) ________________ clear up and be a beautiful day. I think we (b) ________________ be able to have a picnic this afternoon.

Wally: But the grass (c) ________________ be wet; and we (d) ________________ be able to sit down.

Wife: Relax, the sun will dry it out, Wally!

2. Wally on Vacation

Friend: Are you going to try skiing, Wally?

Wally: I (a) ________________. On second thought, the slopes (b) ________________ be icy, and I (c) ________________ fall and break my neck! I think I'll stay in the lodge and drink hot chocolate!

Friend: You (d) ________________ miss a great experience. . . .

Wally: But I won't break any bones!

3. Wally on the Traffic from his Cell Phone:

Wally: Hello, honey. I (a) ________________ be home in time for dinner tonight. The traffic is awful. I'm afraid I (b) ________________ have an accident. I (c) ________________ have enough gas to get home! You (d) ________________ need to come get me.

4. Wally on His New Job

Wally: I (a) ________________ last long at this new job, honey.

Wife: Why not?

Wally: Well, I (b) ________________ like it. And my boss (c) ________________ like me. The salary (d) ________________ be too good.

Wife: You'll be fine. Don't worry so much, Wally.

EXERCISE 14

STEP 1 **What are your plans for the future? Interview your partner and answer your partner's questions. Complete the chart with your partner's information. Then report your partner's plans to the class.**

Example: You: *What are you going to do this evening?*
Your partner: *I'm going to see a movie this weekend.*

	BASE VERB	*WILL/BE GOING TO*	*MAY/MIGHT*
1. this evening	see a movie	✔	
2. this weekend	study at home		✔
3. tomorrow night			
4. a week from today			
5. in three months			
6. next summer			
7. in five years			

STEP 2 **Use the information from Step 1 to write statements about your partner's definite or possible plans.**

EXERCISE 15

Look into your crystal ball again. What is our future ten years from now? Make statements with affirmative or negative forms of *will, be going to, may,* or *might*.

Example: Europe / be a superpower
In ten years, Europe will be a superpower.

1. People / want to go back to the simple days before computers
2. People around the world /move away from big cities
3. China and India / become superpowers
4. Solar energy / be the most common source of energy
5. Students in classrooms all around the world / be able to see and talk to each other
6. Books / disappear completely
7. There / be cures for cancer, bird flu, and other fatal diseases
8. The planet Earth / be 10 degrees warmer

Use Your English

ACTIVITY 1 writing/speaking

What do you think the world will be like in 2050? Think about changes in the environment, the family, in science, health, and technology. With your group, write down ten changes. Discuss your group's ideas with the rest of the class.

ACTIVITY 2 speaking

Role-play the Optimist and the Pessimist. Work with a partner. Make pessimistic statements about your future OR the future of the world. Your partner tries to make you feel better by making more optimistic statements about you / the world.

Example: You: *I will never learn English!*
Your partner: *It may take you a little longer, but you will learn!*

ACTIVITY 3 listening

CD Track 19

Every year, Americans make New Year's Resolutions. They promise to do something to change their lives in the future. Listen to three people from this unit talk about their New Year's resolutions. Identify the person who is speaking. Choose from the people in the box.

Wally the Worry Wart	A chef	Fanny the Fortune Teller
A doctor	A homeless man	A teenage rock star
Person 1: ______________		
Person 2: ______________		
Person 3: ______________		

ACTIVITY 4 writing

STEP 1

Sit in a circle with your whole class or a group of six to eight people. On the top of a blank piece of paper, write:

On ______________ *in the year 2020,* ______________

(today's date) (your name)

STEP 2

Pass the sheet of paper to the person on your left. This person writes a prediction about you for the year 2020. Then he or she passes the paper to the left for the next person to write a second prediction.

STEP 3

Continue until everyone has written their predictions. At the end of the activity, you will have a list of predictions. Read the predictions and choose the best one. Read it aloud to the class.

ACTIVITY 5 research on the web

Search the Internet for the weather forecast for a city you want to visit next week. Use a search engine such as Google®, Ask®, or Yahoo® and enter the keyword: *weather* and the name of your city or town. Share the seven day or next week's weather prediction for your city with a partner. Tell your partner about any special items you will bring for your trip.

Example: *Next week, it will rain in Seattle. It's going to be 60 degrees. I'm going to bring my umbrella and raincoat.*

ACTIVITY 6 reflection

STEP 1 Make yourself a Learning Plan using the table below. Write a list of goals, and decide when you will reach each goal (next week, in two months, next year, in June…). Discuss your Learning Plan with a partner.

My Learning Plan

MY GOALS	WHEN I WILL ACCOMPLISH MY GOALS
1. I will learn fifty new vocabulary words.	in four months
2.	
3.	
4.	
5.	
6.	
7.	

STEP 2 Write an entry in your Learning Journal about your goals and when you will accomplish them.

UNIT 21

PHRASAL VERBS

UNIT GOALS

- Understand the meaning of common phrasal verbs
- Know which phrasal verbs are separable and inseparable phrasal verbs
- Learn which phrasal verbs take objects and which do not take objects

OPENING TASK

What's a Technophobe To Do?

STEP 1

A *technophobe* is someone who is afraid of/not good with technology. Create a questionnaire to identify the technophobes in your class. Complete each question with a word from the box. You may use a word more than once.

out	up	call
give	take	back
away	wake	break
turn	on	

Questionnaire

When your computer doesn't work,

1. Do you bring it ________________ to the store?
2. Do you throw it ________________ and buy a new computer?
3. Do you back ________________ all your files?
4. Do you ________________ up a computer specialist?
5. Do you ________________ out the computer manual and read it?
6. Do you try to figure ________________ what to do by yourself?
7. Do you ________________ off the computer?
8. Do you turn it ________________ again?
9. Do you ________________ up and do your work by hand?
10. Do you ________________ down and cry?

STEP 2

Who are the technophobes in your class? Give your reasons.

form

FOCUS 1 Phrasal Verbs

EXAMPLES	EXPLANATION
(a) **Turn on** the lights. (b) **Take out** the garbage.	Phrasal verbs are special verbs that have two parts: a verb + a particle. The combination of the verb and particle creates a new meaning. *turn* + *on* *take* + *out*

EXERCISE 1

Go back to your questionnaire in the Opening Task on page 345. List all the phrasal verbs.

meaning

use

FOCUS 2 Phrasal Verbs

EXAMPLES	EXPLANATIONS
(a) Plants **grow**. (*grow* = to increase in size) (b) Children **grow up**. (*grow up* = to become an adult)	The verb + particle have a specific meaning. This new meaning can be different from the meaning of the verb or the meaning of the particle.
(c) The speaker **sat down**.	Sometimes the meaning of a phrasal verb is clear from the verb + particle.
(d) I **ran into** Joe on the street the other day. It was great to see him again after so many years.	Sometimes it is difficult to guess the meaning of a phrasal verb. Sometimes the context of the sentence can help you. The meaning of *run into* is not the combination of *run* and *into*. *Run into* means "to meet someone by chance."
(e) I **filled out** the college application. (f) Richie **filled up** the tank with gas.	The same verb can have a different meaning with a different particle. *fill* + *out* = to complete *fill* + *up* = to fill
(g) Please **put out** your cigarette, Jake. (h) Please **extinguish** your cigarettes, ladies and gentlemen.	In informal English, phrasal verbs are more frequent than one-word verbs with the same meaning. In (g), you are talking to a friend. In (h), an announcer is speaking to passengers at a train station.

EXERCISE 2

Read each statement on the left to your partner. Your partner chooses a response from the right.

Statement

1. I don't want to cook tonight.
2. It's hot in here.
3. It's so quiet in here.
4. I can't read the map. The print is too small.
5. I can't do my homework with the TV on.
6. I'm bored.
7. My feet hurt.
8. I'm sleepy.
9. I'm really upset about our argument today.
10. I'm tired of sitting on this plane.

Response

a. Let's calm down and talk about it.
b. Call up a friend.
c. Stand up and walk around for a few minutes.
d. Sit down for a while.
e. Lie down and take a nap.
f. Take off your jacket.
g. Put on your glasses.
h. Turn off the TV.
i. Let's eat out.
j. Turn on the radio.

EXERCISE 3

Work with a partner. Underline the phrasal verbs in the sentences below. Then try to guess the meaning of each phrasal verb in the context of the sentence.

1. A procrastinator puts off chores until tomorrow.
2. A healthy eater doesn't fill up on sweets.
3. A clown cheers up his audience.
4. A saver never throws away anything.
5. A good reader doesn't look up every word in the dictionary.
6. A quitter never sees through any of his projects.
7. A champion never gives up.
8. A neat person always hangs up his clothes.

EXERCISE 4

Circle the phrasal verbs. Then match each phrasal verb with a one-word verb.

Sentences with phrasal verbs

1. I called 911 Emergency. The firefighters will be here soon to put out the fire. __d__
2. Don't just stand at the door. Come in. ______
3. Fill out the application. ______
4. We're going to practice some phrasal verbs. Henry, can you please hand out this exercise? ______
5. I left my book at school. I don't remember the homework for tonight. I'll call up Manny and ask him. ______
6. I can't talk to you now. Please come back in fifteen minutes. ______
7. I can't concentrate! Would you please turn down the music! ______
8. I am freezing in this house. Please turn up the heat. ______
9. Please take off your wet shoes. ______
10. Hold on a minute. I'm not ready yet. ______

One-word verb with same meaning

a. raise
b. remove
c. telephone
d. extinguish
e. enter
f. distribute
g. complete
h. wait
i. lower
j. return

form

FOCUS 3 Separable Phrasal Verbs

EXAMPLES				EXPLANATIONS
				Many phrasal verbs take direct objects. When the direct object is a **noun**, it can go:
	Verb	Particle	D.O.	
(a) The teacher	handed	out	the exercise.	after the particle
	Verb	D.O.	Particle	
(b) The teacher	**handed**	the exercise	**out.**	between the verb and the particle
(c) The teacher handed **it** out. (d) NOT: The teacher handed out **it.**				When the direct object is a **pronoun**, it always goes between the verb and the particle.

Common Separable Phrasal Verbs

SEPARABLE PHRASAL VERBS	EXAMPLES	MEANING
calm down	(a) She is very upset about the accident. We can't **calm** her **down.**	Become quiet or calm
call up	(b) I **called** my friend **up** the other night to ask about the homework.	telephone
cheer up	(c) My friend failed her final exam, so I brought her flowers to **cheer** her **up.**	become happy, make someone happy
clean up	(d) Your room's a mess. **Clean** it **up**!	clean
figure out	(e) This puzzle is very confusing. I can't **figure** it **out.**	solve, understand
fill out	(f) Here's an application. **Fill** it **out** for a new license.	complete
fill up	(g) **Fill** it **up** with regular gas, please.	fill

Continued on next page

Continued

SEPARABLE PHRASAL VERBS	EXAMPLES	MEANING
hand out	(h) The teacher **handed** the tests **out** to the class.	distribute
hang up	(i) My husband never **hangs** his clothes **up.** (j) Please **hang up** the phone.	place on a hanger or a hook
look up	(k) I didn't know his telephone number, so I **looked** it **up** in the phone book.	search for in a reference book
pick up	(l) In my neighborhood, they **pick** the garbage **up** every Tuesday. (m) What time do you **pick** your children **up** from school?	collect, lift
put away	(n) My kids are neat! They always **put** their toys **away.**	put in its usual place
put off	(o) Do it now. Don't **put** it **off** until tomorrow.	postpone
put on	(p) It's really cold outside, so **put** your coat **on.**	dress yourself
put out	(q) It took firefighters a few hours to **put** the fire **out.**	extinguish
take off	(r) **Take** your shoes **off** before you come into the house.	remove
take out	(s) Will you please **take** the garbage **out**?	put something outside
throw out/away	(t) I have a lot of old things in the garage. I need to **throw** them **out.**	dispose of, put in garbage
turn down	(u) It's 2:00 in the morning. **Turn** that stereo **down!**	lower the volume
turn off	(v) There aren't any good programs on TV tonight. **Turn** it **off.**	stop the power
turn on	(w) I always **turn** the radio **on** in the morning.	start the power
turn up	(x) When I hear my favorite song, I **turn** the volume **up.**	increase the volume
wake up	(y) It's 7:00. Time to **wake up!** (z) The baby's sleeping. Don't **wake** him **up.**	to become awake

EXERCISE 5

Sergeant Strict is giving orders to his new soldiers. He's losing his patience and getting very frustrated. Repeat the Sergeant's orders in a different way each time.

1. a. "Take off your civilian clothes."
   b. "I said, take your civilian clothes off."
   c. "Come on, take them off!"
2. a. "Hand out these uniforms."
   b. "I said, ______________________."
   c. "Come on, ______________________!"
3. a. "Put on your new Army clothes."
   b. "I said, ______________________."
   c. "Come on, ______________________!"
4. a. "Turn down that radio."
   b. "I said, ______________________."
   c. "Come on, ______________________!"
5. a. "Put away your old clothes."
   b. "I said, ______________________."
   c. "Come on, ______________________!"
6. a. "Throw out that junk food from home."
   b. "I said, ______________________."
   c. "Come on, ______________________!"
7. a. "Clean up this mess."
   b. "I said, ______________________."
   c. "Come on, ______________________!"
8. a. "Turn off the lights!"
   b. "I said, ______________________."
   c. "Come on, ______________________!"

EXERCISE 6

Fill in the blanks with the phrasal verbs below. Use a pronoun in the second blank of each dialogue.

Example: (clean up)

Mother: Danny, don't forget to (a) ___clean up___ the mess in your bedroom.

Danny: Mom, I (b) ___cleaned it up___ this morning.

figure out	pick up	cheer up	hand out	throw out	fill out

1. **Counselor:** You need to (a) ________________ this application for college.
   Abdul: Can I (b) ________________ at home?
2. **Susie:** Danny, I think it's time to (a) ________________ all these old newspapers.
   Danny: I'm (b) ________________ right now.
3. **Jackie:** Could you please (a) ________________ that paper on the floor for me?
   Mark: I'll (b) ________________ in a minute!
4. **Ms. Wagner:** Can you help me (a) ________________ these exams, John?
   John: Sure, I'll (b) ________________ right now.
5. **Mom:** Please try to (a) ________________ your sister. She's in a bad mood!
   Bobbie: No one can (b) ________________. She's always in a bad mood.
6. **Liz:** Can you (a) ________________ the directions for this software program, Felicia?
   Felicia: I can't, but I'm sure that Sayeed could (b) ________________.

form

FOCUS 4 Inseparable Phrasal Verbs

EXAMPLES	EXPLANATIONS
(a) I **ran into** an old friend on the street. (b) I **ran into** her on the street. (c) NOT: I **ran** an old friend **into** on the street. (d) NOT: I **ran** her **into** on the street.	Some phrasal verbs are inseparable. The direct object—noun or pronoun—always goes after the particle.

Common Inseparable Phrasal Verbs

INSEPARABLE PHRASAL VERBS	EXAMPLES	MEANING
get in *get out of*	(a) I **got in** my car and drove away. (b) I dropped my bag when I **got out of** the cab.	enter and leave a vehicle (car, taxi, truck)
get on *get off*	(c) I **got on** the train at 42nd Street. (d) I **got off** the bus in front of the school.	enter and leave other forms of transportation (bus, plane, train)
go over	(e) How many times did you **go over** your notes before the test? (f) I **went over** them three times before the test. I **went over** them all morning.	review
run into	(g) I **ran into** an old friend the other day.	meet by chance

EXERCISE 7

Fill in the blanks with the correct inseparable phrasal verb. Refer to Focus 4 on page 353 if necessary.

Mandy: It's strange that we live in the same neighborhood, but we never (1) __________ __________ each other.

Sharon: Our schedules are so different.

Mandy: I know! When you (2) __________ __________ __________ work, I go in. When I (3) __________ __________ the bus, you (4) __________ __________.

Sharon: We need to make a date. (5) __________ __________ your calendar and give me a call.

form meaning

FOCUS 5 Phrasal Verbs Without Objects

Some phrasal verbs do not take an object. These phrasal verbs are inseparable.

PHRASAL VERBS	EXAMPLES	MEANING
break down	(a) My car **broke down** last night, so I walked home.	stop working
come back	(b) He left home and never **came back.**	return
come in	(c) **Come in** and make yourself comfortable.	enter
eat out	(d) I hate to cook, so I often **eat out**.	eat in a restaurant
grow up	(e) I **grew up** in the United States.	become an adult
show up	(f) After two hours, he finally **showed up.**	appear
sit down	(g) I feel tired, so I think I'll **sit down** for a while.	sit
stand up	(h) In some countries, students **stand up** to show respect when the teacher enters the room.	stand

EXERCISE 8

Fill in the blanks with a phrasal verb from the box.

stand up	sit down	break down	eat out
show up	come in	come back	grow up

What do you say when . . .

1. you are very late for an important date?
   You say: "Oh, I'm so sorry. Please forgive me, my car _________________."
2. your friend's dog runs away from home?
   You say: "Don't worry, Elliot; I'm sure she'll _________________ home very soon."
3. your child is sitting and an elderly man is standing on the bus?
   You say: "_________________ and give that man your seat."
4. your 30-year-old friend is acting like a child?
   You say: "Come on, Matt, _________________. You're not a child anymore."
5. you are a car salesperson and you are trying to get people into your showroom?
   You say: "Please _________________, folks. We have many new models and great prices this year."
6. you and your roommate are hungry, but you're too tired to cook?
   You say: "Let's _________________."
7. your friend Cheryl is crying about her date last night?
   You say: "What happened, Cheryl? Don't tell me your date didn't _________________ last night."
   Cheryl: "Oh, he did! That's why I'm crying!"
8. you are a receptionist in a very busy doctor's office and an angry patient is complaining about waiting so long?
   You say: "Please _________________, Mr. Brody. The doctor will be with you in a few minutes."

EXERCISE 9

STEP 1 Make a story by putting the pictures in the correct order. Write the number for the order of each picture next to the letter.

a. ______

b. ______

c. ______

d. ______

STEP 2 **Then fill in each blank below with a phrasal verb from the box. Check verb tenses carefully.**

fill up	look up	break down
figure out	wake up	calm down
turn on	get out of	take out

It was a cold and lonely night. Forgetful Phil was on his way to visit his mother when his car suddenly (1) ________________. He was angry and upset, but after a while, he (2) ________________. It was dark, so Phil (3) ________________ a flashlight from the glove compartment. Then he took out his car manual. He tried to (4) ________________, "*What to do when your car breaks down in the middle of nowhere*," but he didn't find anything in the manual. Next, he (5) ________________ the car and looked under the hood. He wasn't able to (6) ________________ what the problem was. Then Phil began to understand. He asked himself, "Did I (7) ________________ my tank with gas?" The answer, of course, was no.

Luckily there was a house nearby. He knocked on the door and shouted, but nobody answered. There were no other houses. There was no telephone. "What now?" thought Phil. Then, just as he turned around to go back to his car, another car crashed into the back of his car. Suddenly, the people in the house (8) ________________ and (9) ________________ the lights. Poor Phil felt like crying.

Use Your English

ACTIVITY 1 writing/speaking

Work with a partner. Write a story or dialogue about the situation below, using the phrasal verbs in the box. You may use other phrasal verbs if you want to. Then role-play the situation for the class.

Situation: It is 11:00 P.M. You are sleeping very deeply. Suddenly, you hear some noise coming from the apartment downstairs. Your neighbor's stereo is very loud.

wake up	throw out	turn down	turn off
turn on	go back	calm down	call up

ACTIVITY 2 speaking

Work in a group or as a whole class. The first person begins a story. He or she says, "I woke up . . ." and completes the sentence. The second person repeats the first sentence and adds a second sentence using a phrasal verb. The third person repeats the first two sentences and then adds a third, and so on. Try not to write anything down. Use your memory! Refer to the phrasal verbs in this unit.

Examples: Player 1: *I woke up early.*
Player 2: *I woke up early, and turned off the alarm clock.*
Player 3: *I woke up early, turned off the alarm clock, and took off my pajamas.*

ACTIVITY 3 speaking/writing

STEP 1 Work in a group. Put numbers 1 to 12 in a bag. Pick a number from the bag. Read the sentence in the box that corresponds to your number and then do the action.

STEP 2 After the group has done all the actions, write sentences about the things you did.

Examples: *Mario put on Marcela's cap.*
José turned off the light.

1. Put on a piece of a classmate's clothing or jewelry.	2. Turn off the light.	3. You spill a cup of hot coffee on yourself and on the floor. Clean it up.
4. Call up a friend and tell him or her you are sick.	5. Draw a picture of yourself on a piece of paper and hang it up on the wall.	6. Stand up. Put your hands on your head. Then sit down.
7. Cheer a classmate up.	8. Hand your phone number out to all the people in the group.	9. Take something out of your pocket and throw it away.
10. Take off an article of clothing and put it on someone else.	11. Turn on something electrical (CD player, printer, light, etc.) and then turn it off.	12. Pretend you find a word whose meaning you don't know. Look it up in the dictionary.

ACTIVITY 4 listening/speaking

CD Track 20

STEP 1 Listen to the conversation. Write down the problem.

Conversation 1: ____________________

Conversation 2: ____________________

Conversation 3: ____________________

STEP 2 Listen to the conversation again, and complete the phrasal verbs you hear below:

Conversation 1:	Turn ________	Turn ________	Put ________
Conversation 2:	Clean ________	Fill ________	Put ________
Conversation 3:	Figure ________	Call ________	Turn ________

STEP 3 For each problem, add a solution of your own.

ACTIVITY 5 writing

STEP 1 Work with a partner. Look back at the phrasal verbs in this unit. What phrasal verbs do you associate with the contexts below? Write them in the appropriate circle or redraw these circles in your notebook.

At school

At home

At a party

STEP 2 Choose one of the contexts. Write a dialogue using as many phrasal verbs as you can.

ACTIVITY 6 research on the web

Search the Internet for the meanings of the following phrasal verbs. Use a search engine such as Google® or Yahoo® or Ask® and enter the keywords: *dictionary* and *search* plus the phrasal verb. Write the meaning in the chart below. Then write a sentence that shows the change in meaning with each different particle.

		SENTENCE	MEANING
	over		
take	away		
	up		
	over		
look	into		
	up to		
	out		
give	into		
	back		

ACTIVITY 7 reflection

STEP 1 Give an example of a time when:

- communication broke down
- you figured out the meaning of a new word
- you felt frustrated and gave up

STEP 2 Explain what happened each time. What will you do next time?

Example: *I had a problem with my rent. I talked to my landlord on the phone. I didn't understand what he was saying. I was embarrassed, so I hung up the phone. Next time I'll let him I don't understand. I'll ask him to say it a different way.*

UNIT 22

COMPARISON USING ADJECTIVES

UNIT GOALS

- Use the (regular and irregular) comparative form of adjectives in statements
- Ask questions using comparative adjectives
- Express similarities and differences with adjectives using *as . . . as*
- Make polite comparisons

OPENING TASK

Comparison Shopping for an Apartment

STEP 1

You are a college student looking for an apartment. Look at the two apartment ads and compare them using the adjectives on the next page.

FOR RENT

Studio Apartment. 400 square feet. Centrally located. Close to bus stop and downtown. Fully furnished. $800/month plus utilities.

FOR RENT

One bedroom apartment in brand new building. 900 square feet. Quiet neighborhood. Lots of light. Furnished. $1,200/month including utilities.

small

close to public transportation

far away from downtown

expensive

spacious

quiet

safe

new

sunny

furnished

STEP 2

In your opinion, which apartment is better? Give reasons for your choice.

I think the ______________________________ *is better because . . .*

FOCUS 1 Comparative Form of Adjectives

Regular Comparatives

There are two regular comparative forms of adjectives in English.

1. For adjectives with one syllable or those ending in *–y*:

   X *is* __________________ *er than* Y.

EXAMPLE	ADJECTIVE	COMPARATIVE	RULE
(a) This neighborhood is **safer than** that one.	*safe*	*safer than*	For adjectives ending in *-e*, add *-r*.
(b) The one-bedroom apartment is **bigger than** the studio.	*big*	*bigger than*	For adjectives ending in consonant-vowel-consonant, double the consonant, add *-er*.
(c) The studio is **noisier than** the one bedroom.	*noisy*	*noisier than*	For adjectives ending in *-y,* change the *-y* to *i*, add *-er.*
(d) The studio is **smaller than** the one-bedroom.	*small*	*smaller than*	For all other adjectives, add *-er*.

2. For adjectives with two or more syllables:

   X *is (more/less)* __________________ *than* Y.

EXAMPLE	ADJECTIVE	COMPARATIVE	RULE
(e) The studio is **more economical than** the one-bedroom.	*economical*	*more economical than*	Use *more* or *less* before the adjective.
(f) The studio is **less expensive than** the one-bedroom.	*expensive*	*less expensive than*	

Notes	
Some adjectives with two syllables can take either *-er* or *more/less*.	My apartment is **quieter than** yours. OR My apartment is **more quiet than** yours.
The forms we use in formal and informal English may be different.	In formal English we say: Joe is taller than **I** (am). In informal English we sometimes say: Joe is taller than **me**.
When you make a comparison, be sure to compare two **like** things.	**My hair** is longer than **Rita's (hair)**. NOT: **My hair** is longer than **Rita.**

Irregular Comparatives

EXAMPLES	EXPLANATIONS
(g) This neighborhood is **better than** that one. (h) This year's winter was **worse than** last year's (winter). (i) The one-bedroom is **farther** away from the bus stop **than** the studio is.	The comparative forms of *good, bad,* and *far* are irregular. *good—better* *bad—worse* *far—farther*
(j) This apartment is **much better than** that one. (k) This apartment is **much farther than** the other one.	Use *much* to make a comparison stronger.

EXERCISE 1

Complete the statements using the comparative form of each adjective in parentheses + *than*. Then make a logical conclusion for each set of sentences.

Examples: a. E-mail is (fast) ___faster than___ regular mail.
b. E-mail is (easy) ___easier than___ regular mail.
c. E-mail is (practical) more practical than regular mail.

1. Online shoppers say:
   a. Shopping online is (convenient) ______________ shopping in a department store.
   b. Shopping online is (relaxing) ______________ shopping in a store.
   c. Therefore, shopping online is (good) ______________ shopping in a store.
2. Small car owners say:
   a. Big cars are (difficult) ______________ to drive ______________ small cars.
   b. Big cars are (economical) ______________ small cars.
   c. Therefore, big cars are (desirable) ______________ small cars.

3. People who live in small towns say:
   a. Big cities are (crowded) ________________ small towns.
   b. Big cities are (expensive) ________________ small towns.
   c. Life in big cities is (difficult) ________________ life in small towns.
4. Healthy people say:
   a. Fast food is (nutritious) ________________ health food.
   b. Fast food is (fattening) ________________ health food.
   c. Health food is (safe) ________________ fast food.

EXERCISE 2

Fill in the blanks with the comparative form of the adjective.

Jane: Kevin, I found these two apartment ads in the newspaper this morning. There's a studio and a one-bedroom. I think the one-bedroom sounds nice. What do you think?

Kevin: Well, the one bedroom is definitely (1) (large) ________________ than the studio, but the studio is (2) (cheap) ________________. You know you only have a part-time job. How can you afford to pay $1,200 a month for rent?

Jane: I know the one-bedroom is (3) (expensive) ________________, but I have so much furniture. The one-bedroom is (4) (big) ________________ and I want to invite guests and it will be much (5) (comfortable) ________________. Besides, maybe someday I'll have a roommate, and I'll need a (6) (spacious) ________________ apartment, Kevin.

Kevin: Well, maybe, but you need to be realistic. The studio is in the center of town. You'll be (7) (close) ________________ to transportation, stores, the library, and the college.

Jane: You're much (8) (practical) ________________ than I am, Kevin. But the studio is directly over a nightclub, so it will be (9) (noisy) ________________ than the one-bedroom. I will need peace and quiet so I can study.

Kevin: Listen—the studio is small, but it's much (10) (cozy) ________________ than the one-bedroom and you'll spend much less time cleaning it!

Jane: True, but I think the one-bedroom will be much (11) (safe) ________________ and (12) (good) ________________ for me than the studio.

Kevin: It seems to me your mind is made up.

Jane: Yes, it is. By the way, Kevin, I'm going to see the one-bedroom later today. Can you come with me?

Kevin: Sure.

EXERCISE 3

Write an advertisement for each product on the left. In your advertisement, compare one product to the product on the right. Use the adjectives below.

Example: *Hassenflas Ice Cream tastes richer than Momma Millie's Frozen Yogurt.*

1. **Product:** Hassenflas Ice Cream
   Compare with: Momma Millie's Frozen Yogurt
   Adjectives: rich, creamy, delicious, sweet, fattening, healthy

2. **Product:** Serenity Vacation Cruise
   Compare with: Adventure Package Vacation
   Adjectives: luxurious, expensive, enjoyable, relaxing, long, exciting, active, adventurous

3. **Product:** Sportso Compact Car
   Compare with: Big Boy SUV
   Adjectives: fast, comfortable, fuel-efficient, safe, sporty, cheap, expensive

EXERCISE 4

Miyuki wants to study English in the United States. She knows about an English program in Brattleboro, a small town in Vermont. She also knows about a program in Los Angeles, California. She needs to decide where she wants to live. Here is some information about the two places.

	BRATTLEBORO, VERMONT	LOS ANGELES, CALIFORNIA
1. rent for a one-bedroom apartment	$750 a month	$1,500 a month
2. population	12,000	3.8 million
3. weather	very cold in winter hot in summer	warm in winter hot in summer
4. public transportation	bus	bus, metro
5. quality of life		
a. air quality	clean	not so clean
b. the crime rate	1.7 crimes per 1,000 people	12.7 violent crimes per 1,000 people
c. lifestyle	quiet	exciting
d. traffic	light	heavy

Make comparative statements about Brattleboro and Los Angeles using the adjectives in parentheses.

1. crime rate (low/high) *The crime rate is lower in Brattleboro than in Los Angeles. The crime rate is higher in Los Angeles than in Brattleboro.* __________
2. city (populated) __________
3. apartments (cheap/expensive) __________
4. public transportation (good/bad) __________
5. winters (cold) __________
6. city streets (dangerous/safe) __________
7. air (clean) __________
8. traffic (heavy/light) __________
9. lifestyle (quiet/exciting) __________
10. In your opinion, which place is better for Miyuki? Why?

____

____

form

FOCUS 2 Questions with Comparative Adjectives

EXAMPLES

Yes/No Questions

(a) **Are** private universities **more expensive than** public universities?
(b) **Are** private universities **better than** public universities?
(c) **Are** public universities **less expensive than** private universities?

Information (*Wh*-Questions)

(d) **Who** is **more serious** about school: you or your friend?
(e) **Which** is **more affordable:** a public university or a private university?
(f) **Whose** grades are **higher:** yours or your friend's?

EXERCISE 5

Refer to the Opening Task on pages 362–363 and ask a partner *yes/no* questions about the studio and the one-bedroom apartment. Answer the questions.

Example: economical
You: *Is the studio more economical than the one-bedroom?*
Your partner: *Yes, it is.*

1. practical
2. far from the downtown area
3. small
4. cheap
5. sunny
6. comfortable
7. economical
8. roomy
9. quiet
10. convenient
11. close to the bus stop
12. pretty
13. large
14. good

EXERCISE 6

Work with a partner. Interview each other about your impressions of the United States in comparison with your native country. Ask *yes/no* questions with the cues below.

Example: children in the United States/spoiled
You: *Are children in the United States more spoiled than children in your country?*
Your partner: *Yes, they are.* OR *No, they aren't.* OR *I'm not sure.*

1. people in the United States/friendly
2. educational opportunities/good
3. the cost of a college education in the United States/expensive
4. the American population/diverse
5. American citizens/safe
6. American food/tasty
7. Americans/happy
8. families in other countries/close
9. gasoline in the United States/cheap
10. Americans/generous
11. American women/independent
12. the divorce rate in the United States/high

EXERCISE 7

Ask a partner questions with *who, which,* or *whose* and the words in parentheses. Answer each other's questions.

Examples: (popular) *Who is more popular, Ricky Martin or Bono?*
(practical) *Which is less practical, a regular phone or a cell phone?*

1. (wise) you or your parents?
2. (difficult) giving a speech or writing an essay English?
3. (hard) a man's life or a woman's life?
4. (bad) ironing or vacuuming?
5. (cheap) a public American university or a private American university?
6. (interesting) a taxicab driver's job or a scientist's job?
7. (delicious) vanilla or chocolate ice cream?
8. (dangerous) a motorcycle or a car?
9. (sensitive) a man or a woman?
10. (neat) your handwriting or your partner's handwriting?
11. (delicious) Chinese food or Italian food?
12. (spicy) Indian food or Thai food?

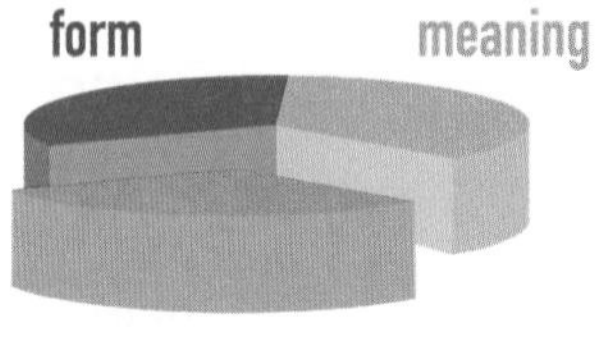

FOCUS 3 Expressing Similarities and Differences with *As . . . As*

EXAMPLES	EXPLANATIONS
(a) Mark is **as tall as** Sam. (b) Tokyo is **as crowded as** Seoul.	To say two things are equal or the same, use *as* + adjective + *as*.
(c) Mark **isn't as tall as** Steve. (= Steve is taller than Mark.) (d) A walkman **isn't as expensive as** an MP3 player.	To say there is a difference between two things, use *not as* + adjective + *as*.

EXERCISE 8

Read the conversation between Tommy and his mother about the choice between a car and a motorcycle. Write the correct form of the comparative in the blanks. Use *-er, more than, less than,* and *as . . . as.*

Mother: Tommy, I don't want you to buy a motorcycle. Why don't you buy a car instead? A car is (1) __more convenient than__ (convenient) a motorcycle, and it's (2) ______________ (practical), too.

Tommy: Maybe it is, Mom, but a car isn't (3) ______________ (economical) a motorcycle. I can get 50 miles to a gallon with a motorcycle! And a motorcycle's (4) ______________ (cheap) a car.

Mother: Listen to me. You live in a big city. There are a lot of crazy people out there on the streets. A car is (5) ______________ (safe) a motorcycle.

Tommy: Mom, I'm a good driver. I'm (6) ______________ (good) you are! Besides that, it's (7) ______________ (easy) to park a motorcycle in the city than it is to park a car.

Mother: Well, you're right about that.

Tommy: And all my friends are getting motorcycles, Mom. I won't look (8) ______________ (cool) my friends.

Mother: I don't care, Tommy. Maybe their mothers aren't (9) ______________ (nervous) I am. Let me think about it . . .

Tommy: Well, don't think about it too much, Mom . . . I'm already 35!!

EXERCISE 9

Work with a partner. You are selling Product #1, and your partner is selling Product #2. Make comparative statements using *–er, more than, less than,* and *as…as.* Try to make the most convincing advertisement!

Example: You: *Headstrong Headache Relief is* ***stronger than*** *Mogain Headache Relief.*
Your partner: *Headstrong Headache Relief is* ***not as strong as*** *Mogain Headache Relief.*

ADJECTIVES	PRODUCT 1	PRODUCT 2
1. effective stronger expensive fast-acting long-lasting	HEADSTRONG Headache Relief is …	MOGAIN Headache Relief is …
2. economical clean safe for the environment expensive fast	A hybrid car is …	A gasoline-powered car is…
3. soft clean shiny natural-looking beautiful	SHIMMER Shampoo will leave your hair …	GLIMMER Shampoo will …
4. white bright clean healthy fresh	With SWISH toothpaste, your teeth will be …	With SWIRL toothpaste, . . .

EXERCISE 10

Look at the idiomatic expressions with comparisons. Then complete the sentences with one of the expressions below.

1. as snug as a bug in a rug.

2. as cool as a cucumber!

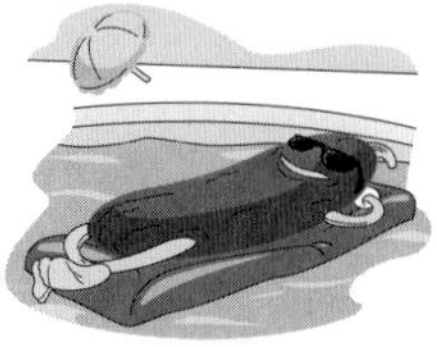

3. as busy as a bee!

4. as strong as an ox

5. as light as a feather

1. Look at that baby sleeping in his stroller. He's ____.
2. How can you carry those heavy books to school every day? Don't worry. I'm ____.
3. I'm sorry, John. I won't be able to have lunch with you today. I have so much to do. I'm ____.
4. **Liz:** I think I need to go on a diet, Karen. I'm gaining weight.
   Karen: Are you crazy? You're ____!!!
5. I really admire our new boss. She always stays calm under stress. She's ____.

FOCUS 4 Making Polite Comparisons

use

EXAMPLES	EXPLANATIONS
(a) Hamid is **shorter than** Marco. (b) Hamid is **not as tall as** Marco.	Sentence (b) is more polite. To make a polite comparison, use *not as* + adjective + *as*.

EXERCISE 11

Work in pairs. One student is "Blunt Betty." This person's statements are very direct and a little impolite. Read a statement from Column A. The other student, "Polite Polly," makes a statement with the same meaning, using *not as* + adjective + *as* to make the first statement more polite.

Column A: Blunt Betty	Column B: Polite Polly
1. Marco is fatter than Jonathan	(thin) *Marco is not as thin as Jonathan.*
2. Tom's watch is cheaper than Ray's.	(expensive)
3. Your handwriting is sloppier than mine.	(neat)
4. Henry's computer skills are worse than Jack's.	(good)
5. American coffee is weaker than Turkish coffee.	(strong)
6. Amy's neighborhood is more dangerous than Sarah's.	(safe)
7. Your apartment is smaller than ours.	(spacious)
8. Chris is sadder than his brother.	(happy)
9. Your child is lazier than mine.	(ambitious)
10. He is older than I am.	(young)

EXERCISE 12

Make true statements about yourself. Use each of the categories below. Add more categories of your own.

Examples: *My partner's older than I am. My partner's older than me.*
I'm not as old as he is. I'm not as old as him.

Categories	Me	My Partner
1. Age	19	24
2. Height	______	______
3. Hair length	______	______
4. Hair color	______	______
5. Personality	______	______
6. Other	______	______

EXERCISE 13

Correct the errors in the following sentences.

1. John is more tall than Mary.
2. Seoul is more safer than Los Angeles.
3. Paul is as intelligent than Robert.
4. Mary is not beautiful as Kim.
5. My test scores were more worse than Margaret's.
6. Lorraine's eyes are darker than me.
7. Jeff is more handsomer than Jack.
8. My parents' life was hard than mine.
9. Is New York exciting as Paris?
10. Is Lake Ontario cleaner that Lake Erie?
11. The Hudson River is not polluted as the Volga River.
12. Mexico's capital city is more crowded than the United States.
13. My typing skills are faster than her.

Use Your English

ACTIVITY 1 speaking

How much do the following things cost in your country? In your notebook write the cost in U.S. dollars for each thing in your country. Ask a partner the prices of the same things in his or her country. Add three items of your own. Present your comparisons to the class. Example: *A gallon of gas is more expensive in Malaysia than in Indonesia.*

a gallon* of gas	a pair of jeans	rent for a one-bedroom apartment
a movie ticket	a cup of coffee	
a CD	cell phone service	

* one gallon = about 4 liters

ACTIVITY 2 writing/speaking

Work in a group. Write six statements comparing cities, countries, or other places in the world. Make three statements that are true and three statements that are false. Read the statements to the class. The class decides if they are true or false.

Examples: *Canada is larger than the People's Republic of China.* (False)
The Pacific Ocean is bigger than the Atlantic Ocean. (True)

ACTIVITY 3 writing/speaking

Work with a partner. Find a product or service you want to sell. Create a name for it. Then create a print ad or a 30-second radio or TV commercial for the product or service. Present your ads or commercials to the class.

ACTIVITY 4 research on the web

Search the Internet for the meaning of five of the idiomatic expressions listed below. Use a search engine such as Google® or Yahoo® or Ask® and enter the keywords: *meaning* and *phrase* plus the idiomatic expression. Find a picture on the Internet, or draw one to illustrate it.

Example: keywords: *"as cute as a button" meaning phrase*
Hint: Put idioms between quotation marks to search.

1. as cute as a button
2. as clean as a whistle
3. as easy as pie
4. as solid as a rock
5. as happy as a clam
6. as clear as day
7. as sick as a dog
8. as proud as a peacock
9. as fresh as a daisy
10. as good as gold

ACTIVITY 5 listening/speaking

STEP 1 Shelly is trying to decide what kind of computer to buy. Listen to her conversation with her friend Anna. List the advantages and disadvantages for the laptop and the desktop computers.

CD Track 21

	ADVANTAGES	DISADVANTAGES
LAPTOP 	more practical	harder to use
DESKTOP 		

STEP 2 Work with a partner. Discuss which computer Shelly finally decides to buy and why? Do you agree with her?

UNIT

23 COMPARISON USING ADVERBS

UNIT GOALS

- Use the (regular and irregular) comparative form of adverbs in statements
- Express similarities and differences with adverbs using *as . . . as*
- Ask questions with *how*

OPENING TASK

Differences Between Men and Women

Work in groups of three. Do men and women behave differently? Make a statement comparing men and women for each behavior below.

1. behave aggressively
____
2. drive safely
____
3. take risks confidently
____
4. work hard
____
5. teach children patiently
____
6. express their feelings openly
____
7. learn math easily
____
8. spend money freely
____
9. solve problems well
____
10. think clearly in emergencies
____

Talk about your answers with your classmates.

FOCUS 1 Comparative Forms of Adverbs

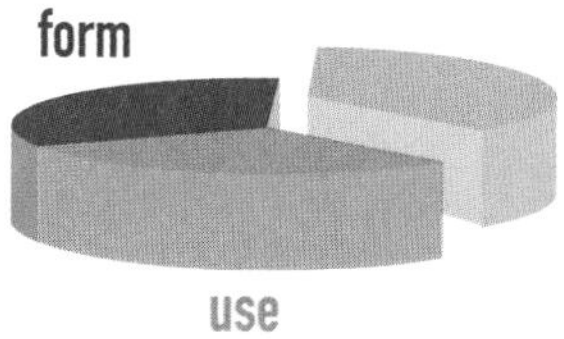

EXAMPLE	ADVERB	COMPARATIVE	RULE
(a) Women live **longer than** men.	*long*	*longer than*	For short adverbs, add *-er* + *than.*
(b) Do women drive **more safely than** men?	*safely*	*more/less safely than*	For adverbs with two or more syllables, use *more/less* + adverb + *than.*
(c) Do men drive **less carefully than** women?	*carefully*	*more/less carefully than*	
(d) Men eat out much **more often than** women.	*often*	*more/less often than*	With adverbs of frequency, use *more/less* + adverb + *than.*
(e) Do women cook **better than** men?	*well*	*better than*	With irregular adverbs, use the irregular form + *than.*
(f) Do boys do **worse** in school **than** girls?	*badly*	*worse than*	
(g) Can a man throw a ball **farther than** a woman can?	*far*	*farther than*	

EXAMPLES	EXPLANATIONS
(h) Jason can climb higher than his sister **can.** (i) She's better in school than I **am.**	Sometimes, the auxiliary verb, for example *can* or *will*, follows the subject after *than.* *Be* can also follow the Subject after *than.*
(j) I type faster than my friend **does.** (k) We speak Spanish better than they **do.**	If there is no *be* or auxiliary verb, you can use *do.*
(l) I type faster than she **does.** (m) I type faster than **her.**	In formal English speech and writing, the subject pronoun follows *than.* In informal English speech, the object pronoun (*me, you, him, her, us, them*) sometimes follows *than.*

EXERCISE 1

Write statements comparing men and women for each behavior below.

Example: run fast

Men run faster than women (do).

1. take care of elderly parents compassionately

______

2. play games competitively

______

3. drive aggressively

______

4. make friends easily

______

5. say "I love you" willingly

______

EXERCISE 2

Work with a partner of the opposite sex, if possible. Write statements comparing yourself with your partner. Use the verbs and adverbs in the chart. Compare your answers with your classmates' answers. Do the men and women in your class behave differently?

VERB	ADVERB	COMPARISONS
1. cry	easily	My partner cries more easily than I (do).
2. listen to others	carefully	
3. watch sports on TV	frequently	
4. exercise	regularly	
5. ask for directions	willingly	
6. study	hard	
7. talk	freely	
8. participate in class	actively	
9. cook	well	
10. read maps	accurately	

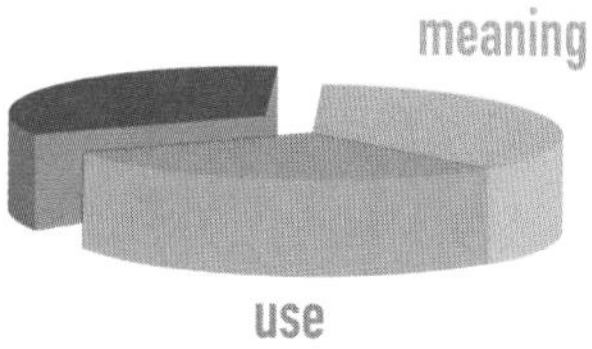

FOCUS 2 Expressing Similarities and Differences with *As . . . As*

EXAMPLES	EXPLANATIONS
(a) A woman can work **as hard as** a man. (b) A man can dance **as gracefully as** a woman.	To show similarities, use *as* + adverb + *as*.
(c) He doesn't speak **as clearly as** I (do). (d) = I speak more clearly than he (does). (e) = He speaks less clearly than I (do).	To show differences, use *not as* + adverb + *as*. Remember that (c) is more polite, more tactful than (d) or (e). (See Focus 4 in Unit 22 on page 374.)

EXERCISE 3

Sally Miller and Bill Benson are applying for a job as director of an art company. Decide who is better for the job. Make comparative statements about each person.

Examples: *Sally works as hard as Bill.*
Bill draws better than Sally. / Sally doesn't draw as well as Bill.

WORK HABITS	SALLY MILLER	BILL BENSON
1. works hard	✔	✔
2. draws well		✔
3. thinks creatively	✔	✔
4. communicates openly	✔	
5. plans carefully		✔
6. works well with others	✔	✔
7. treats the staff fairly	✔	
8. solves problems successfully		✔
9. deals with clients tactfully	✔	✔
10. works efficiently		✔

EXERCISE 4

Imagine you are the president of the art company. You want to compare Sally and Bill. Write some questions to ask about their abilities.

Examples: *Does Sally work as hard as Bill?*
Does Bill draw better than Sally?

EXERCISE 5

Discuss these questions before you read.

1. Do you think boys and girls grow up differently?
   In what ways do they grow up differently?
2. Do you think boys and girls talk to each other differently?
3. Do you think boys and girls play differently? In what ways?

Now, read the following:

Boys and girls grow up in different worlds. Research studies show that boys and girls act very differently. For example, when children play, boys don't play with girls, and girls don't play with boys. Some of their activities are similar, but their favorite games are different. Also, the language they use in games is different.

Boys usually play outside in large groups. The group has a leader. The leader gives orders. There are winners and losers in boys' games. Boys frequently brag about how good they are at something and argue about who is the best.

Girls, on the other hand, play in small groups or pairs. The most important thing for a girl is her best friend. Closeness is very important to girls. Girls like to sit together and talk. In their games, like jump rope, everyone gets a turn. In many of their activities, such as playing together with their dolls, there are no winners or losers. Girls don't brag about how good they are at something. They don't give orders. They usually make suggestions.

Does this text match your answers to the three questions above? What information is the same? What information is different?

EXERCISE 6

To test your understanding of the reading, check *True* or *False* for the statements below.

	TRUE	FALSE
1. Boys and girls play differently.		
2. Boys and girls play together.		
3. Girls act more aggressively than boys.		
4. Girls play more competitively than boys do.		
5. Boys brag about how good they are at something more frequently than girls.		
6. Girls talk to each other more intimately than boys do.		
7. Girls give suggestions more readily than boys.		
8. Boys play more cooperatively than girls do.		
9. Girls play more fairly in their games than boys.		
10. Girls and boys speak to each other differently.		

EXERCISE 7

Read each statement aloud. For each statement you read, your partner says how he or she is similar or different.

Example: You: *I (can) cook well.*
Your partner: *I can cook as well as you.*
I can't cook as well as you.
I can cook better than you.

1. speak clearly
2. dance gracefully
3. sing sweetly
4. jump high
5. run far
6. add numbers quickly
7. meet new people easily
8. tell a joke well
9. study hard
10. learn English independently

EXERCISE 8

Write statements comparing men and women. Use *more/less/as . . . as*. Add two statements of your own. Then discuss your answers with the class. The first one has been done for you.

1. think creatively

   Men think less creatively than women.

   Women think as creatively as men (do).

2. run fast

   ____

   ____

3. behave responsibly

   ____

   ____

4. grow up quickly

   ____

   ____

5. ask for directions willingly

   ____

   ____

6. listen supportively

   ____

   ____

7. act independently

   ____

   ____

8. think logically

   ____

   ____

9. make friends easily

   ____

   ____

10. take care of their parents better

    ____

    ____

11. ______________________________

    ____

12. ______________________________

    ____

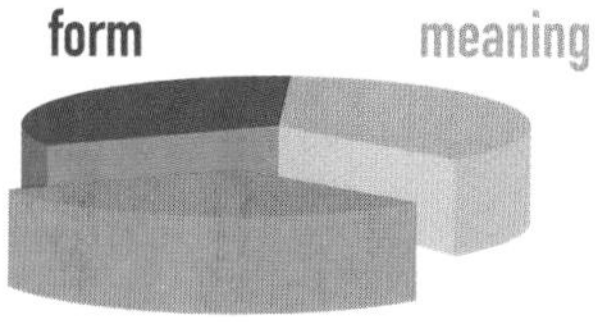

FOCUS 3 Questions with *How*

EXAMPLES	EXPLANATIONS
(a) **How old** are you? (b) **How well** do you speak English?	An adjective (*old, tall*) or an adverb (*well, far*) is often used in a *how* question.
(c) **How far** is it from here to the park? It's about five blocks.	*How far* asks about distance.
(d) **How long does it take** to fly from New York to Saigon? It takes about twenty-four hours. (e) **How long does it take** you to prepare dinner? It takes me an hour.	*How long does it take* asks about time.

EXERCISE 9

Ask a partner questions with *how*. Fill in your partner's answers on the right. Your partner asks you the same questions, and fills in your answers on the left.

Examples: *How far do you live from school?*
How well can you cook?

	YOU	YOUR PARTNER
1. how far/live from school	5 miles	4 blocks
2. how well/cook	very well	very well
3. how easily/fall asleep at night		
4. how far/run		
5. how hard/study		
6. how fast/type		
7. how late/stay up at night		
8. how early/get up in the morning		
9. how well/know your classmates		
10. how often/speak to your best friend		

EXERCISE 10

Compare yourself with your partner for each of the questions in Exercise 9.

1. I live farther away from school than my partner (does).
2. My partner cooks as well as I (do).
3. ______________________________.
4. ______________________________.
5. ______________________________.
6. ______________________________.
7. ______________________________.
8. ______________________________.
9. ______________________________.
10. ______________________________.

EXERCISE 11

Fill in the chart. Say how much time it takes you to do each of the activities below. Then interview a partner. Say how long it takes you both to do these activities.

Examples: *It takes me longer to do my homework.*
I get dressed faster than you (do) in the morning.

	YOU	YOUR PARTNER
1. do your homework	1 hour	45 minutes
2. get dressed in the morning		
3. get to school		
4. clean your room/apartment/house		
5. have breakfast		
6. take a shower		
7. cook dinner		
8. fall asleep at night		
9. read your e-mail every day		

Use Your English

ACTIVITY 1 writing

Write statements comparing two cities or places that you know. Add two sentences of your own.

Example: *The trains run more smoothly in Montreal than in New York.*

1. trains/run smoothly
2. buses/run efficiently
3. people/work hard
4. taxi drivers/drive recklessly
5. traffic/move slowly
6. people/talk fast
7. people/talk to foreigners readily
8. stores/stay open late
9. people/drive fast
10. families/take vacations frequently

ACTIVITY 2 writing

Compare yourself with someone you know—a family member, a friend, your boyfriend/girlfriend, etc. Write a paragraph with a topic sentence.

Example: *I am more emotional than my best friend. I cry more easily than she does. . . .*

ACTIVITY 3 speaking/miming

STEP 1 Here is a list of adverbs and a list of actions. Write each adverb and each action on a separate card.

Adverbs	Actions
slowly	eat spaghetti
sadly	put on your clothes
nervously	make the bed
angrily	cook dinner
fast	write an e-mail
carefully	brush your teeth
seriously	comb your hair
happily	paint a picture
secretly	play tennis
enthusiastically	shake someone's hand
shyly	do exercise

STEP 2 Mix up each group of cards separately. With a partner, take one adverb card and one action card.

STEP 3 Both of you mime the same action and adverb. The class guesses the action and the adverb.

STEP 4 The class compares your two performances.

Example: angrily/eat spaghetti
Paola ate spaghetti more angrily than Maria.

ACTIVITY 4 speaking

Planning a Vacation

Here is a map of the southwestern United States. You and your friend want to take a two-week vacation to visit four national parks. You will start and end your trip in Las Vegas, Nevada.

Approximate Mileage Between National Parks and Las Vegas

	LAS VEGAS	BRYCE CANYON	DEATH VALLEY	GRAND CANYON	ZION NATIONAL PARK
Las Vegas	______	245	130	275	145
Bryce Canyon	(245)	______	365	300	100
Death Valley	130	365	______	405	275
Grand Canyon	275	300	405	______	250
Zion National Park	145	100	275	250	______

STEP 1 Use the map and the mileage chart. Ask each other questions to find out the distances between parks. Fill in the information in the chart below. **Example:** *How far is it from Las Vegas to Death Valley? It's 130 miles.*

DEPART FROM LAS VEGAS	DISTANCE	TIME
Stop 1: Death Valley	130 miles	2 hours
Stop 2: Zion National Park		
Stop 3: Bryce Canyon		
Stop 4: Grand Canyon		

STEP 2 Calculate the time required to go from one place to another, and fill in the information in the chart. Remember you will travel by car, and the average speed limit is 65 miles per hour. All distances are in miles. Take turns asking and answering questions about travel time.

Example: *How long does it take to get from Las Vegas to Death Valley? It takes about two hours.*

ACTIVITY 5 listening/speaking

CD Track 22

STEP 1 Imagine that you have a problem. Do you want to discuss your problem with a male or a female friend? Work in groups of three. Give reasons for your choice.

STEP 2 Listen to the conversation. Take notes on Iris and Josh's ideas about male and female friends.

STEP 3 Do a survey. Ask the question in Step 1 to four people outside of class and write down their answers. In class, compare all the answers you collected. Is there a difference between male and female friends when you have a problem?

ACTIVITY 6 reflection

Self-Assessment

Write statements comparing your language behavior now to your language behavior at the beginning of this course.

BEHAVIOR	COMPARATIVE STATEMENTS
use a dictionary frequently	
read slowly	
express my ideas simply	
make friends quickly	
participate actively in conversations	
express my personality easily	
speak confidently	
respond to others nervously	
read and write regularly	
ask questions timidly	
understand others well	
use the language comfortably	

UNIT 24

COMPARISON USING SUPERLATIVES

UNIT GOALS

- Understand the meaning of superlatives
- Know how to form regular and irregular superlatives
- Express facts and opinions using the expression *one of the* + superlative + plural noun

OPENING TASK

Geo-Quiz

STEP 1

Check your knowledge of geography. Circle the correct answer. Then work with a partner and compare your answers.

1. Which is the largest ocean?
   a. Pacific b. Atlantic c. Indian
2. Which is the highest mountain in the world?
   a. Everest b. K2 c. Kangchenjunga
3. Which is the most widely spoken language in the world?
   a. English b. Hindi c. Chinese
4. Which is the hottest place in the world?
   a. Australia b. Israel c. Ethiopia
5. Which is the tallest office building in the world?
   a. the Sears Tower (Chicago, U.S.A.) b. the Taipei 101 (Taipei, Taiwan)
   c. the Petronas Tower (Kuala Lumpur, Malaysia)
6. Which is the biggest island in the world?
   a. Greenland b. New Guinea c. Borneo
7. Which is the longest river in the world?
   a. Amazon b. Yangtze c. Nile
8. Which is the wettest place in the world?
   a. Hawaii b. India c. Jamaica
9. Which is the most populated city in the United States?
   a. Los Angeles b. Chicago c. New York City
10. Which is the smallest state in the United States?
    a. Connecticut b. Delaware c. Rhode Island

STEP 2

Now write three similar questions. Quiz your classmates.

11. ______________________________
12. ______________________________
13. ______________________________

FOCUS 1 Superlative

form meaning

EXAMPLES	EXPLANATIONS
(a) **The tallest** building in the world is the Taipei 101 in Taiwan. (b) Rosa sings **the most beautifully** of all. (c) **The least expensive** food on the menu is a hamburger.	Superlatives compare one thing or person to all the others in a group. **Least** is the opposite of **most.**
(d) Dr. Diaz is the most respected teacher **at the school.** (e) George Washington University is the most expensive university **in the United States.** (f) Diane cooks the best **of all the chefs.**	Use prepositional phrases after superlatives to identify the group.

EXERCISE 1

Go back to the Opening Task on page 393. Underline all the superlative forms in the questions.

Example: *Which is the largest ocean?*

form

FOCUS 2 Regular and Irregular Superlative Forms

Regular Forms

EXAMPLES	ADJECTIVE	ADVERB	SUPERLATIVE FORM	RULE
(a) The Sears Tower in Chicago is **the tallest** building in the United States.	*tall*		*the tallest*	One-syllable adjectives or adverbs: *the* + adjective/adverb + *-est*
(b) My grandfather worked **the hardest** of his three brothers.		*hard*	*the hardest*	
(c) Jupiter is **the largest** planet.	*large*		*the largest*	One-syllable adjectives or adverbs ending in *-e:* add *-st.*
(d) I get up **the latest** in my family		*late*	*the latest*	
(e) **The hottest** place in the world is Ethiopia.	*hot*		*the hottest*	One-syllable adjectives ending in consonant-vowel-consonant: double the final consonant, add *-est.*
(f) **The easiest** subject for me is geography.	*easy*		*the easiest*	Two-syllable adjectives or adverbs ending in *-y:* change *-y* to *-i;* add *-est.*
(g) She arrived **the earliest.**		*early*	*the earliest*	
(h) **The most nutritious** fruit is the avocado.	*nutritious*		*the most nutritious*	Adjectives or adverbs with two or more syllables: use *the* + *most/least.*
(i) **The least expensive** food on the menu is a hamburger.	*expensive*		*the least expensive*	
(j) Of all his friends, he drives **the most carefully.**		*carefully*	*the most carefully*	
(k) She danced **the least gracefully** of all the students.		*gracefully*	*the least gracefully*	

Common Irregular Forms

ADJECTIVE	SUPERLATIVE	ADVERB	SUPERLATIVE
He is a **good** dancer.	He is **the best** dancer of the group.	He dances **well.**	He dances **the best** of all.
That was a **bad** movie.	That was **the worst** movie I saw last year.	She acts **badly.**	She acts **the worst** of all the actors.
The station is **far.**	That station is **the farthest.**	He ran **far.**	He ran **the farthest.**

EXERCISE 2

Here are some interesting facts from the *Guinness Book of World Records.* Write the superlative form of the adjective in parentheses in the blanks.

Example: (cold) Antarctica is ___the coldest___ place on earth.

1. ________________ (large) pizza was 122 feet and 8 inches and was made in South Africa in 1990.
2. ________________ (successful) pop group of all time was the Beatles.
3. ________________ (heavy) baby at birth was a boy of 22 pounds, 8 ounces. He was born in Italy in 1955.
4. ________________ (fat) person was a man in Seattle. He weighed almost 1,400 pounds.
5. ________________ (productive) painter was Pablo Picasso. He produced about 13,500 paintings, 100,000 prints, 34,000 book illustrations, and 300 sculptures.
6. ________________ (long) attack of hiccups lasted sixty-eight years.
7. ________________ (big) omelet was made of 160,000 eggs in Yokohama, Japan, in 1994.
8. ________________ (hot) city in the United States is Key West, Florida.
9. ________________ (active) volcano in the world is Kilauea, on Hawaii.
10. ________________ (old) man in the world was from Japan. He was 120 years and 237 days old.

EXERCISE 3

Information Gap. Work with a partner. One person looks at Chart A below, and the other person looks at Chart B on page A-21. Ask your partner questions to find out the missing information in your chart. Write the answers in the chart.

Example: **Student A:** *What is the longest river in North America?*
Student B: *The Mississippi.*

Chart A

	NORTH AMERICA	SOUTH AMERICA	ASIA	EUROPE	AFRICA	THE WORLD
long river		The Amazon		The Volga		The Nile
large country	Canada		The People's Republic of China		Sudan	
populated country		Brazil		Russia		The People's Republic of China
high mountain	Mt. McKinley		Mt. Everest		Mt. Kilimanjaro	
small country		Suriname		Vatican City		Vatican City

EXERCISE 4

Express your own opinion. Fill in the name of a student in your class and the superlative form of each adverb.

	Name		Adverb	Superlative
1.	Juan	does his homework	(carefully)	the most carefully.
2.	____________	writes	(well)	____________.
3.	____________	arrives in class	(early)	____________.
4.	____________	guesses new words	(fast)	____________.
5.	____________	makes us laugh	(often)	____________.
6.	____________	expresses opinions	(open)	____________.
7.	____________	communicates in English	(effectively)	____________.
8.	____________	participates in class	(actively)	____________.
9.	____________	raises his/her hand	(frequently)	____________.
10.	____________	works	(hard)	____________.

Add two statements of your own.

11. ____.

12. ____.

EXERCISE 5

Play this game in two teams. Look at the game board on the next page. Choose one student from each team to come to the front of the room and act as questioner. Team 1 chooses a category and a dollar amount. The questioner from the other team asks the question with the superlative. Team 1 has one minute to choose an answer from the Answer Box. If the answer is correct, they "win" the money. If the answer is not correct, Team 2 answers the question and wins the money. The team with the most money at the end wins.

Example: Team 1: *"Animals" for $20.*
Reader: *dangerous animal: "What is the most dangerous animal?"*
Team 1: *The most dangerous animal is the mosquito.* (Some mosquitoes carry malaria and other diseases that kill many people each year.)

Gameboard

AWARD	PLANETS	ANIMALS	OTHER
$10			
$20			
$30			
$40			
$50			

Categories

Planets
$10 large planet/in the solar system?
$20 hot planet/in the solar system?
$30 close planet/to the Sun?
$40 light planet/in the solar system?
$50 close planet/to Earth?

Animals
$10 tall animal?
$20 dangerous animal?
$30 fast land animal?
$40 valuable animal?
$50 large and heavy animal?

Other
$10 cold place/on Earth?
$20 large desert/in the world?
$30 high court/in the United States?
$40 old mountain range/in the world?
$50 short day/of the year?

Answer Box (Choose the answers to the questions from this box.)

PLANETS	ANIMALS	OTHER
Neptune	the mosquito	the Supreme Court
Mercury	the blue whale	the Sahara
Venus	giraffe	the winter solstice (first day of winter)
Jupiter	cheetah	Antarctica
Saturn	race horse	the Urals

FOCUS 3 *One of the* + Superlative + Plural Noun

EXAMPLES	EXPLANATION
(a) Bach was one of the greatest composers of all time. (There are several composers we think of as the greatest composers of all time. Bach is one of them.)	***One of the*** **+ superlative + plural noun** • is common with the superlative form • means that there are several people or things in a group we see as the best or worst. The people or things we are talking about are part of this group.
(b) Tim is one of the least popular students in the school. (There are several students we think of as the least popular students in the school. Tim is one of them.)	

EXERCISE 6

Fill in the blanks with *one of the* + superlative + plural noun. Use the words in parentheses. Then check *Fact* or *Opinion* for each statement.

Example: A Rolls Royce is <u>one of the most expensive cars</u> you can buy. (expensive car)

FACT **OPINION**

1. Ice hockey is ________________ you can play. (exciting sport)

2. Graduation was ________________ of my life. (proud moment)

FACT OPINION

3. The Four Seasons is ________________ in the United States. (expensive hotel)

4. Drinking and driving is ________________ you can do. (bad thing)

5. The Guggenheim in Bilbao, Spain, is ________________ in the world. (good museum)

6. Dr. Jones is ________________ in the hospital. (fine doctor)

7. Louis Armstrong was ________________ in America. (great jazz musicians)

FACT OPINION

8. This is ________________ in the museum. (beautiful sculpture)

9. The tsunami in Asia in 2004 was ________________ in history. (tragic natural disaster)

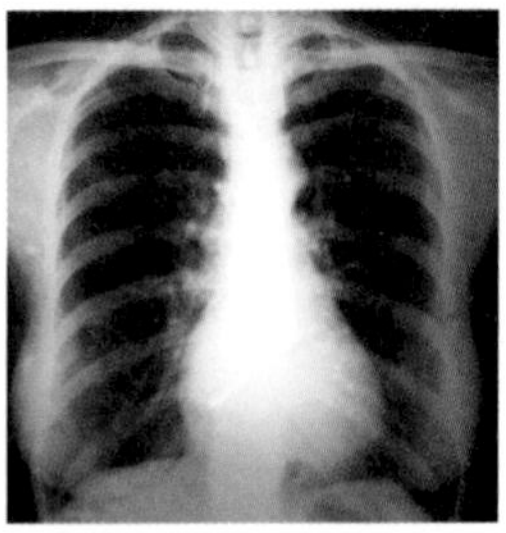

10. Heart disease is ________________ in the United States. (high cause of death)

EXERCISE 7

Make statements with *one of the* + superlative + plural noun. Compare your opinions with your classmates' opinions.

Example: 1. *Prague is one of the most beautiful cities in the world.*

1. a beautiful city in the world
2. an interesting place (in the place you are living in)
3. a good restaurant (in the place you are in)
4. a famous leader in the world today
5. a deadly disease of our time
6. a serious problem in the world
7. a popular food (in the country you come from)
8. a funny show on television
9. a difficult language to learn
10. a dangerous career
11. a useful electronic device
12. an expensive city in the world

Use Your English

ACTIVITY 1 writing/speaking

Write ten questions to ask another student in the class about his or her home country or a country he or she knows. Use the superlative form of the words below, or add your own to the chart.

Examples: *What's the most crowded city in your country?*
What's the most popular sport in your country?
What's the most unusual food in your city?
Who's the most famous person in your country?

crowded city	popular sport	common food	hot month	important holiday
polluted city	expensive sport	unusual food	big problem	highly paid job
beautiful city	big city	popular music	famous person	popular vacation spot

ACTIVITY 2 speaking

In groups, discuss the following opinions. Tell your group if you agree or disagree and explain why.

1. Money is the most important thing in life.
2. AIDS is the worst disease in the world today.
3. English is the most difficult language to learn.
4. Poverty is the biggest problem in the world today.
5. Democracy is the best form of government.

ACTIVITY 3 speaking

Interview a partner about his or her life experience. Use the adjectives below to write questions with superlatives. Tell the class about the most interesting things you learned about your partner.

Examples: *What was the best experience you had this year?*
What was the most embarrassing moment in your life?

unusual	sad	exciting
embarrassing	interesting	frightening
happy	dangerous	beautiful
funny	good	bad

ACTIVITY 4 research on the web

Many of the facts in this unit are from the *Guinness Book of World Records.* Go to a search engine such as Google® or Yahoo® or Ask®, and enter the keywords: *Guinness Book of World Records*. Find five facts that have superlatives, such as the oldest person or the highest mountain on earth, and write them in your notebook. Compare your facts with those of other students in the class. Choose the most interesting or the most unusual facts.

ACTIVITY 5 writing

Write a paragraph on one of the topics below:

a. The most embarrassing moment in my life.

b. The most frightening moment in my life.

c. The funniest moment in my life.

ACTIVITY 6 listening/speaking

CD Track 23

STEP 1 Listen to the quiz show. Circle the letter of the correct answer.

Quiz Choices:

1. a. North America	b. Asia	c. Africa
2. a. the elephant	b. the turtle	c. the bear
3. a. banana	b. avocado	c. orange
4. a. Chinese	b. French	c. English
5. a. North America	b. Asia	c. Antarctica
6. a. The United States	b. China	c. Canada
7. a. ruby	b. diamond	c. emerald
8. a. The Himalayas	b. The Andes	c. The Rockies
9. a. Spain	b. The United States	c. Italy
10. a. Van Gogh's *Sunflowers*	b. Leonardo da Vinci's *Mona Lisa*	c. Rembrandt's *Self Portrait*

STEP 2 Discuss your answers with your classmates.

ACTIVITY 7 reflection

STEP 1 What is the most challenging skill for you in English? Circle one answer and explain why. Write your explanation on the line below.

a. Listening b. Speaking c. Reading d. Writing

____

STEP 2 Read the list of language learning strategies for the **one** language skill you said was the most challenging for you. Rate how frequently you use these strategies. Then talk to a partner. Compare the strategies you use for the skills you chose. Give each other advice about how to be a better language learner.

LISTENING	NEVER	SOMETIMES	FREQUENTLY	THE MOST FREQUENTLY
Use my own knowledge to understand meaning				
Hear words and sentences clearly				
Make predictions				
Guess meaning in context				
Get the global meaning first				
Check my comprehension while listening				
Listen more than once				
Ask the speaker questions				
Don't worry if you don't understand every word				
SPEAKING	**NEVER**	**SOMETIMES**	**FREQUENTLY**	**THE MOST FREQUENTLY**
Use words from my native language				
Rehearse what I want to say before speaking				
Listen and try to imitate correct English pronunciation				
Think about grammar when speaking				
Try my best to express my meaning				
Use body language				
Ask others for help				
Don't worry about making errors				
Learn expressions, idioms, routines for conversation				

READING	NEVER	SOMETIMES	FREQUENTLY	THE MOST FREQUENTLY
Use my own knowledge to understand meaning				
Look at the text to get the global meaning first				
Think of questions I want the text to answer				
Guess meaning in context				
Use a dictionary				
Make predictions				
Check my comprehension while reading				
Re-read when necessary				
Don't worry if you don't understand every word				
WRITING	**NEVER**	**SOMETIMES**	**FREQUENTLY**	**THE MOST FREQUENTLY**
Take time to think and get ideas for writing first				
Think about who will read my writing				
Understand how writers organize their thinking				
Read a lot				
Try my best to express my meaning				
Be ready to revise / re-write				
Learn to check my writing				
Learn useful phrases for connecting ideas				
Ask others for help				

UNIT 25

FACTUAL CONDITIONALS

If

UNIT GOALS

- Use factual conditionals to express relationships that are always true and never change
- Use factual conditionals to express relationships based on habit
- Understand the order of clauses in factual conditionals

OPENING TASK

Test Your Knowledge of Science: What do you know about water?

STEP 1

Work in groups of three. Complete each statement with a scientifically correct answer.

1. If you heat water to 212°F, it ______________________________
2. If you cool water to 32°F, it ______________________________
3. When you boil water, it ______________________________
4. When water freezes, it ______________________________
5. When you put an ice cube in a glass of water, the ice cube ______________
6. When you add sugar to water, the sugar ______________________
7. Water boils faster when you ______________________________
8. You cannot survive if you ______________________________

STEP 2

Reread each statement in Step 1, and choose the correct answer from below.

a. don't have water
b. expands (gets bigger)
c. freezes
d. dissolves
e. boils
f. turns into a gas
g. floats
h. are at a high altitude (height above sea level)

How many did you answer correctly?

form meaning

FOCUS 1 Expressing Relationships That Never Change

Factual conditionals express relationships that are always true and never change. This type of conditional is often used in scientific writing.

EXAMPLES		EXPLANATIONS
Clause 1 (*If* Clause)	**Clause 2 (Main Clause)**	
(a) If you heat water to 212° (degrees) Fahrenheit,	it boils.	Use the simple present in both clauses.* Place a comma after the *if* clause.
(b) If you don't water a house plant,	it dies.	
(c) When (ever) you add sugar to water,	the sugar dissolves.	You can use *when* or *whenever* in place of *if*. Also add a comma after the *when* (*ever*) clause.

* Note: A **clause** is a group of words containing a subject and verb which forms part of a sentence.

EXERCISE 1

Circle the correct medical answer.

Example:

1. If you eat too much salt,
   a. your blood pressure goes down.
   (b.) your blood pressure goes up.

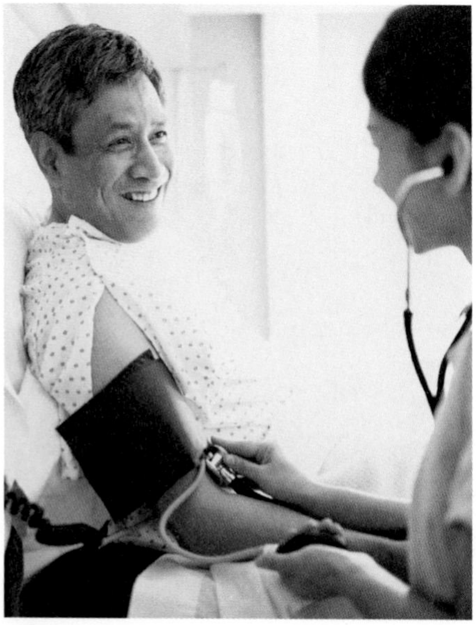

1. If you eat too much,
   a. you lose weight.
   b. you gain weight.
2. If you smoke,
   a. your health suffers.
   b. your health improves.
3. If you stay in the sun a lot,
   a. your skin stays young and smooth.
   b. your skin looks old faster.
4. If you wash your hands often,
   a. you get sick more frequently.
   b. you get sick less frequently.
5. If you brush your teeth every day,
   a. you get cavities.
   b. you prevent cavities.
6. If you don't sleep enough,
   a. you have a lot of energy.
   b. you feel tired.
7. When you get a flu shot,
   a. you protect yourself against the flu.
   b. you get the flu.
8. If you don't exercise regularly,
   a. your muscles become stronger.
   b. your muscles become weaker.
9. If you listen to loud music regularly,
   a. your hearing becomes worse.
   b. your hearing becomes better.
10. When you feel depressed in winter,
    a. bright light makes you sadder.
    b. bright light makes you happier.

EXERCISE 2

Test your knowledge about food and health. Find the *If* clause below that correctly completes each statement. Write the clause in the correct box. Discuss your answers with a partner.

If Clauses

a. If you eat different-colored fruits and vegetables,
b. If you eat small amounts of chocolate,
c. If you eat 3,200 extra calories,
d. If you don't get enough calcium in your diet,
e. When you go on a low-calorie diet,
f. If you eat too much sugar and too many fats and carbohydrates,

1. _______ you gain one pound.
2. _______ you can increase your risk for having diabetes.
3. _______ your bones get weak.
4. _______ your body thinks you are starving; so your body uses up calories more slowly.
5. _______ you can prevent cancer and heart disease.
6. _______ you feel happier and stay healthy.

EXERCISE 3

Proverbs are statements that express basic truths. Read the proverbs below. Discuss the meaning of each proverb with a partner. Then, rewrite each proverb as a factual conditional statement.

Example: The early bird catches the worm. ___If you get up early, you succeed.___

1. Practice makes perfect. ______________________
2. An apple a day keeps the doctor away. ______________________
3. Too many cooks spoil the broth. ______________________
4. Out of sight, out of mind. ______________________
5. Absence makes the heart grow fonder. ______________________
6. Easy come, easy go. ______________________

FOCUS 2 Expressing Relationships Based on Habit

EXAMPLES		EXPLANATIONS
Clause 1 (*If* Clause)	Clause 2 (Main Clause)	
(a) If I **cook**,	my husband **washes** the dishes.	Factual conditionals also express present or past habitual relationships. Habitual conditionals are common in everyday conversation. Use the same tense in both clauses.
(b) If I **lied**,	my mother **punished** me.	
(c) When (ever) it **snowed**,	we **stayed** home from school.	You can use *when* or *whenever* in place of *if*.

EXERCISE 4

Make sentences with *if, when,* or *whenever.* Use the words in bold below or your own words in the main clause. Say your sentences aloud and compare your answers.

Example: you take a vacation every year/feel
If you take a vacation every year, you feel happy and refreshed.

1. you never take a vacation/**feel**
2. you have elderly parents/**worry**
3. you live with a roommate/**share**
4. you don't pay your credit card bill on time/**pay**
5. you exercise regularly/**stay**
6. someone sneezes/**say**
7. you don't want to cook/**eat**
8. you don't own a car/**use**

EXERCISE 5

In some cultures, people say, "If you find a four-leaf clover, you have good luck." We call these kinds of statements "old wives' tales." They are not always true, but people believe them and repeat them. Read the following "old wives' tales," and decide in your group if they are true or not.

1. If you go outside with wet hair, you catch a cold.
2. If your ears are ringing, someone is talking about you.
3. If you eat chicken soup, your cold gets better.
4. If you hold your breath, your hiccups go away.
5. If you eat spinach, you get big and strong.
6. If you break a mirror, you have seven years of bad luck.
7. If children drink coffee, they don't grow tall.
8. If you go swimming right after you eat, you can get cramps and drown.

Now add a few old wives' tales from your home country and tell your group about them.

EXERCISE 6

Complete the *if/whenever* clauses with a statement of your own.

Example: If I feel very tired when I come home, I take a nap for ten minutes.

1. Whenever I can't fall asleep, ____________________.
2. Whenever I get angry, ____________________.
3. If I get a headache, ____________________.
4. If I am late for an appointment, ____________________.
5. If I gain weight, ____________________.
6. If I fail an exam, ____________________.
7. Whenever I have money to spend, ____________________.
8. If I eat too much, ____________________.
9. If I get very worried, ____________________.
10. Whenever I feel blue, ____________________.
11. Whenever I have a day off, ____________________.

    Add two statements of your own:

12. ____________________.
13. ____________________.

EXERCISE 7

Think of the definition for each word in italics. Find the phrase on the right that completes each statement. Say your statements aloud.

1. If you live in a *democracy,* you can	a. want to be independent.
2. If you're *patient,* you don't	b. go to bed late.
3. If you're a *night owl,* you	c. teach in a school or college.
4. If you're a *teenager,* you	d. lose your temper.
5. If you're a *member of the faculty,* you	e. work in a factory.
6. If you're a *pediatrician,* you	f. have any money.
7. If you're a *blue-collar worker,* you may	g. treat sick children.
8. If you're *broke,* you don't	h. vote in elections.
9. If you're a *shopaholic,* you	i. get up early in the morning.
10. If you're *polylingual*, you	j. love to buy things.
11. If you're an *introvert,* you	k. speak more than two languages.
12. If you're an *early bird*, you	l. like to be alone or with a few friends/family members.

EXERCISE 8

Work with a partner. Ask each other questions about your childhood. Then, compare your different childhoods.

Example: told a lie
You: *When you were a child, what happened if you told a lie?*
Your partner: *If I told a lie, my mother yelled at me.*

1. got sick
2. disobeyed your parents
3. did well in school
4. got a bad grade on your report card
5. came home very late
6. had a serious personal problem
7. fought with your brother or sister
8. got into a fight with a classmate
9. had a bad dream

FOCUS 3 Order of Clauses in Factual Conditionals

EXAMPLES	EXPLANATIONS
(a) **If you study hard,** you get good grades.	The *if* clause is usually first.
(b) How do you get an A in this class? You get an A **if you do all the work.**	When the *if* clause contains new information, the *if* clause can be second. When it is second, there is no comma between the two clauses.
(c) How do you get extra credit? You get extra credit **when(ever) you do extra work.**	With *when* or *whenever,* you can also change the order of the clauses.

EXERCISE 9

Answer the questions below.

Example: When do you feel nervous?
I feel nervous if I have many things to do and little time.
I feel nervous whenever I have a test.

1. When do you feel nervous?
2. When do you get a headache?
3. How do you catch a cold?
4. When do you have trouble sleeping?
5. When did your parents punish you?
6. When were your parents pleased with you?
7. When do you get angry?
8. When do you feel excited?
9. How do you know if you're in love?
10. When do you miss home/feel homesick?
11. When do you feel disappointed?

Use Your English

ACTIVITY 1 writing/speaking

Psychologists say there are two personality types: A and B. *Type A* people worry, get nervous, and are under stress all the time. *Type B* people are calm and try to enjoy life.

STEP 1

Which personality type are you? Complete the statements.

1. Whenever there is a change in my life, I . . .
2. If I have a test, I . . .
3. When I get stuck in traffic, I . . .
4. When I enter a room with people I don't know, I . . .
5. When another driver on the road makes a mistake, I . . .
6. If a friend hurts my feelings, I . . .
7. If I don't hear from my family and friends, I . . .
8. When I have a lot of things to do in one day, I . . .
9. When I don't succeed at something, I . . .
10. When someone criticizes me, I . . .

STEP 2

Discuss your results in your group. Decide which students in the group are *Type A* personalities and which are *Type B*. Explain why. Make a chart in your notebook like the one below. Fill it in with your group's information.

NAME	TYPE A PERSONALITY	NAME	TYPE B PERSONALITY
Stefan	If he has a test, he worries a lot.		
	When he doesn't succeed at		
	something, he gets angry		
	at himself.		

ACTIVITY 2 writing/speaking

Do you have any unusual habits or problems eating certain foods? Make a list. Share your list of unusual habits with your group. Try to find the person with the most unusual habits.

Examples: *Whenever I feel anxious, I clean my closets.*
If I eat chocolate, I get a headache.

ACTIVITY 3 writing

Think about your childhood. Write five factual conditional statements about past habits or behaviors in your childhood.

Examples: *If my sister hit me, I hit her back.*
Whenever it snowed, we stayed home from school.

ACTIVITY 4 listening/speaking

About 70 percent of Americans have problems sleeping. Listen to some recommendations from the National Sleep Foundation. As you listen, match each recommendation to a statement with the same meaning.

CD Track 24

Recommendation 1: ______	a. Create a restful place to sleep.
Recommendation 2: ______	b. Go to sleep only when you feel sleepy.
Recommendation 3: ______	c. Cut down on drinks with caffeine.
Recommendation 4: ______	d. Keep regular hours.
Recommendation 5: ______	e. Develop a sleep routine.

ACTIVITY 5 speaking

STEP 1 Work in a group of four. Compare customs in different countries. Write the name of a country in the left column, and complete the main clause for each *if/when(ever)* clause.

Example: *In Italy, when you have dinner in a restaurant, you leave a tip.*

COUNTRY	*IF/WHEN(EVER)* CLAUSE	MAIN CLAUSE
Italy	you have dinner in a restaurant	you leave a tip
	someone gives you a compliment	
	someone gives you a gift	
	you greet an old friend	
	you greet an older person	
	a baby is born	
	someone sneezes	
	someone invites you to dinner	
	you want to refuse someone's invitation	

STEP 2 Add two more customs to the list and make statements about them.

ACTIVITY 6 reflection

Discuss the following with a partner.
What do you do when . . . .

a. **you are reading a text in English and**
   - you don't understand some of the vocabulary?
   - you don't get the main idea?
   - you don't know anything about the topic?

b. **you are having a conversation with someone and**
   - you don't understand what he/she is saying?
   - you can't express what you want to say?
   - he or she doesn't understand you?

c. **you are watching TV or a movie and**
   - you don't understand what someone is saying?

d. **you are speaking to someone and**
   - you don't know the word for something in English?
   - you don't know how to express your idea in English?
   - you are afraid your pronunciation is bad?

e. **you are writing and**
   - you don't have any ideas to write about?
   - you don't have enough vocabulary to write?
   - you don't know how to organize your writing?

ACTIVITY 7 research on the web

Many of our beliefs about food are based on "myths." You can find examples of food "myths" below:

If you eat bread and other carbohydrates, you gain weight.
If you eat eggs and red meat, you have heart problems.
If you eat grapefruit, you burn calories.

STEP 1 Work in groups of three. Use a search engine such as Google® or Ask® or Yahoo®. Type in "the truth about food myths" or "food myths debunked." Find three food myths and read about them. Write each myth in the same type of sentence as the examples above (using Factual Conditionals.) Then explain in writing why they are not true.

STEP 2 Share what you've learned about these three food myths with your classmates.

Appendices

APPENDIX 1 Forming Verb Tenses

Appendix 1A *Be:* Present Tense

I	am	from Japan.
He She It	is	
We You They	are	
There	is	a student from Japan in our class.
There	are	students from all over the world in this class.

Appendix 1B *Be:* Past Tense

I He She It	was	happy.
We You They	were	
There	was	a party yesterday.
There	were	a lot of people there.

Appendix 1C Simple Present

I You We They	work.
He She It	works.

Appendix 1D Present Progressive

I	am	working.
He She It	is	
We You They	are	

Appendix 1E Simple Past

I He She It We You They	worked	yesterday.

Appendix 1F Future Tense with *Will*

I He She It We You They	will work	tomorrow.

Appendix 1G Future Tense with *Be Going To*

I	am	going to work in a few minutes.
He She It	is	
We You They	are	

Appendix 1H *Can/Might/May*

I He She It We You They	can might may	work.

Appendix 1I *Be Able To*

I	am	able to dance.
He She It	is	
We You They	are	

Appendix 2A Plural Nouns

NOUNS	SINGULAR	PLURAL
Regular	book table	books tables
Ends in vowel +*y*	toy	toys
Ends in vowel +*o*	radio	radios
Ends in consonant +*o*	potato tomato	potatoes tomatoes
Ends in consonant +*y*	city	cities
Ends in -*f* or -*fe*	thief wife	thieves wives
(Except)	chief chef	chiefs chefs
Ends in -*ss*, -*ch*, -*sh*, -*x*, or -*z*	class sandwich dish box	classes sandwiches dishes boxes
Irregular plural nouns	man woman child foot tooth mouse	men women children feet teeth mice
Plurals that stay the same	sheep deer fish	sheep deer fish
No singular form		scissors pants shorts pajamas glasses clothes

Appendix 2B Simple Present: Third Person Singular

RULE	EXAMPLE
1. Add *-s* to form the third person singular of most verbs.	My brother **sleeps** 8 hours a night.
2. Add *-es* to verbs ending in *-sh*, *-ch*, *-x*, *-z*, or *-ss*.	She **watches** television every evening.
3. When the verb ends in a consonant *+y*, change the *y* to *i* and add *-es*.	He **hurries** to class every morning.
4. When the verb ends in a vowel *+y*, do not change the *y*. Add *-s*.	My sister **plays** the violin.
5. Irregular Forms:	
have	He **has** a good job.
go	He **goes** to work every day.
do	He **does** the laundry.

Appendix 2C Present Progressive

1. Add *-ing* to the base of the verb.	talk study do agree	talking studying doing agreeing
2. If the verb ends in a single *-e*, drop the *-e* and add *-ing*.	drive	driving
3. If a one-syllable verb has a consonant, a vowel, and a consonant (c-v-c), double the last consonant and add *-ing*.	(c-v-c) sit run	 sitting running
Do not double the consonant if the verb ends in *-w*, *-x*, or *-y*.	show fix play	showing fixing playing
4. In two-syllable verbs that end in a consonant, a vowel, and a consonant (c-v-c), double the last consonant only if the last syllable is stressed.	beGIN LISten	beginning listening
5. If the verb ends in *-ie*, drop the *-ie*, add *-y* and *-ing*.	lie die	lying dying

Appendix 2D Simple Past of Regular Verbs

1. Add *-ed* to most regular verbs.	start	started
2. If the verb ends in an *-e*, add *-d*.	like	liked
3. If the verb ends in a consonant +*y*, change the *y* to *i* and add *-ed*.	study	studied
4. If the verb ends in a vowel +*y*, don't change the *y* to *i*. Add *-ed*.	enjoy play	enjoyed played
5. If a one-syllable verb ends in a consonant, a vowel, and a consonant (c-v-c), double the last consonant and add *-ed*.	stop show	stopped showed
Do not double the last consonant if it is *w*, *x*, or *y*.	fix play	fixed played
6. If a two-syllable word ends in a consonant, a vowel, and a consonant (c-v-c), double the last consonant if the stress is on the last syllable.	ocCUR LISten	occurred listened

APPENDIX 3 Pronunciation Rules

Appendix 3A Regular Plural Nouns

/S/	/Z/		/IZ/
After voiceless sounds (*p, t, k, f, th*)	After voiced sounds (*b, d, g, v, m, n, l, r, ng*) and vowel sounds		After *s, z, sh, ch, ge/dge* sounds. (This adds another syllable to the word.)
maps	jobs	pens	classes
pots	beds	schools	exercises
books	rugs	cars	dishes
cuffs	leaves	rings	sandwiches
months	rooms	days	colleges

Appendix 3B Simple Present Tense: Third Person Singular

/S/	/Z/	/IZ/
After voiceless sounds (*p, t, k, f*)	After voiced final sounds (*b, d, g, v, l, r, m, n, ng*)	Verbs ending in *sh, ch, z, s*. (This adds another syllable to the word.)
He sleeps.	She drives a car.	He teaches English.
She works.	He prepares dinner.	She rushes to class.

Appendix 3C Simple Past Tense of Regular Verbs

/t/	/d/	/Id/
After voiceless sounds (*p, k, f, s, sh, ch*)	After voiced final sounds (*b, g, v, l, r, m, n*)	Verbs ending in *-t* or *-d*. (This adds another syllable to the word.)
He kissed her once.	We learned a song.	She painted a picture.
She asked a question.	They waved goodbye.	The plane landed safely.

APPENDIX 4 Time Expressions

Appendix 4A Simple Present

ADVERBS OF FREQUENCY	FREQUENCY EXPRESSIONS	TIME EXPRESSIONS
always	every { morning / afternoon / night / summer / winter / spring / fall / day / week / year }	in { 1997 / October / the fall }
often	all the time	on { Monday / Sundays / January 1st / the weekend }
frequently	once a week	at { 6:00 / noon / night / midnight }
usually	twice a month	
sometimes	3 times a year	
seldom	once in a while	
rarely		
never		

Appendix 4B Present Progressive

now	this semester
right now	this evening
at the moment	this week
today	this year
these days	
nowadays	

Appendix 4C Past

YESTERDAY	*LAST*	*AGO*	*IN/ON/AT*
yesterday morning afternoon evening	last night week month year summer	an hour two days 6 months a year ago	in 1988 June the evening on Sunday December 1 weekends at 6:00 night midnight

Appendix 4D Future

THIS	*NEXT*	*TOMORROW*	*OTHER*	*IN/ON/AT*
this morning afternoon evening	next week month year Sunday weekend summer	tomorrow morning afternoon evening night	soon later a week from today tonight for 3 days until 3:00	in 15 minutes a few days 2 weeks March 2005 on Tuesday May 21 at 4:00 midnight

APPENDIX 5 Pronouns

Appendix 5A Subject Pronouns

SUBJECT PRONOUNS		
I	am	happy.
He She It	is	
We You They	are	

Appendix 5B Object Pronouns

		OBJECT PRONOUNS
She	loves	me. him. her. it. us. you. them.

Appendix 5C Demonstrative Pronouns

This That	is a grammar book.
These Those	are my classmates.

Appendix 5D Possessive Pronouns

This book is	mine. his. hers. * ours. yours. theirs. **It* does not have a possessive pronoun.

Appendix 5E Reflexive Pronouns

I You We You They	love	myself. yourself. ourselves. yourselves. themselves.
He She It	loves	himself. herself. itself.

Appendix 5F Reciprocal Pronoun: *Each Other*

Friends They Brad and Liz We	help are yelling at love e-mailed	each other.

APPENDIX 6 Possessives

Appendix 6A Possessive Nouns

Bob's Thomas' Thomas's The teacher's The students' The children's Bob and Andrea's	house is big.

Appendix 6B Possessive Determiners (Adjectives)

My His Her Its Our Your Their	eyes are big.

Appendix 6C Possessive Pronouns

The house is	mine. yours. his. hers. * ours. yours. theirs.

*_It_ does not have a possessive pronoun.

APPENDIX 7 Comparisons with Adjectives and Adverbs

Appendix 7A Comparative Form (to compare two people, places, things, or actions)

Betsy	is	older	than	Judy.
		bigger		
		busier		
		later		
		more punctual		
		less talkative		
	plays the violin	faster		
		more beautifully		
		better		

Appendix 7B Superlative Form (to compare one thing or person to all the others in a group)

Betsy	is	the oldest	of all her sisters.
		the biggest	
		the busiest	
		the most practical	
		the most punctual	
	plays the violin	the fastest	
		more beautifully	
		the best	

Appendix 7C *As . . . As* (to say that two people, places, or things are the same)

Betsy	is	as	old	as	Judy.
			big		
			busy		
			practical		
			punctual		
	plays the violin		fast		
			beautifully		
			well		

APPENDIX 8 Past-Tense Forms of Common Irregular Verbs

BASE FORM	SIMPLE PAST	PAST PARTICIPLE
be	was	been
become	became	become
begin	began	begun
bend	bent	bent
bite	bit	bitten
blow	blew	blown
break	broke	broken
bring	brought	brought
build	built	built
buy	bought	bought
catch	caught	caught
choose	chose	chosen
come	came	come
cost	cost	cost
cut	cut	cut
dig	dug	dug
do	did	done
draw	drew	drawn
drink	drank	drunk
drive	drove	driven
eat	ate	eaten
fall	fell	fallen
feed	fed	fed
feel	felt	felt
fight	fought	fought
find	found	found
fly	flew	flown
forget	forgot	forgotten
get	got	gotten
give	gave	given
go	went	gone
grow	grew	grown
hang	hung	hung
have	had	had
hear	heard	heard
hide	hid	hidden
hit	hit	hit
hold	held	held
hurt	hurt	hurt
keep	kept	kept
know	knew	known
lead	led	led

BASE FORM	SIMPLE PAST	PAST PARTICIPLE
leave	left	left
lend	lent	lent
let	let	let
lose	lost	lost
make	made	made
meet	met	met
pay	paid	paid
put	put	put
quit	quit	quit
read	read*	read*
ride	rode	ridden
ring	rang	rung
run	ran	run
say	said	said
see	saw	seen
sell	sold	sold
send	sent	sent
shake	shook	shaken
shoot	shot	shot
shut	shut	shut
sing	sang	sung
sit	sat	sat
sleep	slept	slept
speak	spoke	spoken
spend	spent	spent
stand	stood	stood
steal	stole	stolen
swim	swam	swum
take	took	taken
teach	taught	taught
tear	tore	torn
tell	told	told
think	thought	thought
throw	threw	thrown
understand	understood	understood
wake	woke	woken
wear	wore	worn
win	won	won
write	wrote	written

*Pronounce the base form: /rid/; pronounce the past-tense form and the past participle: red.

UNIT 1

Unit 1, Opening Task (Page 1)

Go back to your guesses in the chart in the Task. Compare your guesses with the correct information below. Are your first impressions of each person correct?

NAME	AN PHAN	NAKISO MOYO	JACKIE VERAS	YOUNG MIN AND MI JUN KIM
Country	Vietnam	Zimbabwe	Dominican Republic	Korea
Nationality	Vietnamese	African	Dominican	Korean
Age	22	28	34	Young Min 50 Mi Jun 50
Single/Married/ Divorced	single	single	divorced	married
Occupation	student	Web designer	secretary	shopkeepers

UNIT 3

Unit 3, Activity 1 (Page 42)

CATEGORIES					
	Monuments	Famous Places	Countries	Rivers, Mts, Deserts	Capitals
Question	*Where is/are. . . ?*	*Where is/ are. . . ?*	*Where is. . . ?*	*Where is/ are. . . ?*	*What's the capital of. . . ?*
$10	People's Republic of China	Australia	Afghanistan	South America	Washington D.C.
$20	Greece	Zimbabwe and Zaire	Brazil	Mongolia and China	Santiago
$30	Moscow, Russia	The U.S.	Cuba	India	Rangoon
$40	Paris, France	Egypt	Greece	Nepal	Helsinki
$50	New York	Peru	India	Vietnam	Rabat

UNIT 3

Unit 1, Activity 2 (Page 43)

Top row: Kofi Anan and Bono, The Dalai Lama, The Grand Canyon, Petronas Tower in Malaysia

Bottom row: Angkor Wat, Rio de Janeiro

APPENDIX 10 Exercises and Activities (Second Parts)

UNIT 1

Unit 1, Exercise 6 (Page 6)

List B

MEN	COUNTRY	NATIONALITY
1. Mario		Peruvian
2. Mohammed	Morocco	
3. Hideki and Yoshi		Japanese
4. Leonardo	the Dominican Republic	
5. Oumar		Senegalese

WOMEN	COUNTRY	NATIONALITY
6. Lilik	Indonesia	
7. Krystyna		Polish
8. Liisa and Katja	Finland	
9. Belen		Spanish
10. Margarita and Dalia	Brazil	

11. I		
12. You		

Unit 2, Exercise 4 (Page 18)

EXAMPLE:

1\.

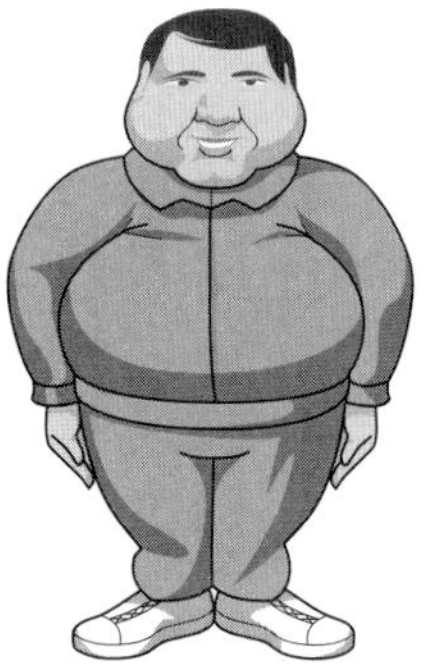

2\.

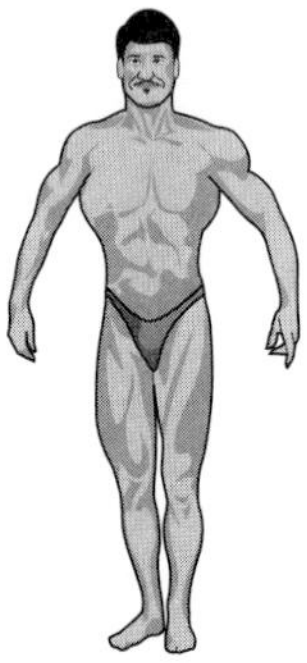

3\.

4\.

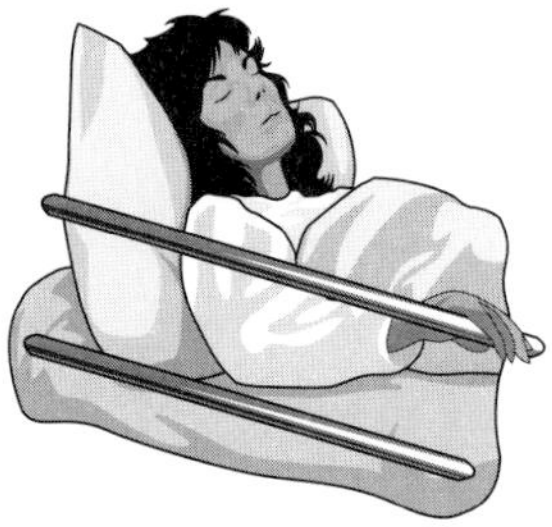

5\.

6\.

7\.

UNIT 3

Unit 3, Exercise 7 (Page 34)

MAP B

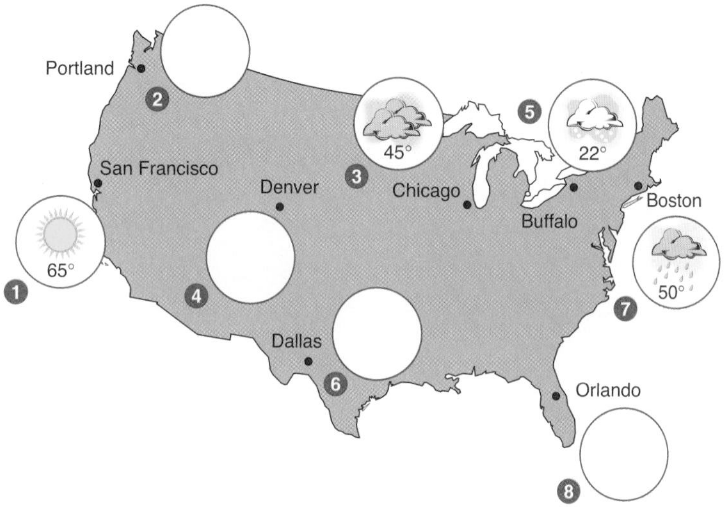

Unit 3, Exercise 8 (Page 36)

Chart B

STEP 1

1. 10:30 2. 6:15 3. 8:35 4. 11:45

STEP 2

5. 2:55 6. 4:10 7. 1:40 5. 3:20

Unit 3, Exercise 10 (Page 39)

PICTURE B

7.

sunglasses

8.

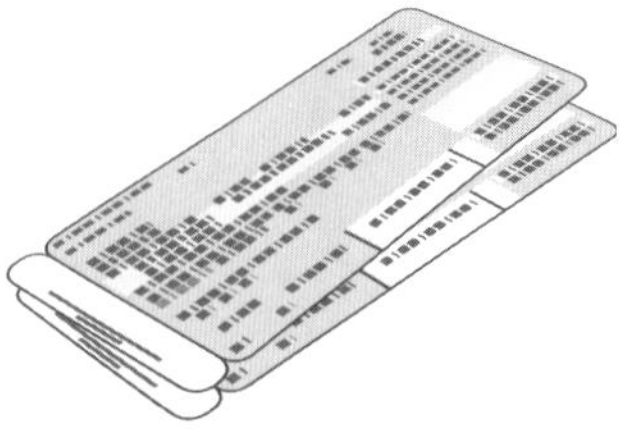

plane tickets

9.

address book

10.

guide book

11.

suitcase

12.

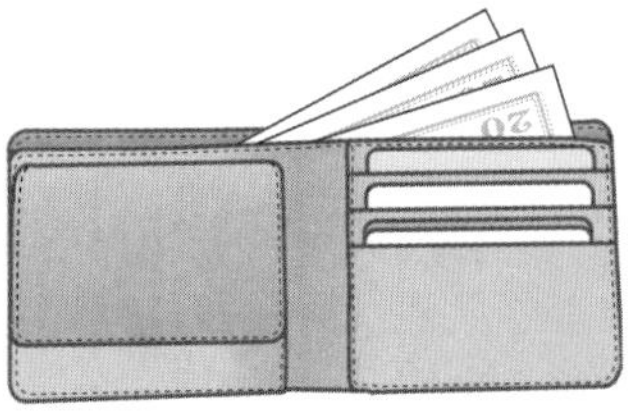

wallet

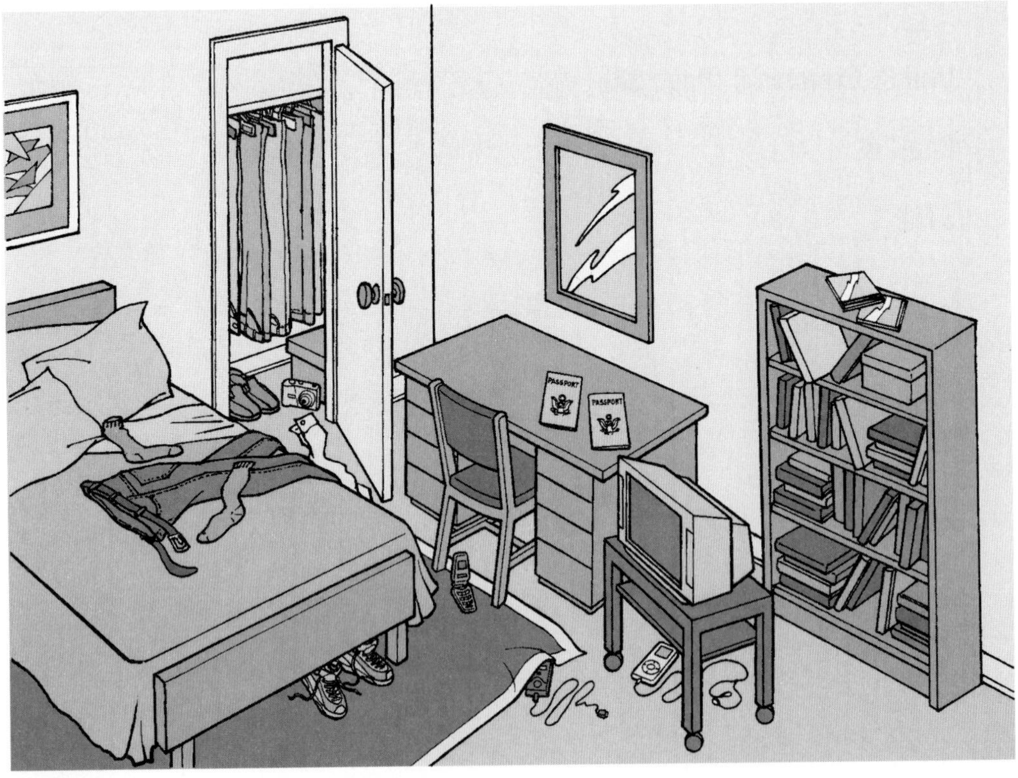

UNIT 9

Unit 9, Exercise 3 (Page 141)

Student B:

	ADRIANA		SANG-WOO	
	YES	NO	YES	NO
1. like to learn English			✔	
2. want to meet English-speaking people	✔			
3. feel nervous when speaking English			✔	
4. like to work in groups	✔			
5. need grammar rules to learn English			✔	
6. learn by speaking and listening to English	✔			
7. learn by reading and writing English			✔	
8. learn slowly, step by step		✔		
9. try new ways of learning				✔

UNIT 11

Unit 11, Exercise 10 (Page 181)

Yearly Consumption per Person in the United States in 2000

Chart B

CATEGORY	QUESTION
1. Meat (beef, pork, veal, lamb)	a. 195 pounds
2. Chicken	b.
3. Fish	c. 15 pounds
4. Milk	d.
5. Cheese	e.
6. Eggs	f. 250
7. Fats and Oils (vegetable oils, butter, margarine)	g. 74.5 pounds
8. Grain Products (bread, bakery items, etc.)	h.
9. Sugar	i. 152 pounds
Source: USDA	

Unit 17, Exercise 9 (Page 281)

Chart B

1. Anne Frank		a. a young victim of the Nazis during World War II b. because she was Jewish c. her diary
2. Susan B. Anthony & Elizabeth Cady Stanton	d. who e. what/famous for f. when/famous	
3. Amelia Earhart		g. the first female aviator h. the first woman to fly across the Atlantic Ocean i. in 1928
4. Indira Gandhi	j. what/famous for k. whose daughter l. what/her father/famous for	

Unit 18, Exercise 15 (Page 307)

Text B

1. Doina grew up in ______________________ (where).
2. She married a government official.
3. She was pregnant in 1976. She had ______________________ (what).
4. Doina was unhappy ______________________ (why).
5. She thought of ways to escape every day.
6. She taught her daughter ______________________ (what).
7. On October 9, 1988, she and her daughter swam across the Danube River to Serbia.
8. ______________________ (who) caught them.
9. Doina and her daughter went to jail.
10. They tried to escape ______________________ (when) from jail.
11. Finally, they left Romania on foot in the middle of the night.
12. They flew to ______________________ (where) in 1989.
13. Doina went to school to learn English.
14. She wrote ______________________ (what) in her ESL class.

Unit 18, Exercise 12 (Page 303) and Activity 3 (Page 310)

The conclusion of Jerry's story:

Unit 18, Activity 6 (Page 311)

(Only the Host looks at this game board.)

Game Board

$$$	CATEGORY 1 PEOPLE	CATEGORY 2 *WH*-QUESTIONS	CATEGORY 3 *YES/NO* QUESTIONS
$10	Ms. Kudo	A flash drive	Yes, she did.
$20	Leo	On the first day of the new semester	Yes, he did.
$30	The Director	In her school bag	No, he didn't.
$40	Mr. Dim	Because he was jealous	No, he didn't.
$50	The students	She noticed grammar mistakes in the note.	Yes, they did.

Unit 24, Exercise 3 (Page 397)

Chart B

	NORTH AMERICA	SOUTH AMERICA	ASIA	EUROPE	AFRICA	THE WORLD
long river	The Mississippi		The Yangtze		The Nile	
large country		Brazil		Russia		Russia
populated country	The United States		The People's Republic of China		Nigeria	
high mountain		Mt. Aconcagua		Mt. Elbrus		Mt. Everest
small country	Bermuda		Macau		the Seychelles	

APPENDIX 11 Learning Journal

These are the words and phrases used in Unit 1 to greet, introduce, and say good-bye. Remember to add new phrases you hear to your Learning Journal.

Section 1: Words and Expressions

GREETINGS	RESPONSES	GOOD-BYES
Hello.		Have a good day.
Good morning.		Good-bye.
How do you do?	Very well, thank you.	So long.
How are you?		Take care.
How's everything?		See you later/tomorrow/next week.
How are you doing?	Fine, thank you.	Bye!
How's it going?	Great, thanks.	
What's happening?	Pretty good.	
Hi!	I'm okay.	
What's up?	I'm good.	
Hey!	So-so.	
What's new?	Not bad.	

Photo Credits

Page 0: All photos © Royalty-Free/Corbis
Page 8: (Top) © PhotoDisc Green/Getty/RF, (Top Middle) © PhotoDisc Green/Getty/RF, (Bottom Middle) © IndexOpen/RF, (Bottom) © Hans Neleman/zefa/Corbis
Page 9: (Top) © M. Thomsen/zefa/Corbis, (Middle) © Royalty-Free/Corbis, (Bottom) © Charles Gullung/zefa/Corbis
Page 13: © IndexOpen/RF
Page 28: © Photos.com/RF
Page 29: (Top to Bottom) © Photos.com/RF, © Pascal Le Segretain/Getty Images, © Steve Winter/National Geographic/Getty Images, © Photos.com/RF, © Photos.com/RF, © IndexOpen/RF
Page 33: © MARTIN BERNETTI/AFP/Getty Images
Page 43: (Top Left) © SZENES JASON/CORBIS SYGMA, (Top Left Middle) © RAVEENDRAN/AFP/Getty Images, (Top Right Middle) © IndexOpen/RF, (Top Right) © IndexOpen/RF, (Bottom Left) © PhotoDisc Red/Getty/RF, (Bottom Right) © PhotoDisc Red/Getty/RF
Page 46: © Joseph Sohm; ChromoSohm Inc./CORBIS
Page 47: (Top Row Left to Right) © IndexOpen/RF, © PhotoObjects.net/RF, © PhotoObjects.net/RF, © PhotoObjects.net/RF (Middle Row) © PhotoObjects.net/RF (Bottom Row Left to Right) © PhotoObjects.net/RF, © PhotoObjects.net/RF, © Photos.com/RF, © PhotoObjects.net/RF
Page 50: (Top Left) © Royalty-Free/Corbis, (Top Right) © Royalty-Free/Corbis, (Top Middle Left) © Tobbe/zefa/Corbis, (Top Middle Right) © Royalty-Free/Corbis, (Bottom Middle Left) © Christie & Cole/CORBIS, (Bottom Middle Right) © Jim Craigmyle/Corbis, (Bottom Left) © Royalty-Free/Corbis, (Bottom Right) © Royalty-Free/Corbis
Page 51: (Top Left) © Jim West/Alamy, (Top Right) © Royalty-Free/Corbis, (Bottom Left) © Ariel Skelley/CORBIS, (Bottom Right) © Photos.com/RF
Page 64: (Top Left) © Caroline Penn/CORBIS, (Top Right) © Christopher J. Morris/CORBIS, (Bottom Left) © Wolfgang Kaehler/CORBIS, (Bottom Right) © Rob Howard/CORBIS
Page 68: (Left) © Richard T. Nowitz/CORBIS, (Left Middle) © Lindsay Hebberd/CORBIS, (Right Middle) © David Turnley/CORBIS, (Right) © KEVIN LAMARQUE/Reuters/Corbis
Page 73: © Royalty-Free/Corbis
Page 74: (Top Left) © Patrik Giardino/CORBIS, (Middle Left) © PhotoAlto/Getty/RF, (Bottom Left) © Royalty-Free/Corbis, (Top Right) © Stockbyte Platinum/Getty/RF, (Middle Right) © VEER Michael Grecco/Photonica/Getty, (Bottom Right) © Brad Wilson/Iconica/Getty
Page 79: © Keren Su/Corbis
Page 80: All photos © IndexOpen/RF
Page 81: (Top Left) © Royalty-Free/Corbis, (Top Right) © IndexOpen/RF, (Top Middle Left) © Photos.com/RF, (Top Middle Right) © PhotoObjects.net/RF, (Middle Left) © Photos.com/RF, (Middle Right) © ian nolan/Alamy, (Bottom Middle Left) © Photos.com/RF, (Bottom Middle Right) © Photos.com/RF, (Bottom Left) © Photos.com/RF, (Bottom Right) © Philip Bramhill/Alamy
Page 85: © Photodisc Green/Getty/RF
Page 86: (Top) © Photodisc Red/Getty/RF, (Top Middle) © Photodisc Green/Getty/RF, (Middle) © Photos.com/RF, (Bottom Middle) © Charles Gupton/CORBIS, (Bottom) © IndexOpen/RF
Page 87: (Top) © Creatas/SuperStock, (Top Middle) © Ty Allison/Taxi/Getty, (Bottom Middle) © Zubin Shroff/Stone+/Getty, (Bottom) © Rainer Holz/zefa/Corbis
Page 92: (Top Left) © Gandee Vasan/Stone+/Getty, (Top Right) © Mauro Speziale/Photonica/Getty, (Bottom Left) © Stuart McClymont/Stone/Getty, (Bottom Right) © G K & Vikki Hart/Iconica/Getty
Page 93: © PhotoObjects.net/RF
Page 94: (Top Row Left to Right) © JupiterMedia/Alamy, © Steve Skjold/Alamy, © Royalty-Free/Corbis, © Photos.com/RF, (Top Middle Row Left to Right) © PhotoObjects.net/RF, © PhotoObjects.net/RF, ©BrandXPictures/RF, ©BrandXPictures/RF, (Middle Row Left to Right) © Photos.com/RF, © PhotoObjects.net/RF, ©BrandXPictures/RF, © PhotoObjects.net/RF, (Bottom Row Left to Right) © PhotoObjects.net/RF, © PhotoObjects.net/RF, © PhotoObjects.net/RF, © BrandXPictures/RF
Page 95: © IndexOpen/RF
Page 97: © PhotoObjects.net/RF
Page 107: © PhotoObjects.net/RF
Page 110: © Photos.com/RF
Page 116: (Top) © Adamsmith/Taxi/Getty, (Bottom) © Royalty-Free/Corbis
Page 130: © Paul Barton/CORBIS
Page 131: (Top) © Photos.com/RF, (Bottom) © Darren Padgham/Stone/Getty
Page 132: (Top) © David Young-Wolff/Alamy, (Top Middle) © Clarissa Leahy/Stone/Getty, (Bottom Middle) © BananaStock/Alamy, (Bottom) © Grace/zefa/Corbis
Page 136: (Top Left) © Patrik Giardino/Corbis, (Top Right) © Royalty-Free/Corbis, (Middle Left) © Channel Island

Pictures/Alamy, (Middle Right) © Comstock Images/Alamy, (Bottom Left) © archivberlin Fotoagentur GmbH/Alamy, (Bottom Right) © Matthias Clamer/Stone/Getty
Page 138: © Bruce Laurance/The Image Bank/Getty
Page 140: © Royalty-Free/Corbis
Page 141: © ImageState/Alamy
Page 142: © Royalty-Free/Corbis
Page 148: © LWA-Dann Tardif/CORBIS
Page 156: © Royalty-Free/Corbis
Page 157: © Stockbyte Silver/Getty/RF
Page 159: (Left to Right) © Digital Vision/Getty/RF, © David Pollack/CORBIS, © Photos.com/RF
Page 188: © David Pollack/CORBIS
Page 198: © Photos.com/RF
Page 199: All photos © PhotoObjects.net/RF
Page 200: © Photos.com/RF
Page 205: © Brand X Pictures/Alamy
Page 219: ©Eastcott-Momatiuk/The Image Works
Page 224: © Lebrecht Music and Arts Photo Library/Alamy
Page 228: © Simeone Huber/Photographer's Choice/Getty
Page 230: © Photos.com/RF
Page 239: © IndexOpen.com/RF
Page 251: © Art Kowalsky/Alamy
Page 252: © Peter M. Wilson/CORBIS
Page 273: (Top to Bottom) © Consolidated News Pictures/Getty, © Hulton Archive/Getty Images, © Ken Goff//Time Life Pictures/Getty Images, © Fox Photos/Getty Images, © Agence France Presse/Agence France Presse/Getty Images, © Photos.com/RF
Page 275: © Bettmann/CORBIS
Page 279: © Bettmann/CORBIS
Page 280: © David Keaton/CORBIS
Page 281: (Top to Bottom) © Anne Frank House, Amsterdam/Getty Images, © Hulton Archive/Getty Images, © Evening Standard/Getty Images, © Central Press/Getty Images
Page 297: © Rich LaSalle/Photographer's Choice/Getty
Page 312: © Royalty-Free/Corbis
Page 322: © Johner/Johner Images/Getty
Page 329: (Left) © Paul Burns/Digital Vision/RF, (Right) © David McGlynn/Taxi/Getty
Page 344: © Sean Justice/The Image Bank/RF
Page 362: © Iconpix/Alamy
Page 377: (Top) © Judith Collins/Alamy/RF, (Bottom) © sciencephotos/Alamy
Page 378: All photos © Photos.com/RF
Page 383: © Daniel Pangbourne/Digital Vision/RF
Page 392: © Louie Psihoyos/Science Faction/Getty
Page 394: © IndexOpen.com
Page 400: (Top) © Paul Viant/Taxi/Getty, (Bottom) © Nancy R. Cohen/PhotoDisc Red/Getty/RF
Page 401: (Top to Bottom) © Adam Eastland/Alamy, © Stock Connection Distribution/Alamy, © Donald Nausbaum/Alamy, © PHOTOTAKE Inc./Alamy
Page 402: (Top to Bottom) © Hulton Archive/Getty Images, © STR/AFP/Getty Images, © Medical-on-Line/Alamy
Page 408: © ImageState/Alamy
Page 410: © Wendy Ashton/The Image Bank/Getty
Page 414: © D. Hurst/Alamy/RF
Page 420: © mediacolor's/Alamy

INDEX

C

D

K

L

M

N

O

P

Q

U

V

W

Y